MY FATHER IS A BOOK

BOOKS BY
JANNA MALAMUD SMITH

*Private Matters: In Defense
of the Personal Life*

*A Potent Spell: Mother Love
and the Power of Fear*

*My Father Is a Book: A Memoir
of Bernard Malamud*

My Father Is a Book

A MEMOIR OF

BERNARD MALAMUD

Janna Malamud Smith

Houghton Mifflin Company

BOSTON · NEW YORK

2006

For information about permission to reproduce selections from
this book, write to Permissions, Houghton Mifflin Company,
215 Park Avenue South, New York, New York 10003.

Visit our Web site: www.houghtonmifflinbooks.com.

Library of Congress Cataloging-in-Publication Data
Smith, Janna Malamud.
My father is a book : a memoir of Bernard Malamud /
Janna Malamud Smith.
p. cm.
ISBN-13: 978-0-618-69166-1
ISBN-10: 0-618-69166-9
1. Malamud, Bernard. 2. Novelists, American — 20th century —
Biography. 3. Novelists, American — 20th century — Family
relationships. 4. Malamud, Bernard — Family. I. Title.
PS3563.A4Z887 2006
813'.54 — dc22   2005024736

Book design by Robert Overholtzer

PRINTED IN THE UNITED STATES OF AMERICA

QUM 10 9 8 7 6 5 4 3 2 1

Lines from "The Blue Swallow" by Howard Nemerov reprinted by
permission of Margaret Nemerov. Excepts from *Dubin's Lives* by Bernard
Malamud, copyright © 1979 by Bernard Malamud. Reprinted by
permission of Farrar, Straus and Giroux, LLC.

For Peter Malamud Smith
and Zachary Malamud Smith

CONTENTS

For one thing love and death have in common more than those vague resemblances people are always talking about, is that they make us question more deeply, for fear that its reality will slip away from us, the mystery of personality.

—MARCEL PROUST, *Swann's Way*

PREFACE

THIS MEMOIR tells my story about my father, the writer Bernard Malamud. I wasn't sure I'd ever write it. My initial reaction to having any of his intimate letters and journals made public was intense and negative. I wrote a piece, published in the *New York Times Book Review* in 1989,[1] in which I explored his complex sense of privacy and my own. I noted Dad's pleasure in reading biographies and the fact that he'd written a novel, *Dubin's Lives*, about a biographer. But I also described how fiercely he guarded the personal sources of his fiction and how he delighted in Shakespeare's relative biographical anonymity. Troubled by "pathographies"—biographies that gain their sales by demeaning their subjects—I applauded James Joyce's grandson, Stephen Joyce, for publicly claiming a family's right to destroy material as they saw fit. I ended by stating that I thought it most unlikely that I'd ever make the contents of my father's early journals public.

Now I am doing so. How do I justify my own change of heart? I'm not sure I can. In part I have to laugh at myself: when I finally read the notebooks, I realized their content didn't need my protection. But the larger answer is that time has passed. Dad has been dead for nearly two decades. My grief has abated. I am older. Our family past has come to feel distant enough to approach. When I wrote my first book, *Private Matters*, I broadened my own understanding of privacy — and subsequently needed less of it. So, too, as my mother moved through her eighties, a balance tipped for me between shielding her and capturing her knowledge.

One day I realized that my father's life had shifted from something overshadowing into something disappearing from view. With the aging of my mother and the deaths of so many of their friends, my own witness had become one of a few remaining membranes holding the boundary between life and void. Writing more also altered my perspective. Years practicing allowed me insight into his effort, and left me with a better understanding of him. My loyalties gradually shifted.

WRITING A MEMOIR — the process of remembering, together with conversations and the reading of letters and journals — has been pleasurable and painful, even more moving than I expected. The revisiting, the learning, and the daily work of describing have all brought an unexpected acceptance: yes, this is who he was; this is who I am. I realized when I finished the book that he had somehow become mine again: a muddle had cleared, and I could feel a simpler love for him. Meanwhile, I have struggled to speak frankly without harming living people or violating their privacy. Honoring familial requests, I have removed some names and a few bits of text.

In the process of writing, I read or reread Dad's novels and stories. Like every writer's work, my father's fiction grew out of his experience, his thoughts, and his fantasy. Although his characters' views diverge from his own in many places, there is no doubt that they sometimes speak his mind. For that reason, I occasionally quote their voices to articulate his feelings. To disarm his ghost's irritation, or at least to amuse him, I have taped on the refrigerator a line clipped from a newspaper: "May your house be free of memoirists. They cause such trouble."

This book was preceded by an essay of the same title, which I wrote in 2001.[2] As I explained in the essay, the phrase "My father is a book" came to me many years ago when I read Vardaman's exclamation, "My mother is a fish," in William Faulkner's novel *As I Lay Dying*. I am reusing the title because it captures several pleasing condensations about my father — the pull he felt between the everyday world and his art making, the depth of his belief in the transformative power of books, and the way some ever animate part of him is stored within their pages. It also says something, more fully elaborated in the chapters that follow, about the particular psychic pleasure and confusion of being his daughter.

MORE THAN A FEW people have suggested to me that the absence of a biography has worked to my father's disadvantage. What once was a trio — Saul Bellow, Bernard Malamud, and Philip Roth — became a dyad, partly because Malamud died first, but also because biographies are a way we designate writers as significant and keep their fiction alive. I have felt some guilt for my part in discouraging such undertakings, and my family is now cooperating with Philip Davis, a British literary critic who is writing a life. His acceptance of the harder assignment has left me free to write this more personal story.

Chapter 1 ⤙

Early Stories

⤙ ⤙ FOR SOME PERIOD of years starting when I was little, my father used to put salve along my eyelids at night before I went to bed. The tiny prescription tube of medicine was meant to treat an inflammation that the adults could see but of which I was oblivious. Seated on the couch in the living room of our small house in Corvallis, Oregon, I would lean my head back, and he would carefully, gently, steadying his hands on my face, lower my lid and squeeze a thin line along its inner edge. I liked his care, but I disliked the ritual, and particularly the way the ointment temporarily disarmed me — Vaseline on a camera lens. I disliked, too, the requirement that I stay still while it melted in.

To ease my impatience, he would tell me stories. Some were short; others were serial creations, miniature novels or movie segments that unwound across nights. As a boy, he had loved silent films, studied them to learn about storytelling and America. His first glimpses of a landscape beyond Brooklyn had likely been brought to him by the flickering reels that each week miraculously projected comic melodrama and then left the audience hanging, eager for seven days to pass. One episode would end starkly with a villain harassing a maiden he'd bound to the tracks, a train steaming toward her around a blind curve. The next, the following Saturday, would begin with the knot-cutting hero galloping onto the scene. Dad had captured their technique and knew how to hold my attention.

When, as an adult, I once asked about his childhood, he started telling me how he had relished going to the movies as a boy. When penniless, he sometimes half conned, half stole tickets to get into a local theater. Quickly embarrassed, he stopped himself midway through the recollection. I was in my thirties. Even then, he remained reluctant to talk about his early life, its pains and contradictions still unmanageable on his tongue. He wanted to be an exemplary father. He taxed himself hard to provide his children with what he had not had: stability, comfort, protection from the worst emotional horror. He worked to get daughter-love completely right; he took on his duties earnestly, repeatedly considered how one might frame the world to a child. His real memories were often too broad for the archway of his paternal propriety, his code of acceptable self-revelation; few squeezed through.

ON A SATURDAY MORNING when I was four and my mother and brother had gone out, he was writing at the dining room table, and I was amusing myself. Morning gave way to noon, and I became hungry and bored. I interrupted to ask for a snack. No, it was nearly lunchtime, he said, and my mother would return soon. The kitchen adjoined the dining room in our small house, but the swinging door between the rooms was shut. Entering the kitchen from the opposite hall, tiptoeing quietly, I opened a drawer and stealthily reached a hand into the crinkly cellophane bag of bread. I grabbed two slices and retreated to the sanctuary of the staircase.

"Janna," my father called. "Come here." I dropped the half-eaten bread on the stair, swallowing my mouthful while crossing the few steps through the living room and into the dining room. A black Royal typewriter sat temporarily on the table where we ate; beside it a pad of paper, a pen, a typewriter eraser.

"What were you doing?" he asked.

"Nothing."

"Were you eating?" He'd given me a second chance.

"No."

He pulled his chair back away from the table and invited me to climb into his lap. He seemed as he was, serious and kindly. I liked him and his lap. He no doubt saw a parenting opportunity that helped him accept the end of the morning's writing. For me it was binary: caught or not caught?

"George Washington," he began, "was the first president of the United States, and a very great man." He paused to retrieve the Parson Weems fabrication that had lain dormant in his mind for decades. "When he was a little boy, his father gave him an ax."

I was interested. I was becoming an outdoor Oregon girl, and axes were attractive. Maybe telling the story would distract him from my situation. He kept on and described how the boy, excited with his new ax and eager to try it out, chopped down his father's cherry tree. Having built suspense, he marched the angry father onto the scene, and in a mock deep-bass voice boomed the great question: "George, what happened to my cherry tree?" Then, in a higher octave, the famous answer: "I cannot tell a lie, Father. I chopped it with my little ax."

"You see," my father carefully explained, lest I get distracted by thoughts of axes, cherries, or maybe cherry jam on bread, "George Washington was a great man because he always told the truth."

He must have sensed that I was holding out. Almost without pausing, he started in on Lincoln and how, when Abe worked in a little grocery store, he accidentally overcharged a woman by a nickel or a dime, and, barefoot in the snow, ran after her to return the coin.

Finishing this second tale, he looked at me and asked, "So, Janna, did you take some bread?"

"No." I shook my head and slipped off his lap, grabbing the crusts on the stairs as I retreated up to my bedroom.

I MAY HAVE resisted him at that moment, but the two stories set themselves in my conscience like granite ledge. And it is an amiable irony that my father cornerstoned my appreciation for truth by using chapbook tall tales that were complete biographical lies. He did not turn to his own life, to his Russian Jewish tradition, or to the literature he loved to instill a primary sense of right and wrong. He chose the popular American vernacular. If he knew Yiddish tales — Yiddish had been the language spoken in his home — he never told me one during my childhood. With a lesson to teach, he picked stories he'd likely heard in grade school, as his own teachers molded an American boy.

When, after writing this memory, I reread his novel *The Assistant*, I realized that our conversation had a further dimension. In the spring of 1956, when I was four, Dad would have been finishing — or have just finished — writing *The Assistant*, a book about the Bobers, an immigrant Jewish family that owns a grocery store in Brooklyn. An Italian clerk, Frank Alpine, comes to work for them. Frank falls in love with Morris Bober's daughter, Helen. Dad's father, Mendel "Max" Malamud, who died during the time Dad was writing *The Assistant*, had much in common with Morris Bober. In a sense, the book recounts my father's grieving struggle to master his feelings about his own father.

Toward the end of the book, at Morris's funeral, the presiding rabbi, who has never met Morris, tells the gathered mourners this story about him:

"Helen, his dear daughter, remembers from when she was a small girl that her father ran two blocks in the snow to give back to a poor Italian lady a nickel that she forgot on the counter. Who runs in wintertime without hat or coat, without rubbers to protect his feet, two blocks in the snow to give back five cents that a customer forgot? Couldn't he wait till she comes in tomorrow? Not Morris Bober, let him rest in peace. He didn't want this poor woman to worry, so he ran after her in the snow. This is why the grocer had so many friends who admired him."

The rabbi paused and gazed over the heads of the mourners.[1]

Did the novelist remember the Lincoln story he had learned in grade school and drape it over his character? Certainly, the act, a chilly pursuit to return a bit of change, is consistent with Morris, the book's honest and kind-to-the-point-of-ridicule storekeeper. It is consistent, too, with Max Malamud, who has been described as poor, honorable, trusting to a fault, and generous. Had Dad actually witnessed Max return a nickel to a customer? If so, why didn't he tell me about my grandfather? Maybe, in the novel, he wanted to offer the dead storekeeper some of Lincoln's stature. Or maybe, child in lap, he unconsciously wished that his daughter had had Lincoln as her grandfather, and that he had had a great, heroic American, rather than a sad, defeated Jew, as his father.

Putting the chronology together for the first time, I realize that my bread-grabbing antics could have interrupted him just as he was writing the scene. What he imagined as Helen's memory, he set in Janna's, or vice versa. It was exactly the kind of small, private riddle he enjoyed.

Our bread encounter seems to have stayed with Dad, too. A quarter of a century later, he had Calvin Cohn in *God's Grace* tell the cherry tree tale to his chimpanzee "son," Buz. That telling is part of Cohn's futile attempt to reestablish civilization after nuclear war has destroyed the world. Dad's use of the story suggests

not just his memory of having told it to me but also the staying power of his schoolboy experience hearing it. Perhaps it was
linked with his own entry into "civilization" as he moved from
Yiddish family life to the Brooklyn public schools: "I will be
American; honest like Washington."

Honesty is such a basic theme in my father's work that it likely
had multiple meanings to him. In the course of *The Assistant,*
Frank Alpine transforms from petty crook to a man struggling to
live honestly. Storytelling itself lives precariously beside more literal truth. It bothered Dad his whole life that his father had once
called him a "bluffer" for inflating details of a tale. Two years before he died, he wrote about himself as a boy, "I could on occasion
be a good little liar who sometimes found it a burden to tell the
truth. Once my father called me a 'bluffer,' enraging me because I
had meant to tell him a simple story, not one that had elaborated itself into a lie."[2]

As a young man, my father may have wondered if Max-like
honesty would entrap him in an equally claustrophobic life. Or
perhaps his ambition made him feel dishonest — the desire held as
a false claim or a filial disloyalty.

MOST OFTEN the lessons in Dad's stories were gentle. When I
was five or six and struggling with my fantasy life, with the whole
matter of whether the mind's productions were private, I asked
him about it.

"Can people know what other people are thinking?" I ventured
guardedly one night at bedtime. I had lately been dreaming up diverse torments for schoolmates, from which I then heroically res-
cued them.

"Why?" he asked.

He worked to understand me. He was psychologically curious,
admired Freud. His perceptiveness was good and bad — sometimes

soothing, other times contributing to the very sense of being over-exposed I was attempting to broker.

"I don't know," I hedged. He seemed to comprehend.

"Once upon a time," he began, seeking to reassure me by telling me a story he attributed to American "Indians." More likely it was a Malamudian invention in the manner of Rudyard Kipling, but I cannot say for sure, as he read broadly. I recall only its essence: Long ago, people could read one another's minds. Then a crow abused the privilege, violating sacred rules and breaking the contract with his Indian maker that had enabled the power. The god realized that thought reading was not something his creatures could manage and declared that from that day on, no one would ever again be able to know the secrets within anyone else's mind.

"It can't be done anymore, Janna," he announced with just the right amount of authority, and kissed me good night.

WHEN NOT SAD or preoccupied with work or worries, my father had a ready playfulness, a smile that could become a long, full laugh or, more quietly, a chuckle. He relished telling elaborate jokes to guests at dinner parties. He drank little, and I recall only once seeing him tipsy. But a glass of wine and the company of friends relaxed him, and when the conversation paused — or if it didn't and he had to call the table to attention — he'd commence: A Frenchman in Paris is out for a date with a very pretty girl. In the course of the evening, their passions become aroused. In fact, they are so overcome that they dive under the nearest Citroën and go to it making love. Before long, still in the heat of passion, the man feels a tap on his shoulder. He looks up, startled, and sees that a gendarme is standing over him. "Monsieur," says the gendarme, "I am so sorree to disterb you. But it is my duty to tell you that your car has been stolen."

Dad would ham the French accent, gesture in the air with his finger to re-create the shoulder tap. Each time he would savor the punch line as much as his guests.

DAD LOVED Charlie Chaplin, Buster Keaton, and Laurel and Hardy, and he took inspiration from them. The best of his nightly fictional inventions contained hilarious moments. It delighted him when my brother or I giggled helplessly, and he skillfully angled to make it happen. Racky Raccoon, a comic mainstay in his repertoire, lived at the zoo in Avery Park, in our town, Corvallis. The tales about him likely took shape as Dad watched us watch the raccoons during family outings he joined when he was not working his double shift of teaching and writing.

The raccoon cage was concrete, barren except for a dead climbing tree and a cement trough filled with water in which bits of old carrot or lettuce floated. In spite of the little zoo's gray demeanor, worsened by the perpetual wet of the Oregon winter, I loved going there, particularly loved how the masked creatures, disarranged from their nocturnal practices, washed food with their delicate black fingers and paced the floor all day in an odd humping walk. They endured a sorry confinement, but it made them fun for small children to watch.

When tired of the zoo, we would wander through the park to its playground. If the sun came out, the many humid acres would warm and fill the air with the particular evergreen sweetness of cedar and balsam. My brother and I sometimes carried, folded in our pockets, pieces of wax paper to polish the steep metal slide until it became slick.

The playground's glory was a single swing suspended from a high wooden beam between two tall Douglas fir trees. The swing had a spectacular reach. When it was my turn, Dad would push me high and higher, finally running underneath in an "undercut" that careened me up. "Do it agaaiinn!!!" I would beg, and often he would.

I picture him in dark pants and a gray lamb's wool sweater over a dark plaid, collared shirt. Wire-rimmed glasses frame his brown eyes, and he is balding. Although he was skinny in his twenties, by the mid-1950s his five-foot-eight frame carried more weight than it needed; he had a paunch. Aside from the short walk to and from his college office, he was sedentary. And his tiny instructor's salary led my Italian American mother to cook meals with inexpensive local farm ingredients: eggs, butter, cream, cheese. I can see her picking the skin and soft bones out of canned salmon before mixing it with eggs into a loaf, or grating a block of orange Tillamook Cheddar into a soufflé. Dessert for company after we returned in 1957 from a year in Italy was often zabaglione, an Italian pudding of egg yolks, sugar, sherry, and heavy cream poured over canned mandarin oranges and sherry-soaked graham crackers (Oregon's substitute for *amaretti*). What's more, Dad had brought west with him his childhood delicatessen diet: after finishing a sandwich at lunch, he'd cut up a banana in a bowl and pile it with sour cream. (The other visible legacy of his family's grocery store was his index finger missing part of its tip, which he'd accidentally cut off while slicing meat for a customer.) Sometime in the 1960s, his doctor warned him that he was "a candidate for a heart attack" and admonished him to change his habits. He did, taking daily walks, eating less, and losing weight. He possessed unusual self-discipline.

IN MY FATHER'S STORIES, Racky — a resourceful, energetic scamp, a leader among his fellows — spent his days outwitting the rather befuddled but good-natured zookeeper who cared for him. Food was often on the raccoon's mind. Indeed, Racky once attached a hose to a watermelon he had commandeered and then, for some long-forgotten reason, pumped water into the melon until it exploded. Was he ingeniously opening it to eat? Playing a trick on his minder? Or was the rascal getting his comeuppance for his thievery? I no longer remember.

The zookeeper may have possessed qualities Dad attributed to his father, whom he loved but viewed as inept, incompetent in American ways. He respected Max's kindness and endurance, but he was disappointed in Max for getting stuck in an unsuccessful life from which he could not extricate himself. My father struggled to appreciate his father's circumstances: the difficulty of immigrating, of marrying a woman soon beset by mental illness, of trying to survive her, raise two sons, and eke out a living from a tiny, worthless grocery store. Dad's compassion for his fictional characters came not only out of what he had lived and witnessed but also from the unremitting internal struggle this life stimulated. His protective tenderness toward his parents existed side by side with his sense of having been gypped, his anger about it, and then his shame and guilt. "The emotion of my youth was humiliation," Levin tells Pauline in *A New Life*. I believe he was speaking for both character and creator.[3] My father's writing was partly a gesture of repair, grounded in the hope that he might someday redeem his family, or, if not, at least be able to forgive them and himself.

MY GRANDFATHER Max Malamud died at age sixty-nine, in Brooklyn in 1954,[4] two years after I arrived on the scene in Oregon. We never glimpsed each other. Born in 1885, he emigrated from a shtetl near Kamyanets-Podilskyy in Ukraine in the middle of the first decade of the twentieth century. He spent much of the early journey hidden in a hay wagon. He was trying to escape induction into the tsar's army during Russia's war with Japan and to flee the country's terrorizing pogroms. The author Amos Elon writes, "The word *pogrom* — meaning 'devastation' in Russian — was entering the international lexicon to describe violent outrages against a particular ethnic group. From the early 1880s, Russia's recurrent anti-Semitic pogroms were government-inspired diversions from the miseries of daily life. Nearly two million Jews fled Russia between 1880 and 1910."[5]

Although Dad rarely spoke about his past, my interest in it quietly registered with him. When he died, he left a folder of loose notes — letters from relatives and papers covered with names and other information. He had telephoned some cousins and gathered what he could. Names are spelled variously; details are contradictory. On a scrap of paper containing bits of family history collected by one of Dad's cousins, a note implies that Max's father, Shepsil, may have been killed by a Cossack. In Dad's first published piece of fiction, "Armistice" (1940), a Jewish grocer named Morris Lieberman becomes distraught when he hears reports of the rise of Nazism, which trigger his traumatic childhood memory of a pogrom: "When he was a boy, Morris Lieberman saw a burly Russian peasant seize a wagon wheel that was lying against the side of a blacksmith's shop, swing it around, and hurl it at a fleeing Jewish sexton. The wheel caught the Jew in the back, crushing his spine."[6] I do not know whether Shepsil was murdered, what Max witnessed, or what my father knew. But the violent image may capture memories Max carried that his older son sensed or heard told — an Old-World burden of collective and personal horror.

"MOST RUSSIAN JEWS were confined by law to the so-called Pale of Settlement, a region permeated by poverty and hopelessness," Elon writes. "The czar's chief adviser on Jewish affairs was Konstantin Pobedonstsev, a fanatical Slavophile. His formula for solving Russia's 'Jewish problem' was simple: 'one third must emigrate, one third convert, and one third must die.'"[7] Dad thought that the shtetl in which the Malamud family lived was called Zbrizh and that the Jewish homes, along with the remaining inhabitants, had been bulldozed over by the Nazis or Stalin during World War II. Shepsil and his two brothers, Abraham and Kalman, were butchers who supplied meat for the Russian army. My father's cousin Murray Malament wrote in 1976, apparently in response to a question about the family's past on the occasion of my wedding, "Tante Boontsah described the house the family lived in as one of the nicest houses in town, built of brick with a wooden floor. It had two kitchens, a large one used in the summer and a smaller one for winter. The parents, Shepseh [Shepsil] and Zlotta, had a very large bedroom. Our grandmother, Zlotta, owned a general store in which the children worked."[8]

After Dad wrote *The Fixer,* and the Pulitzer Prize he won for it attracted attention from long-lost friends and family, an eighty-year-old cousin, Mathis Silverman, wrote, "[Shepsil] and your Grandmother, Zlatte [Zlotta], lived in a very small town named Zbrizh in Czarist Ukrainia [*sic*] near the Galician border. What they did for a living, I don't know, but they must have been 'fabulously rich' because their house was probably the only one in that town that had a *wooden floor*!"[9] I don't think that Dad knew until then that his father's family might have been slightly better off in the past, however relative wooden-floor wealth was in a shtetl. He may have experienced the Malamuds as even poorer than they were because immigration stripped the older context, and because Max seemed so impoverished to him.

MAX WAS THE SIXTH of seven siblings, all of whom eventually made their way to America, none of whom I met.[10] Even now, as I think about it, there's something too inconsequent for me about this family: kin everywhere, who didn't and don't exist. With his brother Mattes (Morris) Cohen, Max earned his first American living by delivering butter and eggs. The work must have gone well, for as a young married man, Max had prospects. When Dad was about five, Max and his wife, Bertha, lived in Borough Park in Brooklyn. Florence Hodes, my father's cousin, described this as a pleasant neighborhood of new houses, a mixed population (but mostly Jewish), and nice stores. Here, around 1920, Max and a partner named Ben Schmookler opened a grocery store described by Florence as "better than the usual grocery store around." But the situation quickly soured. Bertha, emotionally ill in the years after the birth of her second son, Eugene, too sick to attend the cash register herself, became convinced that Mrs. Schmookler was stealing. However paranoid her perceptions, at some point Ben Schmookler apparently took off with all the partners' jointly invested money, and the store failed.[11] The family's fortunes quickly went downhill and never recovered.

IN *The Assistant,* Dad tells a similar tale about Charlie Sobeloff and Morris Bober. Perhaps he recounts something about how Max himself lost hope.

> Years ago, Charlie, a cross-eyed but clever conniver, had come to the grocer with a meager thousand dollars in his pocket, borrowed money, and offered to go into partnership with him — Morris to furnish four thousand — to buy a grocery Charlie had in mind. The grocer disliked Charlie's nervousness and pale cross-eyes, one avoiding what the other looked at; but he was persuaded by the man's nagging enthusiasm and they bought the store . . . But Charlie's talented nose had sniffed the right sucker. Morris never looked at the books until, two years after they had bought the place, the business collapsed.
>
> The grocer, stunned, heartbroken, could not at first understand what had happened, but Charlie had figures to prove that the calamity had been bound to occur . . . They sold the place for a miserable

price, Morris going out dazed, cleaned out, whereas Charlie in a short time was able to raise the cash to repurchase and restock the store, which he gradually worked into a thriving self-service business.[12]

Max acquired another, smaller store, but the Depression was soon on them. In the meantime, Bertha had become more ill. In *The Assistant*, at Morris's funeral, his daughter Helen observes, "Poor Papa; being naturally honest, he didn't believe that others came by their dishonesty naturally. And he couldn't hold onto those things he worked so hard to get."[13]

Florence Hodes described Max as having been unusually kind. She loved him and remembered that when she was a girl, he would sing sad, poetic Yiddish songs to her. He always took an interest in her and would give her pennies when she visited. She would sometimes confide in him her worries. Once, she had taken a small amount of money from the purse of her ill mother's nurse and felt so guilty that she confessed to Max. He told her not to worry; he would put aside money for her to pay it back.[14]

BERTHA FIDELMAN, my father's mother, was born in 1888. She came separately to New York, also from Ukraine, in 1910, the year she married Max. It's possible they had already met in Russia. Tante Boontsah, one of Max's cousins, told Dad, "Your mother, Bertha, came from a larger town near Zbrizh, Lonscrinya. Your maternal grandfather was a *schochet*." A schochet is a ritual slaughterer, appointed by a rabbi, who offers a prayer, carefully kills the chosen animal, and then examines its health before allowing it to be butchered. He does not do the butchering himself. My father, Bernard, was named for this grandfather, Baruch Fidelman, who was the "chief schochet" of his shtetl. Baruch's father was a rabbi.[15]

Reading about schochets on the Internet, I found the follow-ing humorous story that captures the qualities of piety and holi-ness sought in candidates for the work. Dad would have smiled to hear it.

> The old shochet had retired and the rabbi had to help choose a new one. When one of the people in the town, a friend of the rabbi's, asked about the candidate the rabbi had seen today, . . . the rabbi shook his head. "Did he check the knife for sharpness and nicks?" The rabbi nodded. "Did he slaughter with one smooth, clean stroke?" The rabbi nodded again. "Did he say the proper blessing?" The rabbi nodded. "Did he drain the blood and check the lungs?" The rabbi again nodded. "So, what is the problem?" asked his friend. "The old shochet used to cry afterwards," replied the rabbi.[16]

BERTHA WAS ONE of at least four siblings, and "a gentle, fine, loveable woman," Mathis Silverman wrote to my father. "She had a cousin here, Isidor[e] Cashier, a famous actor, who played in Maurice Schwartz's Jewish [Yiddish] Art Theater. She was a great lady, very friendly. When she married your father she was, like all Jewish mothers, very devoted to her family." Until she became ill, she was said to have kept a very clean house.[17] Such descriptions suggest that few people knew her very well.

Two of Bertha's sisters stayed in Russia. Her parents, if they were still alive, did, too. Dad recalls her speaking frequently of them. Mathis Silverman claims that she was an orphan, so they may have died or been killed before she reached adulthood. Dad's knowledge was vague. He was aware that his mother's side of the family had reared other artists besides the actor Isidore Cashier. He thought that one of Bertha's younger sisters might have been a dancer or an actress. Her brother Casile (Charles) Fidelman, who settled first in Argentina and later in America, worked for a while in New York as a prompter in the Yiddish theater, whispering lines to actors. As a young man in Argentina, he wrote plays that got produced. It may have been Casile from whom Dad took some birthright for storytelling. He saw the Fidelmans as more refined people than the Malamuds, and he believed that his father's slight crassness — spitting, walking around the apartment half dressed — together with his reluctance to venture out, were sources of his mother's misery.

The religious men in Bertha's family are of interest, for although my father was not religious, there was something rabbi-like about him. It is most obvious in his writing but also was evident in other aspects of his life. There seemed to have been a dybbuk inhabiting him from beyond the Pale, suggesting the phantom endurance of disembodied familial traditions, severed during immigration but extant in an invisible continuity with the past. Certainly as he aged, my father had a rabbinic stance about him — the formality, the slight distance from the everyday, the dignity of office, the wish to place himself above the fray. He liked to comfort, make peace, offer wisdom, teach, advise. He was funny and ironic, possessing a particularly Jewish wit. He enjoyed the authority his writing won for him and was fond of situations in which he might assume the relationship of leader to flock.

THE RACCOON ADVENTURE I've remembered for half a century is one in which Racky found some sugar cubes. Perhaps the zookeeper forgot them after he drank his coffee or a visitor tossed them into the cage. Racky gathered them up; he had seen humans enjoy them and was curious. He touched one to his nose and mouth, discovering its delightful sweetness. But of course he could eat nothing, not even sugar, without vigorously washing it in water. First hopeful, then amused, and finally awed, I listened as Racky, over and over, delicately picked up a cube, carried it to the trough, scrubbed it, and lifted his fingers to his mouth — only to find them empty.

My father, brother, and I fancied candy. Mouths watering, we all viscerally understood Racky's desire, and his disappointment. For years in Corvallis, no Christmas or birthday was complete unless we'd bought Dad Aplets & Cotlets from the small candy store downtown. They were an Oregon specialty, apple- or apricot-based, gelatinous squares with bits of walnut inside and coated with powdered sugar: chewy fruit essence.

When I consider the tale of Racky and the sugar cubes now, I feel Charlie Chaplin's influence: the laughter erupting from baffled loss; the comic narrative that shelters something more poignant, sadder, angrier. I read into the story a central question of my father's life: How much could he savor the sweetness that he touched? He was resourceful, but his early circumstances had taught him that nothing is solid.

DAD WAS THIRTEEN years old when he came home from school one day to find his mother, Bertha, alone, insane, sitting on the kitchen floor, an empty can of disinfectant ("something like Drano") in one hand, the poison foaming from her mouth. He took the scene in for an instant, then ran to the neighborhood drugstore for aid — a powder, a medicine — that he and the druggist spooned into her. He credited his quick response with saving her life. We were in his study in the house in Vermont when he told me. I was in my twenties. He said nothing about his feelings at the time, focusing instead on his lifesaving effort. Fifty years later, it may still have been the only bearable cast.

In *The Natural,* Harriet, offering sex, lures the young baseball talent, Roy Hobbs, into her room. As he approaches, she takes out a gun, assures herself through a brief exchange that he is indeed the Roy Hobbs who is about to become the greatest baseball player ever, and then shoots him in the stomach. Later in the book, the moment returns as the recovered Hobbs, making love to a woman, is overcome by the pain of a burst appendix. "He threw up his arms for protection and it socked him, yowling, in the shattered gut. He lived a pain he could not believe existed. Agonized at the extent of it, Roy thudded to his knees as a picture he had long carried in his mind broke into pieces. He keeled over."[18]

In the simplest sense, the picture, shattered before the boy in the kitchen, must have been of a mother who loved him, lived for him; of a primary intimacy that could be trusted. "He lived a pain he could not believe existed" seems a close description of a child's feeling after finding his mother in the midst of destroying herself. In the folder of notes Dad left behind is his recollection of seeing his father weep over his ill mother. He also recalled how much weight she gradually gained, and how once, when she got into someone's car, a cousin observed to him how the car tipped. His tenderness, sadness, and shame were immense. In *A New Life*, Levin recalls, "He had been, as a youth, a luftmensch, sop of feeling, too easy to hurt because after treading on air he hit the pavement head first. Afterwards, pain-blinded, he groped for pieces of reality. 'I've got to keep control of myself. I must always know where I am.' He had times without number warned himself, to harden, toughen, put on armor against love."[19]

ROY HOBBS'S extraordinary native talent is destroyed by a woman. I am inclined to think what was damaged by Bertha's psychosis and despair was not her son's talent, but rather his "natural" being, his ability to live easily, openly, casually in the everyday world. His trust. The moment in the kitchen exploded through him, an immeasurable betrayal. Ever after, the texts hint, approaching women in search of love, comfort, or sex, the old agony would rear up and threaten to overshadow his present moment.

Writing tempered the pain. When you tell stories, you can pack your feelings onto your characters. Meanwhile, your privacy is preserved. You can rewrite; you are not helpless before circumstance. I think of the Roman statue of Romulus and Remus — a figure Dad loved, human infants sucking a she-wolf — and of how both the psychological and actual worlds are filled with endless, awkward, lifesaving mismatches between orphans and their accidental wet nurses. Creative expression is a weird, corkscrew grab for survival; a substitution; human lips on a lupine tit.

BERTHA WAS TAKEN AWAY to an asylum soon after Dad found her on the floor. She died on Mother's Day 1929. His last memory of her was from when he had just turned fifteen. One day he visited the hospital grounds with his father, and she, whom he'd loved, who had loved him more than anyone, waved to him briefly through a barred window. That was it. He wasn't allowed in, nor she out; he could neither speak to her nor touch her, nor tell her goodbye. He was told that pneumonia killed her, but his father's vague and evasive telling made him believe that suicide was more likely. Many years later, he wrote requesting her records, but without luck.

Bertha had lost her first baby, a stillborn boy, probably in 1912. She adored my father. When he was three, his younger brother, Eugene, was born, and Bertha had what was apparently her first psychotic breakdown. So her older son lost her repeatedly — when he was three, then thirteen, then fifteen. Eugene's own mental illness erupted first as "combat fatigue" when he was fighting in the Pacific during World War II. My father survived them both, remarkably, though his childhood shadowed him like a petitioner who wouldn't quit.

He willed himself on. As a little girl in Oregon, I'd hear him shaving in the bathroom, on the bad days cursing quietly to himself, on the good ones announcing to all within range, firmly, audibly, "Someday I'm going to win."

I BELIEVE THE RATTLEDOX stories made their first appearance in 1956–1957, the winter we lived in Rome. Rattledox was a knight, and the tales about him were so enchanting that my mother repeatedly, though fruitlessly, urged my father to write them down. A quixotic fellow, Rattledox had a horse who could talk and a tiny thumb-size companion who would ride in the horse's ear. My mother also read to me that year, in Italian, a version of Tom Thumb, so perhaps I am confused. I suspect Dad borrowed the little fellow for his purposes. My memory is that the unlikely trio traveled from adventure to adventure. I am certain that their constant enemy was a bad witch named Sycorax, on loan from *The Tempest*. Once, Sycorax turned the horse and its tiny rider into stone, and Rattledox freed them.

Here is the single story I recall: One winter day, the milkmen of Rome went on strike. They would not deliver milk. Sycorax had put them up to this nastiness, perhaps cast a spell, and there simply was NO milk. No milk meant fretful, hungry babies. And, naturally, all the mothers in the city were very upset; indeed, they were becoming desperate. As always, the pastured cows chewed grass, and the Italian farmers milked them, stacked full cans in carts and trucks, and hauled them into the city. But then trouble. No one would bottle the milk. No one would carry it from house to house, or even deliver it in cases to neighborhood hole-in-the-wall groceries.

The Roman mothers gathered in crowds in the piazza. Politicians ineptly sought to quiet them. "Signore, per favore," the mayor said, twisting his hands. Carabinieri shrugged their shoulders. Rattledox, hearing the noise, ran to investigate. Entering the vast sea of mamas with their fussing bambini, he quickly became the object of their pleas: "Help us. Our children are miserable and thirsty." The knight suspected Sycorax. (Perhaps uncovering her handiwork was a whole evening's telling; I don't recall.) She was powerful and very bad; how to defeat her? He thought, then he sketched with a stubby pencil on a bit of paper. He whispered to his fellows. Soon they set off in search of . . .

Here the episode broke in suspense.

By evening, the trio had reunited in the piazza, each hauling his day's scavengings. After unloading precarious stacks of pipes from the horse's back, Rattledox grabbed a large wrench and set to work. When he paused occasionally to direct things or to eat a plate of *scaloppine al limone* that Mario brought him (Mario ran a tiny workingman's trattoria where we occasionally ate), he could hear sleepless children whimpering. The night was cold; Rattledox rubbed his hands, then lit candles and a small fire to help himself see. Scrambling to beat the dawn and Sycorax's malevolent eye, the trio labored on.

The winter sun rose late and slowly. Mothers opened shutters, shivered, pulled their wool shawls tighter around their shoulders, and looked out their windows, contemplating, as they did each new dawn, the first long-shadowed pale sunlight setting aglow the carved stone fountain that for centuries had been the piazza's jewel. This morning they could not believe their eyes. They blinked and looked again. Pipes and hoses crisscrossed the ground, tangled and oddly rigged. In their midst stood the grand fountain flowing not water but milk. Milk everywhere — spouting from the dolphins; streaming along the gods' tridents, out the horses' mouths, through the mermaids' hands; jetting high into the air. Glorious milk for all the bambini of Rome.

The mothers cheered, then ran down their apartment stairs and into the street, clasping their pitchers, their house slippers flapping on the cobblestones. Laughing, relieved, they dipped milk out of the pool and hurried home to feed their children. Rattledox and his weary companions sagged into victorious fatigue. Out of sight, Sycorax snarled.

Milk was also on the family mind that year in Rome because I had taken badly to Italy, becoming ill the moment I set foot there. In the hotel room, my parents, hoping to stanch my fever and diarrhea, struggled to grate apple and mix it with hot semolina, as someone had instructed them. Later, a doctor who lived in our apartment building told my mother to boil any milk we drank because the local pasteurization was unreliable.

Another bit of our Roman life present in the tale was the terrible postwar poverty, the raggedy children still visible everywhere around the city. I remember sitting in the back of a car one night when we first arrived in September 1956, being driven by a relative of my mother's past a bunch of makeshift shacks, jerry-built from scrap wood, cardboard, and tin, that were lit only by an occasional bare bulb.

No doubt, too, even as he was falling in love with the city, Dad had quickly discovered the constancy of strikes in Rome and the "can't-do" response of bureaucrats. He might have dreamed up Rattledox while standing in some long line waiting for an official paper to be stamped, or while trying to mail a letter home.

Having Rattledox defeat the milk-withholding witch and deliver the goods seems emblematic of the kind of continual creative act my father must have felt his psychic survival required, albeit often unconsciously. He had to outwit privation, to become the mothering he had not received. From early on, I understood that he was himself maternal, could apply Band-Aids or tuck me in at night, as well as perform the more "fatherly" functions of teaching me how to ride a bicycle and hit a baseball. Not infrequently, I sought out his tenderness and turned to him to soothe me. Between teaching and writing, he was absent a lot. He meted out time in small amounts. When present, he seemed at ease offering care. He liked to make me feel better. Dependence, insecurity, and sadness in women were comfortable for him. Female aggression was completely off-putting. I gathered from him that self-assertion unsexed women, perhaps even ungendered them. As far as I can recall, the only female characters in his bedtime stories were bad witches. Perhaps a coincidence, but his adult stories are also populated by an array of disappointing and destructive women. More than a few are ill, decomposing from the inside out.

MY FATHER AND I were intensely attached, at ease with each other, deeply compatible. Throughout my growing up, I used to sit down on the couch right next to him while he was reading so he would lift his arm and pull me in. I'd stretch mine across his sweatered chest and hold him. Often we'd talk about whatever book was in his hands, and I learned the names of writers long before they had particular meaning. I recall at one point creating a pantheon in my head, where Plato, Socrates, Shakespeare, and Freud ruled, because they each had a single name. Occasionally, he would mention how deprived his own family life had been — empty, bookless. He wanted us to have more. Once, while still a child, he had become very sick with pneumonia and was near death. The sight of the ill, weakened boy, laboring for breath, so moved Max that he'd scraped together money he didn't have and purchased an encyclopedia set, *The Book of Knowledge,* for his son to read as he convalesced. Dad enjoyed buying my brother and me books and looking over the ones we took out of the library.

My father found singular balm in my little girl love and idealization of him. Still now, I encounter people who begin conversations by telling me how much he cared about me. "Your father loved you." When I was little, I relished my position, felt emboldened by knowing he was on my side. I had, still can have, the irritating qualities of someone who believes she has an extra nickel under her heel. My play delighted him. I was often outdoors, often up to something: digging for worms, roller-skating, or returning home from a bicycle outing, a sloshing gallon can full of captured sala-manders precariously balanced in my basket. Catching sight of me, he would stop in his path, greet me with a grin, ask about my proj-ects. He let me know that he approved of them — and of me.

I also understood early and deeply that he was wary, quickly be-trayed, easily hurt. He disliked being challenged, and I protected him instinctively. I felt acutely his massive, silent sadness. The in-tense feeling comes back as I write about him, the momentary ur-gency to tell others — myself — "Leave him alone. Don't you see what he's survived?" One of the few boyhood stories he told on himself was about a time he provoked his usually mild-mannered father, making him so angry that Max gave chase around the apart-ment, yelling and threatening him. Dad hid under the bed, and when Max came near, thrust out a bandaged finger, as if to say "I'm already wounded; how can you hurt me more?" It stopped the pursuer in his tracks. The gesture characterized my father. He believed he had suffered enough, had earned some partial "pass" from contemporary accountability. He wrestled continually with his own conscience; shouldn't he be spared other critics?

He gulped down my little girl admiration, I his fatherly delight. But we became touchy and awkward when, as I grew up, I sought to free myself. Father–female child we grasped; father-woman baffled each of us in different ways. We did not trust that I could go *and* stay. I think he feared that I would try to depart from him completely. I feared that he would somehow tether me. I found his need for me oppressive, felt angry at his oversize, insistent pres-ence. Early in my adulthood, I had a dreamlike vision of him as a large hot-air balloon, at once lifting the family and consuming all our heat to fire his updraft.

*   *   *

DUBIN'S LIVES ends with an imaginary list of books that Dubin, the biographer protagonist, has written. The last, coauthored with his daughter, Maud, is a biography of Anna Freud. It's hard to think of any female child who did righter by a father than Anna Freud — if such are your terms. She continued his life, grafting her own onto it, and was eventually rewarded by being crowned queen of psychoanalysis. He analyzed her himself, and the couch talk may have bound them tighter. She loved Dorothy Burlingham, but no man rivaled his position in her heart. Even before finding it in print, I was acutely aware of the part of my father that longed for such a grown daughter, intelligent, cultivated, who would devote herself to tending him and his achievement. And at moments, I longed to be her, or at least to have her prerogative, to exist unassailably chosen and empowered. I also understood the endpoint of such intense love: some part of me would be forever subsumed. Daphne at the moment Bernini sculpted her, marble leaves growing upon her marble fingers, already half transformed by Apollo into a tree.

Looking back now, it seems no accident that Dad named Dubin's daughter Maud. In one of his earliest letters to a young woman he fell in love with in the 1960s, he argued with her about Maude Gonne, William Butler Yeats's great unconsummated love, and Gonne's deep influence on the poet. Certainly, he knew the resonances of the name.

In college, I lived in a new dormitory, opened in 1970, where each state-of-the-art room had a telephone. It was before the days when you could turn phones off, and I rather impressed the man who, when installing my neighbor's phone, glimpsed the on/off switch I had spliced onto mine to kill its ring. I dreaded that one of my father's lonely calls, unexpected, would shatter the fragile, isinglass screen I had attempted to place between us. The two of us could talk about many things, but one existed within a large, dark silence. When I was eleven, he had fallen in love with a student and had bruised our family in pursuing her. Half a dozen years later, I had developed an intense, passionate crush on a high school teacher my father's age, who left his wife and ended a marriage of some decades partly in the hope that, once separated, I would agree to become his lover. Fat letters from him had arrived daily at our Bennington, Vermont, house throughout one summer. Whichever parent retrieved the mail would place them on the bench beside the door. No one questioned the propriety of such a correspondence. Neither relationship, nor particularly their symmetry, was discussed or deemed directly discussable.

THE UNSPOKEN could become molten. Once, home from college, I said something that wounded Dad, I haven't even a slight memory what. A challenge, a criticism, some bit of verbal nastiness. I had my ways. Tensions, as they often were in our house, must already have been running high. He lashed out back, as furious as I ever saw him, emphasizing each syllable: "NO . . . MAN . . . IS . . . EVER . . . GOING . . . TO MARRY . . . YOU." He hit the words hard. I had defied our tacit unity, and he pronounced me an inadequate woman and wife. Thus, of course unstated, perhaps unintended, forever only his daughter.

I SEE US. The house in Bennington, with its airy lightness, polished hardwood floors, an early-spring sun shining in through the window by the hall staircase, dappling the floor and my bare feet. Me — in old jeans, a faded blue work shirt, gold hoop earrings, my long, wavy, auburn hair clipped back — crouching, sobbing. Him in the living room, livid, speechless, rage crumbling into remorse. My mother opening the upstairs bedroom door, calling down to us.

Chapter 2 ⤙⤙

The Early Journals

My stomach is still bad, just as if I had eaten a quilt
and it stays in me forever.

— *Bernard Malamud, March 1940*

⤙⤙ ⤙⤙ BEFORE HE HELD ME NEWBORN, Bernard Malamud
had lived thirty-eight years. He had passed through the most significant events of his life. Born in 1914 to a poor, Yiddish-speaking, immigrant family in Brooklyn, he had witnessed his mother
go mad and die, his father fail in his work, and his brother drop out
of high school and begin to falter. He had attended Erasmus Hall
High School and had commuted by subway for four years to City
College, graduating in 1936 at the height of the Depression. He
had received a master's degree in English from Columbia, started
writing, and worked in a government agency in Washington and a
factory in New York. In the early 1940s, he had begun to publish
short pieces and stories. He had taught night school at Erasmus;
met and in 1945 married my mother, Ann; and in 1947 fathered my
brother, Paul. In 1949, he'd ridden a train across the country to a
teaching career at an agricultural college in the Pacific Northwest.
Two years later, Harcourt Brace had bought his novel *The Natural*.

*   *   *

I WITNESSED NONE OF THIS. I got to know him in Oregon and mistook his alien landscape for my native ground. I grew up there for most of a decade, largely unaware of his Brooklyn world. Childhood, you might say, is a second act masquerading as a play's beginning. I was born in a small, neat, western American town, with its expansive vistas and neighborly, frontier, Protestant pot-luck ways. Yet it wasn't long before I intuited a gulf between what I was seeing and what I sensed ruled us. I imagine that many peo-ple possess a version of this feeling — of being affected by an ob-scured foreign past, blocked from direct view but still present. Time doesn't simply pass for immigrants; it careens around hair-pin turns expunging any long backward glance. The road from Corvallis to the coast, all switchbacks, was a correlative of my in-heritance. In the belly of the mountains, you could see neither the town from which you'd departed nor the ocean ahead, only the surround of tall evergreen trees.

Besides my father's abandoned world, there was my mother's Italian American immigrant experience — equally tension-filled in its way; their different, formative religions — Jewish and Catholic — both lapsed; their divergent social classes, separate primary lan-guages and countries of origin, and similar absence of proximate kin; and the fact that Oregon was, in the days before casual air-plane travel, far from everywhere. I hadn't thought about it until now, but it makes sense that as a child, when I saw Disney's ver-sion of *Swiss Family Robinson*, I fell for it hard. Like many other second-generation, mongrel, postwar American families, we'd survived shipwreck, too. We'd washed onto a verdant island and set about scavenging and jerry-building, apparently without any sure sense of how one communicates — in the midst of such a re-lieved, effortful scramble — about civilizations left behind.

It seems that for me, as for many, interest in the family past is a midlife acquisition — like bifocals. You can no longer take the fine print for granted, so you bestir yourself. But there are other reasons I've waited to learn more about my father. One motif he conveyed was the relief of departure, the immigrant's assimilative momentum: just keep moving. I appreciated the sentiment. Additionally, by my adolescence, his success had made him flame way too bright. Why burn your eyes staring into the sun? But I'm also trying to capture something else — the sense of "stay away" I felt. It came partly from intuiting his pain and thus joining with him in a silent protection plan. He could use his past for writing, but then he was in control. Otherwise, it was simply too sore for him to touch or have touched. He wrote in *Pictures of Fidelman*, "The truth is I hate the past. It caught me unaware."[1]

AFTER HE DIED in 1986, my mother meticulously sorted through his story drafts, manuscripts, letters, and papers, sending many boxes to libraries. She tore up one or two notes, sequestered letters, and slipped his two earliest notebooks into a manila envelope in her drawer in case my brother or I (perhaps her grandsons) might someday want them. For a decade and a half, I ignored them. I rarely looked at any of his papers or books. I gathered letters about him from several of his childhood friends but put them away in boxes, often without fully reading them first.

I remember thinking about him sometime in the late 1980s and seeing in my mind's eye a large, wet, barnacled, scarred, black whale lying dead on a beach. Pebbles, seaweed, post-storm detritus, damp sand, a wide flat seascape, the sky dark gray with thick low clouds. Wintry. I recall particularly my surprise at finding that I could approach the creature, and how the mirrorlike black skin, upon closer inspection, revealed itself as variegated, spotted with gray-white patches and uneven surfaces, spackled with parasites. My dominant feeling was of muscled energy gone still, of fading awe. Death had lifted him from the water's privacy and placed him before me. The stillness gradually liberated my curiosity, and with it a nascent, but for a while equally inhibiting, sense of guilt: any scamp can poke a dead whale.

In reality, my father was a smallish man, physically undramatic, sometimes funny, often subdued, measured, decent, generous, rarely casual. Many years ago, I visited the concentration camp at Dachau, Germany. In front of the museum stood a bronze memorial figure of a nondescript Jew in a thin overcoat, hands in pockets: an everyman. Though taller and thinner, the figure reminded me of my father. Readers of biographies know about writers' excesses: Hemingway in one of his fits of rage, breaking Steinbeck's beloved walking stick. Dickinson hiding for decades in her room. Mailer marrying six times. Dad was not flamboyant or eccentric. He was responsible, sober, familial. He spent many hours at his desk writing and correcting student papers; many more reading in a chair. He was not one to allow his quotient of destructiveness free rein.

The behemoth in my mind could claim no more physical place in nature than some Elizabethan's illustration of a New World beast. In part it represented my little-girl desire for a powerful father and the excitement of his success. Yet the fanciful creature also captured other accurate perceptions: my father's distrust of women, the true intensity of his carefully managed emotions, the sheer force of his ambition. Fiction writing is nearly impossible without substantial ego. It takes strength to bear the preposterousness of the endeavor, the inevitable defeat. And hungry egos draw their plankton where they can.

I was loath to return to contemplating him. Only slowly did my curiosity outpace my reluctance.

I BORROWED THE TWO notebooks and let them sit for several months on my desk. Then I opened them. As I read them, my feelings changed. I found myself wanting to know everything — curious to understand who he'd been as a child, how he'd become a writer. I regretted all I hadn't asked. No, that's not quite right. I regretted that he had died before I'd felt ready to invite the conversations about his life we might have had.

FOLDED IN ONE NOTEBOOK, I found a few brown-stained pieces of paper, apparently from the late 1940s, on which Dad had listed events from his childhood. They seemed as good a starting point as any. I recognized few names.

GRAMMAR SCHOOL

Aged (6)	1. The Pecker incident: 1A.
Aged (12)	2. The Rappaport lost auto license incident.
Aged (10–11)	3. Proposal to Hilda McDermott
Aged (7–8)	4. Fight with boy — lost
14–15?	5. Lying to Mrs. Snider
8–14?	6. Looking at Mama with the match.

HIGH SCHOOL

Aged 18	1. The cooperation-in-govt episode with Frank Rexjond.
18	2. Borrowing buck from Clara (Same day)

COLLEGE

19–20	1. Doris Milman incident
20	2. Drooling on Mimi
	3. The fight
	4. Bawled out in Pine Hill Dining room
	5. Job: You Stink

AFTER COLLEGE

C. Frankel's Trial
Dr. Burrell Cohen
The Ticket Line — movie — forcing way ahead
Gregory Peck: Huntington Museum

romit biz with rafferran elev + Schmeitzer

1. night Don was here for first time.
2. Reading ch. to him.

3. Reading ch. 12 to Mike and Bud
4. Reading Kafka Review to all assembled
5. Bernadette-Alex incident (forced confession)

I brought the pages with me one evening in the summer of 2003 when I visited my mother. What do you know? I asked, and slowly read her each entry. Very little. She recognized nothing in the "Grammar School" section. Under "High School," she suggested that Clara would have been Clara Molendyke, a teacher at Erasmus Hall, who had befriended Dad and a group of his friends. In "College," Mom knew Doris Milman as one of Dad's lifelong friends; "Drooling on Mimi" referred to his having fallen in love, his devotion painfully unreturned, with Doris's sister, Miriam. In "After College," Mom described how during the summer of 1946, they had traveled to California to visit her mother and stepfather. One afternoon they glimpsed and greeted Gregory Peck in front of the Huntington Museum. She did not know the significance. The last entries seem to have had something to do with reading some of his early writing, perhaps the novel he later burned, to friends — Don Early, Mike Seide, Bud Evslin. Finally, Alex and Bernadette Inkeles were close, lifelong friends of my parents, initially my mother's from Cornell. But "incident"? "Forced confession"? My mother had no memory.

Curious to find out whether, sixty years later, any knowledge remained, I wrote to the Inkeleses, and Alex e-mailed back:

Janna: Neither Bernadette nor I can tell what the reference to forced confession might have been. You know your father insisted on scrupulous honesty in personal relations, and so may have felt he pushed someone — and likely us — too hard in that direction. In some ways he seemed to feel he needed that as a writer, and some people may have been offended to be pressed so hard about intimate thoughts and feelings. He balanced this by often saying "Never destroy the mystery of the human personality."[2]

It seems the list writer may have been ruminating upon a misdeed his friends hadn't noticed. Alex's response captures well an aspect of my father: how his urgencies sometimes dragged the rest of him along. He'd elbow in and then feel awkward. His desire to stare into other people's intimacies heightened his wish to shield himself, to peer out of a blind. A much later example comes to mind. Of the many faculty-student liaisons going on at Bennington College in the 1960s and 1970s, one between a music professor and his student became a particular topic of conversation. Later, in the late 1970s, around the time *Dubin's Lives* was published, the young woman had a housewarming party to celebrate her purchase and restoration of a farmhouse. Mom and Dad were invited. As the hostess walked out of the house and onto the green expanse of lawn toward her gathered friends, a large chilled bottle of champagne in each hand, Dad stopped her and, seemingly unaware of place and moment, said, "I just want you to know you're not the model for Fanny" (Dubin's mistress in the novel). The woman later confided to a mutual friend that it had taken much self-restraint not to bash him with a bottle.

AFTER READING AND REREADING Dad's list, I have come to feel that it is an inventory of embarrassments: lying; prematurely proposing marriage; losing a fight; getting told he stinks; having to borrow money; loving without control ("drooling"), his passion unreturned; pushing ahead in a movie line; rushing a movie star; feeling forced to confess, or forcing others to do so. I imagine he cataloged the memories at a moment when he was trying to corral some troubling sense of self. He wrote lists all the time on pieces of yellow newsprint, always had one on his desk of "things to do," often neatly subdivided: letters, telephone calls, class planning, social engagements, and so on. They were a preferred way of making order, and it wouldn't have been unlike him to write to soothe unmanageable feelings, to steady himself with words. Years later, close to death, he would attempt to quiet panic about his diseased heart by carefully listing symptoms.

"The Pecker incident" might refer to a story I overheard him tell my brother once in Oregon, apparently to help Paul understand why the boys' gym class required jockstraps. Paul and I each had a small, eaved bedroom, the only rooms upstairs in our house. At bedtime, Dad would come up some nights to tuck us in, sitting for a few minutes first with one, then the other. Paul was four years older, and their more substantial conversations sometimes caught my ear. I'd lie still in bed, trying to decode door-muffled words. When too puzzled, I'd sometimes ask Dad to repeat to me what he'd said to Paul. On this evening, he described a bunch of childhood buddies racing each other down a long hill. At the bottom, they stopped quickly, and the winner's erect penis popped out of his open fly, surprising him and provoking considerable amusement among his pals. As the tale was told, the exposed protagonist was some other boy. Maybe not. Or maybe this one was a different pecker incident.

THE MOST HAUNTING PHRASE on the pages is "Looking at Mama with the match"; next to it a large temporal uncertainty — "8–14?" Other memories are attached pretty well to years; this one is singularly inexact, unlocated by age or grade. What was he doing? If I could ask him a single question, this one might be it. I imagine darkness, silence, a late hour, all but my father asleep. He tiptoes to his mother's bed, lights a match, and stares at her for the flame's instant. What does he see? A poor, ill, still youngish Russian Jewish woman sleeping. If I am correct to surmise shame as the list's coalescing affect, what was this moment's contribution? Feeling drawn to examine her secretly or something he saw? Perhaps he hoped her insanity would still itself in sleep, allow him to find his mother beneath its surface. Or maybe, after he'd caught her trying to kill herself, he simply wanted to watch her breathing and felt ashamed of the need. Did he do it more than once? "Mama." *Mama* is a gentle word — plaintive, intimate, evocative, pleading.

What about his mama? In 1982, Dad underwent heart bypass surgery, suffered a stroke on the operating table, and almost died. Several days later, I flew west to his hospital bedside. He was alive but not yet coherent. "What is your name?" a nurse asked him. "William," he confabulated. She noted that he was disoriented. "How old are you?" "Fifty-seven." He was about to turn sixty-eight. He had published *Dubin's Lives* three years earlier, in 1979, dedicating it to his mother, father, and aunt. Through William Dubin, the book's biographer protagonist, he talked some about his past and hinted at his experience of his mother.

The book is a thick tangle of creation and memory. And while Dubin's maternal recollections may have happened only to Dubin, the feelings of anguished shame are of a sort that haunted Dad.

> He remembered when he was twelve, one day walking home from school with his seventh-grade teacher, a broken-nosed knowing nasally talkative young man. As they were walking, this strange reddish-haired woman wearing a green hat trimmed with brown felt flowers approached in excitement from down the block. When William saw his insane mother coming toward them he said goodbye in the middle of somebody's sentence and hurried across the street. When he looked back she was standing alone on the sidewalk, sobbing, crazily waving her fist.[3]

Later in the book:

> He had once, as a child, noticed menstrual blood on her petticoat and she told him she had had a nosebleed. "There on the back, Mama?" "I turned my head to look for something." . . . One day he

asked her to take him to the movies and she had promised. In those days a child had to ask an adult to take him in and Willie didn't like to. He waited all afternoon for his mother to come down and accompany him to the movies. She came down wearing an old hat. They walked half a block, and then she said she couldn't go, and wept, and went back upstairs . . .

When she was dead and he and Charlie Dubin were alone in the house sitting shivah, the waiter sat soaking his purple-veined feet as he read his newspaper. William had felt shame for his father, for his ineffectuality, unwillingness to try to be more than a poor waiter — for hiding his crazy wife in the back bedroom. Without knowing why, as he looked at him, he felt then a sudden keen compassion for the old man. It seemed to the son that whatever else Charlie could or couldn't do, he had done what he had to. The boy was ashamed of having been ashamed of him. Years later he forgave his mother for having lived her insane life in his presence. It was the only life she had to live.[4]

One of two memories Dad told me in 1985, before, a few minutes into it, he asked me to turn off the tape recorder (the only time he let me record him), was of himself as a boy waiting with a friend for his mother to come down and take them to the movies. In spite of her having agreed to do it, she was too ill and couldn't leave the apartment. They waited with growing restlessness and I'm sure, on his part, embarrassment. He'd promised his friend he'd get them in. Time passed; the movie started long before she came; I'm not sure she ever did.

Throughout his adult life, Dad was absolutely, compulsively prompt. He never arrived at a train station or airport less than an hour early, often more. He became agitated, sometimes to the point of fury, if my mother held up their departure for a dinner party, and he was often the first guest to arrive. Friends recall driving to a wedding celebration with my parents one summer in Vermont. My mother had made a large cooked-vegetable salad to contribute, and in the last-minute hurry had forgotten it on the counter. When she realized her mistake — half an hour into the trip — my father refused to return. It would make them late.

I NEXT UNFOLDED, also tucked into one of the journals, the Erasmus Hall Class Day program from February 1932. Course work finished, my father, along with some of his classmates, graduated from high school midway through their senior year. The Class Day ceremony was a closing ritual: a daylong talent show with performances of "Eccentric Dance," "Spanish Dance," and "Jazz Tap," as well as "Songs," "Presentation of Knocks," and "Play." It was also the occasion for awards, and the back page lists twenty-one "Class Celebrities." Bernard Malamud is named three times: He is one of five seniors nominated for the Erasmian Medal. (He did not win it, but he did win the Richard Young Prize for essay writing.) He is also listed as class actor and as Judge Leonard Botal, the male lead in the Anatole France play performed that day, *The Man Who Married a Dumb Wife*.

It was a surprise to find him so prominently celebrated. I had imagined him as slightly bookish and quiet in high school. But not at all; he was gregarious, energetic, and outgoing, with a circle of good pals. Though not particularly coordinated, he was physically active. He played stoopball, street games, even a little tennis. He roughhoused with buddies. He dated girls. Friends from that era recall that he was a known figure in most of his classes. By the time I knew him, the actor had disappeared into his writing — except for slight glimpses one would get when he told stories or jokes. He kept a physical playfulness. Occasionally, he'd wrestle gently with my brother or, when I insisted, with me. He'd give us "horse" rides on his back.

*   *   *

THE ESSAY THAT WON the 1932 Richard Young Prize is titled "Life — From Behind a Counter." In it, the young writer tells how at thirteen he took a part-time job in his father's grocery. He describes neighborhood characters and life lessons drawn from his four years as a clerk. He already writes vividly. You can see the effect of his P.S. 181 and Erasmus education, for in a single paragraph he refers to Hamlet, Wordsworth, and Beethoven. You can also hear the humor and the vernacular that will characterize his fiction. He describes "the old Swedish lady from the home, who speaks in slow tremulous tones, and says — 'De drooble iss ven you get ouldt, you ken't eat so much.'"[5]

The first long anecdote is of the teenage clerk arguing with a wealthy female customer about which cheese she ordered, then being humiliated by her. "A tall woman entered dressed richly in furs," he begins. As he tells the story, she deliberately lets him slice the wrong cheese for her, then castigates him. He argues back. "Finally with a very well enunciated and perfectly pronounced 'Stupid,' she strode haughtily out of the store."[6]

The essay also describes a gunpoint holdup similar to one that occurs in *The Assistant*. One day, when Dad had stepped out to buy a newspaper, two boys, one of whom he knew slightly, pulled a gun on Max and his clerk, locked them in a closet, and emptied the cash register. Not long after, the police caught the thieves. Right before the trial, the younger boy's parents approached Max and begged him to drop the charges, which he did. Eventually, the boy himself appeared and apologized: "About one year later, he came into the store and blushingly introduced himself. He showed my father his bank book. He said that he was working hard and would soon be married. He thanked my father for giving him a chance."[7]

THE CLASS DAY PROGRAM and the essay illustrate my father's good fortune that Brooklyn was the home of both P.S. 181 and

Erasmus Hall High School. In a bit of family history he wrote late in life, listing various childhood addresses, he noted that when he lived at 2700 Albemarle Road, "I went to P.S. 181, the most important school in my life." As a young boy, he'd somehow gotten himself transferred out of district into this outstanding grade school, five miles from his home. To get to P.S. 181, he, as an eight- or nine-year-old, had to make a forty-five-minute trip — two trolleys each way — alone every day. He thrived in the new environment, and, as he later recalled, he began writing: "In grammar school, where I lived in a state of self-enhancing discovery, I turned school assignments into stories. Once I married off Roger Williams of Rhode Island to an Indian maiden, mainly because I had worked up an early feeling for the romantic."[8]

He made lifelong friends — boys from stable, more established families, who admired his pluck and invited him into their homes, creating for him some refuge. One, Herb Wittkin, wrote about Dad as having been unusually adept at capturing the warm interest of adults:

> I marvelled at his composure when he conversed with my parents in my home. And when it came to teachers, he took them captive. All the teachers in the last three years at P.S. 181 — Mrs. McDermott, Mr. Squires and Mrs. Ahner — fell under his spell.
>
> The nature of his attachment to his teachers was unique. It was not truly that of a teacher's pet . . . It was engaging more than ingratiating. He volunteered his services, initiated projects and mixed in a healthy amount of seduction, so that he became more of a child affiliate of the teacher than a pet.
>
> He talked himself into most of the choice positions involving extracurricular activities that provided him with some measure of prominence and authority. This characteristic, this tendency to find his way into his teachers' hearts remained a constant throughout his school years.[9]

The environment also fed his mind. Another friend, Hans Kerber, recalled in a letter to me that the atmosphere was rich. For instance, their fourth-grade teacher would often play classical music records for them.[10]

OCCASIONALLY, during my growing up, Dad mentioned Erasmus Hall. He'd name a teacher or remind me that he still, on visits to New York, saw Erasmian friends. I understood that the school mattered to him, but not why. Only lately, in a conversation with my parents' physician, Norman Selverstone, who attended Erasmus soon after Dad, did I finally grasp how important this school had been in forming the nascent writer.

Erasmus Hall was founded privately by the Dutch in the eighteenth century, given to the city of Brooklyn in the late nineteenth century, and rebuilt and revitalized in the early twentieth century to educate the immigrant flood that included my father. Modeled on Oxford, it comprised a whole campus of buildings clustered around a courtyard. The buildings were stately, covered with ivy and accented with gargoyles and carvings, the architecture pointing unself-consciously toward England and Europe. Look at an old photo, and you glimpse a pure belief in public education that now, seventy years later, has become so tarnished that simply contemplating its older, unembarrassed assertion is moving. It was a fine school, available to penniless kids. The teachers were erudite, often with Ph.D.'s. Selverstone recalled that in his day, seven foreign languages were taught. Dad's notebooks show that he studied French and Latin. His friend Hannah Needle Broder wrote me a reminiscence that also suggests the tone of the place and its impact on Dad — as well as his way of approaching girls:

> I met Bern in Miss Mastin's English class. She was a poet of some note and had an ability to convey her enthusiasm for literature and

creative writing to the members of her class. Learning from her was a rewarding experience and Bern often gave her credit with kindling his original desire to become a writer. One day, Bern came up to me and said, "I like your dress." (It was a pretty dress.) The next day I returned the compliment by telling him, "I like your poem." That is how our friendship began.[11]

Miraculously — considering the mediocrity of many schools now and then — my father received, free, a first-rate "classical" education at P.S. 181, Erasmus, and later City College. I don't think it's an overstatement to say that the schools transformed him, not only by providing daily sanctuary from his home life but also by exposing him to dedicated teaching, books, and ideas. At the very least, his teachers' interest in his talent helped him determine that he would write. His parents repeatedly told him that education would liberate him from their drudgery and secure him opportunity in America, and these schools lit the path of egress. In a fond piece his friend Miriam Milman Lang wrote about him after he died, she recalled how focused he already was during college on becoming a successful writer. The "all consuming belief [that he'd become a famous author] colored his entire outlook, both verbally and non-verbally. I remember his reaction after we visited my cousin, Sidney Kingsley, who, in his late twenties, had recently won the Pulitzer Prize for his first play . . . After we left, Bernie was silent, but I sensed as though he had uttered the words, 'Some day *I'm* going to win the Pulitzer.'"[12]

NOT SURPRISINGLY, my father loved telling this joke: A poor, pious man, who has fallen on hard times, prays to God asking to win the lottery. "Dear God, I am a very poor man. I have suffered greatly. I have many debts and a family I cannot support. Please, use your power to allow me to win the lottery." Nothing happens, and the next week the man prays again. "Dear God, I prayed to you last week and asked to win the lottery. Did you not hear my prayer? My need is large, and yet I have asked you for so little. Why did you not help me?" Another week passes. "I am a patient man, God. But it seems so unjust that I, one of your creatures, should be suffering so, should pray to you to win the lottery, and should have my prayers unanswered." Nothing happens for another week. "God, I find myself getting angrier and angrier at you. I've served you faithfully, prayed to you that I might win the lottery, but silence. Why don't you give me a break?" As he's praying, the sky goes black: thick thunderclouds everywhere; lightning. Suddenly, a voice booms down out of the heavens: "Why don't you give *me* a break? At least buy a ticket."

In the midst of the Great Depression, when he had to worry about having the nickel to ride the subway from the grocery store to school, writing was the lottery ticket Bernard Malamud bought.

MY FATHER KEPT his two early notebooks in tandem, starting the first in 1933, when he was nineteen and a freshman at City College, and the second a year later, when he was twenty. They initially seem intended for different purposes, one more of a commonplace book, the other a "drawer" in which to gather writing projects: stories, plays, poems, novels, book titles. But before long, the entries overlap. Each includes quotations, ideas, personal observations, self-admonitions, transcribed bits of conversations, and letters. There is nothing intimately descriptive about his family and few expansive accounts of his own activities. But they shed light on his inner life and particularly speak to my curiosity about his efforts to make himself into a writer.

Both are composition books, the white parts of their black-and-white-speckled covers now gone yellow, their black bindings torn, their pages brown and brittle. One is larger and thicker than the other. Its label says "Graham A/L Special," and next to "Name" is penned in a careful cursive, "Le Livre de Bernard Malamud." Inside, on the blue-lined first page, a neat handwritten "Table of Contents" lists each of the years covered: 1933–1941. He seems to have felt a need for secrecy as he started, for the first page of text is headlined in a coded Greek-like alphabet, which I made no attempt to decipher. In spite of his high school prize, few around him found him terribly plausible when he said he wanted to be a writer, so the hubris of the undertaking may have heightened his natural inclination to hide.[13]

The serious content of his own reading, and its breadth, immediately stands out. The list of novelists, philosophers, critics, poets, and playwrights whom he quotes includes Longfellow, Swift, William James, Nehru, Samuel Johnson, Rossetti, Bacon, Swinburne, John Stuart Mill, George Bernard Shaw, Homer, Catullus, Verlaine, Protagoras, Buddha, Freud, Victor Hugo, Aldous Huxley, Lord Byron, Aristophanes, De Quincey, Thomas Mann, Edwin Arlington Robinson, Shelley, Shakespeare, Hippocrates, Flaubert, Lucretius, Homer, Matthew Arnold, Ruskin, Spinoza, the Bible, Emerson, Meredith, Melville, Wordsworth, Carlyle, Somerset Maugham, Mencken, Coleridge, Thackeray, Browning, Elinor Wylie, Edna St. Vincent Millay, and John Masefield.

What was this effort about? He possessed pure intellectual curiosity, but something more seems also to have been in play. As I read his entries, I found myself thinking about his much anthologized 1956 short story "A Summer's Reading." In it, a high school dropout, George Stoyonovich, whose mother has died, is jobless while the rest of his impoverished family works. He stays in his bedroom all day and aimlessly wanders the streets after dark. One night, asked about his summer by a neighbor, Mr. Cattanzara, George tells a lie. He claims that he is spending his time reading one hundred books. The news of a scholar-in-the-making spreads quickly through the neighborhood, creating fresh respect for

George and lifting his mood. But as weeks pass and no books are seen, his sister and Mr. Cattanzara separately confront him. He has betrayed them by claiming accomplishment he hasn't earned. The story ends: "One evening in the fall, George ran out of his house to the library, where he hadn't been in years. There were books all over the place, wherever he looked, and though he was struggling to control an inward trembling, he easily counted off a hundred, then sat down at a table to read."[14]

The notebooks reflect a similar undertaking. (George's actual circumstances resemble Eugene's rather than Dad's, and the story in part must reflect my father's longing to see his ill brother leave his room and begin a life.) They document a young man's effort to become his grand claim. By purchasing the two notebooks, Bernard Malamud declared himself an intellectual and a writer, not a grocery clerk. On one level, he must have felt relieved to assume the identity. But the pages also show how troubled he was by his ambition. Was he right to think he had talent? Or was he a fool? He didn't know whether he had donned clothes that fit him or a presumptuous outfit that misled him and others and would finally draw only ridicule. The notebooks record his persistent struggles as he labored to become a writer, to rivet his inflated fantasy to solid practice. They also repeatedly confirm the value he put on books: no matter how mundane his daily reality, he could transform himself by reading them. Repeatedly in his stories and novels, his protagonists — Frank Alpine in *The Assistant,* Yakov Bok in *The Fixer,* Willie Spearmint in *The Tenants* — discover themselves as serious moral beings by reading.

FROM THE FIRST journal entry:

> 1933 — In autumn, as I watch the multi-colored leaves drift sadly to the ground, and as I breathe the bewitching autumn air, and gaze

long at the silver rivers in the heavens — invariably, I feel a lonely exaltation of Spirit and I long vaguely for many things. During that time of year, how thrilling it is to hear the soft rustle of silks in a darkened room, to gaze fascinated at the red lips of ladies who laugh, to breathe in deeply their entrancing perfumes, and, as you dance with them, to feel their silken hair lightly against your cheek . . . How much satisfaction is derived from those scintillating conversations . . . when every lady is seduced by the potency of your imagination. I think I enjoy life so much because I use people according to the Kantian doctrine. I mean "Ding-an-zich" — thing in itself. Kant said to use people as "ends" never as "means." Therefore, when I meet one of these charming young ladies, as we talk — we become spellbound by something intangible within ourselves. And as we discuss its beauties and sorrows, our minds become subservient to one another, and 'though I could, I go no further than the kiss that invariably follows. If I did, I'd be using her as an end to my own personal lust, rather than a companion in ecstasy . . . I guess I'll have to explain this attitude of mine towards people to the emotionally tender soul who marries me. I'll tell her of my deep feeling for people, of my belief that individuality should be retained in marriage. And if she understands — as she will, we will live such a beautiful and happy life.[15]

The callow style, German romantic with a touch of T. S. Eliot, is almost unrecognizable as my father's, yet the nascent writer is already into several of his lifelong themes: morality, ideal love, and how to reconcile marital fidelity with seductive pleasure and lust. It seems he'd had an evening out, met a girl, charmed her, and returned to his room happy, aroused, a little emboldened with success. Perhaps his elation gives him the courage to begin writing.

A day or so later, the ebullience is punctured, and he's copying out sober quotations. Though likely writing most immediately in response to the ups and downs of his pursuit of young women, he seems also to have his mother's death in mind.

Boswell wrote when he heard of Johnson's death, "I was stunned, and in a kind of amaze . . . I did not shed tears. I was not tenderly affected. My feeling was one large expanse of stupor . . . I knew that I should afterwards have sorer sensations."

Tertullian said, "Women thou shouldst ever go in mourning and sackcloth, thy eyes filled with tears. Thou has brought about the ruin of mankind."[16]

THE NOTEBOOKS HOLD my father's own early writing efforts. In November 1933, he copies into one what may be his first sonnet, about lost love, one of the few he wrote: "Now let me weep amidst the dying leaves / These tears to quench the sparks tho' dead, yet glow."[17]

Early in 1935, about to turn twenty-one, he records his first story idea: "Situation: a man loves a woman who is nurse of some kids. On Sundays she meets him on the trolley car. They go places — suppose the kids are left to the nurse somehow. The man likes them to [too] — they have trouble but finally manage to win the kids for themselves?"[18]

In October 1936, the first mention of a play:

October 11, 1936 — Idea for one act play: Dramatize Wm. Wordsworth "Guilt + Sorrow, or Incidents upon Salisbury Plain" 1842[19]

October 12, 1936 — "Her infant Babe / Had from its mother caught the thick of grief, and sighed among its playthings." "The Ruined Cottage" — William Wordsworth[20]

October 16 and 17, 1936 — Begun work on my first play.[21]

HIS ROMANTIC UPS AND DOWNS run through the journals, sometimes recorded fully, more often cryptically. His deepest feelings are for Miriam Milman. I'm unsure exactly when he first fell in love, but by 1934 he is "drooling" over her. In July 1934, beside the initials MM, he writes, "When you speak, it is music in my heart, when you smile, it is laughter in my soul." In April 1935, he copies into the notebook the letter in which she confessed that she does not love him:

> "Bernie, when I said I liked you I meant it sincerely — and it's the kind of feeling that's indestructible. I guess it isn't love — I only wish it was, because love is very beautiful. Almost, I caught beauty, but it has eluded me — as it always does . . . I guess it sounds like 'Cant we be friends?' but its really not as trite as all that. Its an indefinable relationship, much deeper. I know I'm being a trial to you and I'm sorry, awfully sorry, but Bernie, can't we make a go of it in accordance with the way matters stand?" — Written at Wellesley, Wednesday April third. Received by me Friday, April fifth.

From "The answer — written April fifth":

> The moving finger has dotted the two (i)s and underlined the word <u>finis</u>
>
> Perhaps it is better so; you've always been a "mansion unpossessed" and I've always been unsatisfied. Now, at least, there is a certain calm satiety in finality.
>
> I'm glad, both for your sake and mine, that you've had courage enough to stop my being a source of uneasiness to you. I wish also, that you'd utilize this same courage to end difficulties you experience in life — to cleanse yourself of futility, to overtake and possess beauty. Somehow, I should like to see you content, happy. You deserve happiness.
>
> Thanks once more, for your more than kindness to me; at least, I can say that I tried to be worthy of you. There are some debts that remain unpayable — yet, I feel that I was able, in some small measure, to return "something" you gave me.[22]

He tried, when deeply wounded, to be larger than his feelings; he demanded of himself a gracious reply, though its stiffness suggests large effort. The sentences that seem most exactly him begin when he declares himself "glad" that she has been able "to stop my being a source of uneasiness to you" and his more critical admonition that she use this same courage to improve her life in other areas. I hear it as a familiar "teacher/father" voice.

For years after, he wrote occasional short entries about her.

January 6, 1936 — Looking at Mimi to-day, quite dispassionately. Of course, it's psychologic — but she seems a goddess grown human.

February 6, 1936 — Remember when I called her Miriam — I choked?

February 7, 1936 — I continue to suck the vinegar-ice of disappointment, so that my lips are cold, and my tongue is thick with bitterness.[23]

August 14, 1938 — It was August, the August summer day that I've always wanted to describe. I was sitting on a bench on Columbia campus waiting for Miriam and the thought came to me how much I didn't belong, and how much I wanted to belong.

A few days later, I thought of my relations with Irene W. and of how much I wanted love — belonging to someone.[24]

March 14, 1940 — Has loving Miriam passionately conditioned me for a certain type of beauty only? I can't understand Janice and me. Kisses as cold as forgotten cereal.[25]

Friends recalled "Bernie" as a ladies' man from grade school on — eagerly dating, continually speaking with his buddies about girls. Herb Wittkin wrote about himself and Dad as young teenagers, exciting themselves by talking about different girls' and teachers' bodies, then measuring their erections with rulers. During college, my father proposed to Hannah Needle (Broder) as well as Miriam. But "Mimi" evoked his most intense feelings and served as the standard against which others failed. In the piece she wrote for me, Miriam Milman Lang described how they got to know each other in 1930 in Brooklyn "at the Youth Group at Temple Beth Emeth, to which my family belonged." He was sixteen; she was fifteen.

> The first year, Bernie and I didn't actually date . . . As a compromise, we'd arrive separately at the Sunday evening Youth Group meetings, after which Bernie would walk me home along the maple-lined streets of our quiet neighborhood. On the way, he liked to clown with the irrepressible spirit of a Groucho Marx ad-libbing melodramatically in iambic pentameter alternating with a convincing Hebrew chant. Between laughter and embarrassment, I'd try to hush him, for fear of what the neighbors might think.[26]

She found him "strangely silent" about his family. "To all intents and purposes, then Bernie seemed like an orphan in need of family closeness. He enjoyed stopping by our house of an afternoon to visit with anyone who happened to be around: me, my two younger sisters and brothers, even my parents." She recalled how later, as his feelings for her intensified, he admitted to her that he occasionally stood outside her house — after a date, or if she'd been out with someone else — secretly watching, hoping to glimpse her through a window. He was sometimes awkwardly provocative with her about sex, once pulling out a condom and dangling it in front of her face — at a time, she felt, before he had actually used one. Later, he bragged to her about taking another girl into the woods, ending his letter, "And then I honored her with my body." Generally, there was more talk than action: "Since I had all the repressions of my generation and he was inexperienced, our intimacy didn't go beyond primary necking. Actually, I'd say that, based on the fact that he never pressured me, Bernie was remarkably chaste for the era." But, she observed, "he was governed by the age-old male chauvinism: he put the individual woman on a pedestal, while at the same time he regarded sex and the sexual woman as degraded."[27]

Something about his feelings for her stayed with him through the years. When, in the early 1960s, he fell in love with a student, he wrote to Miriam, seemingly out of the blue, asking her to return his old love letters. She explained that they'd been thrown out some years earlier. He expressed relief: "Sometimes I shudder at what a romantic kid I was."[28]

THE NOTEBOOKS are a repository for descriptions of Dad's world, himself, the way his feelings work. He practices recording observations, notes moods, attempts to figure out his life.

> October 29, 1939 — I can't keep track of the many many psychological changes that I have undergone, bit by bit during the last year. All I know is that there is a kind of complete emotional blocking in me. No sense of thrill. No feeling of soaring ambition. No intense feeling of any kind, as if my feelings were chained to earth.
>
> Why? Perhaps Horty [Hortense Batchker], and with her the vision of a prosaic life. The school teacher with a decent salary. The comforting wife, etc. But that's not all, if it is *it*. I'm blocked because I can no longer believe; or if I do believe, I haven't any way — or anything to believe in. The times have stripped me of all my ideals . . .
>
> There may be a way out. I want very much to write, but I haven't picked up my pen these long months. What am I afraid of?[29]

"There may be a way out . . . What am I afraid of?" he asks himself as a twenty-five-year-old. He is circling, unable to settle, reading more than writing. He copies out lines from poems and prose. He continues to assemble himself, gather nerve. Sometimes the entries are hopeful; more often he recounts depression, stomachaches, despair. It seems there was much to fear: a wish not to seem ridiculous in his ambition; reluctance to reencounter old pain; the absence of work prospects that would allow him to write and support a family; a sense that sanity is fragile and quickly lost; a near certainty, examining the artist's odds, that he will fail; and unremitting poverty — "and always want," as he names it. On December 14, 1939, he writes, "Perhaps I ought to remember only that I'm warm this winter. Twelve pounds, one scarf, one pair of green gloves warmer."[30]

A few months later, he copies into the notebook a letter, an agonized cri de coeur written to his friend Ben Loeb. He is badly depressed. He once allowed to me that he'd felt enough despair at some moments during these years to at least glance at suicide. My image/memory is based on a brief account he offered of winter cold — a desolate, skinny, poor young man walking in traffic in the snow, wishing for an accident that would kill him. But he returned to his room.

Dec. 22, 1939. Friday.

Dear Ben,

    School has ended for a while, and I came home to rest to find myself physically sick and spiritually tormented.

    I told you about my new regimen. I haven't got used to it, so my stomach feels worse than ever. Once more the noises of the night — a sleep word from my brother, the drone of an aeroplane following the beam across my house, the cat in the hall, the man upstairs going to work — tear me from my dreams — stuffed sleep into sleeplessness. Once more my eyes have begun to hurt, and the lid of my left eye has begun to twitch. My days are filled with a sort of cream-cheesy pain. A pain that is soft, and can be spread in thin layers over bread — my body.

That's enough to torment anyone, but my life — the rag-like thing it is — adds more agony. I feel bound to emptiness, to disbelief, to the slime of the twentieth century spirit. I feel as though I had eaten something of death's, and that it putrefies me.

What is it? Perhaps the fact that I have no place as yet for next term is worrying me. The future looks so dark. Perhaps it's because I've ceased to believe in anything. Perhaps it's because I'm so everlastingly lonely. Perhaps its the way things are going in the world —

"For this, for everything, we are out of tune; / It moves us not . . ."

It must be all of these things.

I'm trying not to rant, Ben. You've helped teach me sobriety. But I don't know where I'm being blown. I feel like crying out. I feel the strength of my will, like a steel flame from a steel candle, and it is forcing me to live. Bernie.[31]

My heart ached for him when I read the letter. The winter of 1939 into 1940 appears to have dragged his mood to its lowest, loneliest ebb. Why then? Sometimes I read the journals less as a curious daughter and more as an inquisitive psychotherapist or would-be sleuth. And after I'd reread various entries enough times, I came to feel that 1938 was a fulcrum year for my father in his becoming a writer. A balance tipped. His voice shifted. Although there must have been many reasons — he was maturing, he was studying for his master's degree at Columbia, he was tutoring German immigrants in English and expanding his worldview — a key one appears to have been his discovery of Freud's writing, and from it an ability to return more directly to considering his own life, particularly his mother's death.

Freud is now often treated like a slightly demented uncle who drags down the holiday mood by blabbing off-key stories everyone has heard too many times. Many consider him old news. Certainly,

he got lots of things wrong — but then so did Plato. Throughout my childhood, I heard his name spoken with respect and his
ideas pondered. Reading Freud changed my father. What's more,
throughout the 1930s, many German and Austrian psychoanalyti-
cally trained refugees fleeing Hitler settled in New York City, and
Dad found himself in their midst. Psychoanalytic ideas let Dad see
new meaning in his own struggles and were part of what permitted
him to stop fleeing himself and his life.

BEFORE 1938 in the journals, only an occasional "practice" paragraph diverges from a flowery, romantic manner Dad assumes
while writing about desire and loss. When he first decided to become a writer, he left his world and his native tongue. He imitated
and absorbed other writers, keeping much of his actual environment at arm's length. The entries that he produced in this persona
tend to be stilted, far from the tone into which he later settles. Here
is an example from early February 1938. His subject is grief, but he
is self-distanced and mannered.

> February 1, 1938 — Upon me, as upon many others scattered thinly
> by tens and twenties over every thousand years, fell too powerfully
> and too early the vision of life. The horror of life mixed itself al-
> ready in earliest youth with the heavenly sweetness of life; that
> grief which one in a hundred has sensibility enough to gather from
> the sad retrospect of life in its closing stage for *me* shed its dews as a
> prelibation upon the fountains of life whilst yet sparkling to the
> morning sun. I saw from afar and from before what I was to see
> from behind.[32]

Already, in early 1938, as the next entry shows, he is thinking
more about more realistic scenes. But his reference in the next entry to Henry Adams, Matthew Arnold, and T. S. Eliot — three
writers whose defining common characteristic is their intellectual

focus and profound personal and cultural reserve — suggest that he hadn't yet found models who fit him well enough to release his voice and allow his developing narratives to move from mind to paper.

> February 16, 1938 — One scene has been growing in my mind lately: a young man lives by himself in a strange city. His room is small, bare, but clean and contains a few books. The backyard is large and has as its regular inhabitants several cats whom he has come to know and name because he has watched them so often. Of course, their is a woman in the house. She gets to know him only after accidentally opening the door in his room and seeing him sitting on his empty bed, on the springs, burning out the bed bugs from the coiled springs at each end of the spring.
>
> The time is evidently one of some kind of defeat or youthful emptiness.
>
> His stomach is gassy; his food is bad. Eyes are strained and luxury of any kind brings discomfort — because he has become a stranger to living the full life that he, above all, was meant to live. Shall their affair be miserable or cleansing? She could be (A) the usual woman with the usual broken heart which has become petrified, or (B) the woman afraid of becoming an old maid.
>
> Somehow — this whole episode, or the result of this episode should produce the flavor of Henry Adams, Matthew Arnold's poetry and T. S. Eliot's poetry: decay, despair, stoicism.[33]

Then something shifts. For the first time, three entries in February reveal that he has Freud on his mind. In all three, he is trying out psychoanalytic ideas as a new way of thinking about morality, of understanding himself, and also as potential literary material. As he struggles with his sense of failure, one hears harbingers of many of his protagonists, including the soon-to-materialize Roy Hobbs in his novel *The Natural*.

February 13, 1938 — Is morality one of the results of mens tendency towards masochism and sadism:

A) A man fails repeatedly in life

B) Unconsciously he tends to punish himself for his failures

C) One form of doing so is to lose all sense of objectivity and blame the failure on himself because (masochism + sadism — disimilation of psychic energy) he did or did not do something he should or should not have done.

D) Soon he is blaming himself not for failing but for not propitiating these external forces which by now have become a morality.[34]

The entry is convoluted but important. At age twenty-four, he had lost faith in himself. He is not becoming a famous writer. He's not sure he's doing much of anything. Difficult feelings — apparently including his own masochism and sadism — torment and overwhelm him. Reading Freud gives him a new perspective. He grasps that moral codes are not just rules handed down by authorities — tablets delivered from on high. They may actually originate in psychological conflict. They may be internal torments — like his self-blame — writ large. To put it in a Malamudian fashion, it's just possible that God's impossible laws initially sprang from some poor schlemiel's overactive conscience. The step from this discovery to the one that powers his fiction is small: grand moral struggles belong to the common man as much as to the hero. Therefore, a Brooklyn storekeeper's son can take on the big questions by writing about the characters he knows from his days behind the delicatessen counter. By attaching the pain and effort of their familiar, mundane lives to larger mythic or moral frames, he can create resonant, uncanny stories. Dad's religious grandfather and great-grandfather might have pondered, as part of their faith, similar ideas about morality: How much originates in the man? How much is imposed by God? Psychoanalytic theory let Dad re-encounter his Jewish religious roots freshly and secularly. He could make the ancestral tradition his own by integrating psyche with society and soul.

IN THE SECOND STORY I tape-recorded (erased per his request, then scribbled by me onto a note card), he told how, as a boy, he'd once snitched a movie poster from a neighborhood store and placed it in his father's grocery. He knew that displaying the adver-tisement earned a storekeeper free movie tickets. He wanted the tickets and hoped his gambit would work. It's a tiny, innocent tale. Most raconteurs, sixty years later, would have relished their own ingenuity and laughed. Yet it was almost unbearable for him to tell it. Partly, he hated revealing to me moments of less-than-perfect rectitude. But I suspect that his shame and reluctance came from a private recognition that drowned the gesture's innocence. As a boy, he used to sneak under the subway stiles with his buddies to ride the El to Coney Island. He also used to snitch apples from a neighbor's tree. He was exuberant and adventurous, but he also had an angry, deprived kid within him who wanted to grab what he knew wasn't his. And while his inner life was hardly unusual, the persona didn't fit with his larger sense of who he wanted to be. By the time I knew him, he was meticulous about paying what he owed. Yet I wonder if he was able to create Frank Alpine, the petty thief in *The Assistant* in search of his moral being, because he knew intimately the pilfering feelings that frustration raised in a young man and the struggles to resist and overcome them.

What sadism he had, and he mostly checked it, would lead him to humiliate others occasionally, in spite of his more measured wishes. Anytime I brought a boyfriend home, he would instantly light on some word the poor guy misused and set up a formal, pub-lic exam, a show trial for whoever happened to be in the room.

"Which is the correct pronunciation of *exquisite*? How do you spell *cemetery*?" They'd inevitably squirm, often flunk, and he'd set them straight. All described feeling embarrassed — introduced to the famous writer and then publicly dunced.

February 22, 1938 — Can a psycho-analyst fall in love with his beautiful patient, who refuses him on the grounds that a love affair between them would be an intensification of a weakness?[35]

Also on February 22, 1938, he quotes a critic writing about Arthur Hugh Clough: "one can only divine his greatness in his unfulfillment." The quotation must have resonated with his ongoing search for evidence that his ambition was credible. He plumbs the idea by imagining a protagonist who embodies his own struggle: Can he become an artist, or ought he to be fulfilled by teaching well? As he will again several decades later in his novel *Pictures of Fidelman*, he describes an opposition between the development of the artist and that of the man. He also seems to be stringing a safety net he hopes will catch him if his writing fails.

In the light of the above — the protagonist after years of drifting, or in those years — should constantly argue with himself whether he was meant to be an artist. He has many doubts:
1) Lack of self-confidence. Will *ART* let him into her house. His first writings are so immature!
2) The question of experience — travel, etc. Has he learned a truth from life — a truth which he can proclaim?
3) Can he master the techniques of art.
4) Has he the patience to master his art?

Perhaps he doesn't become an artist but he develops himself in to a comprehensive human being. Perhaps that is his victory. At the end (last page of the book) he may (when everything has been defeat) walk into a classroom as a great teacher, even before he starts to teach — because he has acquired

1. Power of self-analysis and criticism
2. The power of experience in life — a sustained search for knowledge
3. The knowledge of a technique; the patience to use it
4. A truth to proclaim — which is that he has found no complete truth.[36]

The first mention in the notebooks of his mother occurs on August 14, 1938, when he is twenty-four. He includes within it a direct link to Freud. Although he nowhere details her condition, the small entry illuminates her loss as an engine of his fiction:

> If I write the inevitable bildungsroman, Id have to start it with my mother's funeral, using flashbacks in the minds of the main characters for expository and descriptive background . . . Lately Freud, and Thomas Wolfe and Thomas Mann have been influencing my thought. Freud because he deepens my sense of perspective and because he actually points out new roads for me to follow; Wolfe because he too tries to belong, to find a kind of object-choice.

He admired Mann's "great knowledge, his sense of calm and self-possession, his patient search for something; his humanitarianism, his lack of fear."[37]

A few months later, on December 4, 1938, he is making notes for a novel: "The death of a father scene (why does that idea persist). The father talks about the loss of his first wife, the boy's mother (whom he didn't mention much since the years of her death) dead since 20 years. He talks long about her; then thinks he hurt her on the wedding night."[38] The first image, the funeral, is of a defining loss; the second is of loss and a father's guilt, the hurt caused by lust or sex — not unlike the blood on Dubin's mama's petticoat. Dad and his father must have struggled silently with the question of who had damaged Bertha and how. In this writing, Dad's answer is Max and sex. My hunch is that his reading of Freud offered him a deflecting mirror in which to contemplate the Medusa's head of his mother's awful illness and her wish to die. To put it another way, Freud offered the possibility that my father could make meaning from his pain; it could drive his art rather than simply baffle and impede him. He could stop running; his writing wouldn't flow from imitating Anglo-centric, highbrow literature — Matthew Arnold, T. S. Eliot, and others — but from exploring his own past.

HARD AS MY FATHER WORKED to channel the debris from his family experience away from us, sometimes his suffering would slip out and catch me off-guard. At one point in the years before he died, I cannot remember when, he carefully explained to me that my arrival into the family had harmed my brother. Paul had been a happy child, the lecture went, but I, four-plus years his junior, had been such a competitive baby and toddler that I had hurt him. Whatever my real malevolence, I now feel that Dad was shifting onto me his own unbearable sense that some behavior of his had been the source of his mother's and brother's more serious troubles. In one of the few autobiographical pieces he wrote, "A Lost Bar-Mitzvah" (an account of his urgency as a twelve-year-old to prepare for a bar mitzvah, and his father's failing to adequately support him, then eventually performing the ceremony himself), he talks remorsefully about his relationship with Eugene:

> I looked after him when I thought of it, but was short of patience and used to sock him in the back when he didn't do what I wanted. He cried. No one told me to cut it out . . .
> My father was too much worried about [my mother], and his

meager place of business, to notice how badly I was treating my brother, or the troubles he was having in school.[39]

Had Eugene not become ill, Dad's typical big brother cuffs and petty meanness would easily have taken their place for what they were — sibling bruises. But because Eugene lived such a miserable life, Dad felt awful guilt. I'm not sure he trusted anyone enough to reveal the whole of his anguish. He let slip bits, but mostly he bore the memories alone, working them out as much as he could in his writing. Yet because he was prosecutor, defendant, judge, and jury, his self-recrimination functioned within a closed system. His imperfections met with the "hanging judge" psychic harshness to which he alludes in his reflection about sadism, masochism, and morality (see page 55).

When one looks for intimate sources of the quest for morality at the center of Malamud's novels — his characters' struggles to live as moral beings and good men — the starting point has to be the psychic board-to-head smash of my father's family life and the constant mental attention and effort required to right himself from its blow. The pain, together with the despair, shame, rage, guilt, and sense of want it stirred in him, led him to contemplate basic questions: Who hurts whom and how? What choices can a man make in living to contain the damage he does both in the public world and to intimates? Where can he turn for guidance? What can he learn, even gain, from suffering? "Gypped" was a word easily on his lips about his own youth. "I was gypped," he said on many occasions. But what to do about it? How to find more for oneself without grasping? How to care for others?

It seems likely, by the proximity of the entries, that when he read Thomas Wolfe, Thomas Mann, and Sigmund Freud, they created a useful synergy. In Freud he found a deeper psychological way to think about his life, one that might allow him to hold his past differently. In Wolfe he saw a "gland"-driven, lusty artist, using family life, however raw and tumultuous, as material for fiction. (He wrote humorously, "I've got a funny theory about Wolfe. It seems to me that all his furious wanderings from place to place, those fitful walks into the night, the search for the stone, the leaf — are all the result of his glands. I imagine that every one of them is enormous.") In Mann he found a mature version of his own virtues and aspirations. Mann represented the wished-for literary future: the humanity and intellectual depth the young writer admired. At the same time, Mann seemed steady, "self-possessed."

FINISHED AT COLUMBIA, Dad wanted to teach high school. The Depression was ongoing, and he couldn't find full-time work. In the spring of 1940, he moved briefly to Washington, D.C., to take a government census job and quickly found that by laboring purposefully in the morning, he could quietly write at his desk in the afternoon. Within a few months, he had published several short nonfiction pieces in the *Washington Post* column "The Post Impressionist." He was paid five dollars for each, his first money made from writing. "The Refugee" — undated, the yellowed newsprint now too brittle to unfold — describes one of the German refugees whom he had tutored.[40] In a letter he wrote around 1938 — recipient unknown, a copy kept in one notebook — he talks about others, including a Dr. R., a German Jewish journalist who'd fought for Germany in World War I:

> Yesterday he showed me his distinguished service cross and his long dagger, on which the words mein Lebensretter, my lifesaver, appeared. Yours, but nobody elses, I said.
>
> I never used it, he said.
>
> How did it get rusty?
>
> Peeling apples he said.[41]

As part of his new life, Dad shared an apartment with his friend Ben Loeb, and it did not go well. The result was a wounding encounter that created an unusually vivid and personal journal entry, which ends one notebook. No doubt the friendship was complicated by Ben's having dated Miriam Milman after Dad. And although she had broken up with him, too, some angry rivalry likely smoldered. The entry captures the degree to which both men were intrigued by Freudian notions, and it indicates how implausible, still in 1940, Dad's ambition was at least to one friend. It also offers a snapshot of him as a twenty-six-year-old.

April 8, 1940 — Washington D.C.

The weather has been improving, and sometimes spring fills the air with clean fragrance. I've been happy just resting — somehow dreams and desires have been suspended. The apathy I felt in New York has become less depressing . . . I've been fairly content.

But last night, Ben, after a week of side swipes at me, let me have both barrels at once. For a long time he has railed against my set of values and last night he made me sit up and take notice. He seems to know more about psychology and its explanations than I do, and he was able to get me to . . . see lots of things that were happening to me as part of the past pattern or fabric of my life.

He says in effect that I have to learn the discipline of new living or I'll carry my symptoms around with me forever. God knows I'm sick of them, but according to him, I have to give up my present way of living before I shall get rid of them.

1. He accused me of having a tremendously exagerrated ego — the basis of an inferiority complex.
   a. I use knowledge for show to compensate for my inferiority
   b. I talk too much, and am not modest
2. The inferiority came in my childhood for some reason.
   a. (I remember being ashamed of my parents when I was very young. Its only within the last few years that I've gotten over this)

      b. For years its manifested itself in different ways.
          1. Sex — lack of experiences: Irene
          2. Social life — manners: until quite recently a feeling that
             I was with my betters
          3. Writing — the fear that I shall never be [have?] food if
             I write
          4. Financial — never having the things others had. (I got
             my first bathrobe and slippers last week)
          5. Wanting school kids (everyone) to like me
   3. Naturally, the result of these inferiorities has been an adop-
      tion of a superior attitude
      1. also a romanticizing of other elements — e.g. I'm one of
         the lost generation — and loving it. Being satisfied to find
         a category for myself to hibernate in
         A. This showed itself in
            1. Dramatizing things — mostly situations I've been in
            2. wanting to write
            3. tremendous ambition
            4. calling it a search for tradition
   4. Other results were my physical symptoms . . . [and a] narrow
      kind of living so that I began to deprive myself of a good
      deal of joy in life . . .
   5. Ben's way out
      a. Fight all symptoms. Don't give into them or to my egois-
         tic drive for self-assertion
      b. Don't try to write a novel — only objective pieces for
         magazines, etc.
      c. Sleeping with women.
      d. Drop correspondence with my adolescent school children
         (Clara's Situation).
      e. More exercise
   6. Naturally I was shaken by his rather drastic pronouncements.
      I must confess that I have been looking forward to healing
      myself with the writing of a novel. If I were to fail, perhaps

this whole business would recur with worse symptoms. Perhaps success, unless I could achieve the objectivity of a Mann (which Ben says I can't because I'm not built as tough as Mann? In other words — don't write, you can't pay its price. Youre not strong enough) I would die like Thomas Wolfe. What misery he had.

He speculates a little about Ben's psyche, then ruefully adds, "I understand things much better now. I hope that I'll be able to attack these symptoms viciously — get rid of them. But I still would like to write if I can. I wonder if its worth trying. I must live as I write — or I'm sunk."[42]

The men continued to room together for several more weeks until Dad's summer work ended and he returned to Brooklyn to teach evening high school at Erasmus. In 1986, after Dad died, Ben wrote a letter to Miriam Milman Lang about him, answering one from her: "Your early impressions of his talent were much like my own. While he was in Washington he made some noises about wanting to be a writer and I remember my reaction was very skeptical. I liked him a lot as a friend but thought he was a phony in his artistic pretensions. I don't know why I belittled him. Maybe it was because he didn't seem very intellectual. Maybe it was some ego thing of my own."[43]

Perhaps another way to put it is that artists sometimes feel consumed by their urgency to create before others see them as plausible and before they themselves can begin to realize their ambitions. The quintessential statement of this feeling is Keats's great sonnet "When I have fears that I may cease to be / Before my pen has glean'd my teeming brain . . . ," a poem I fell for hard at sixteen and used to recite sometimes to my father, who had long loved it, too.

Chapter 3 ⊰⊱

Courtship

⊰⊱ ⊰⊱ MY PARENTS MET in February 1942 at a small party at their mutual friend Ruth Batchker's family's apartment on the west side of Manhattan. My mother, after studying Romance languages and graduating from Cornell in 1939, was living in the city with her mother, Ida (Ettari) Barbieri, and stepfather, Gino Barbieri, and working at Young & Rubicam, an advertising agency. She had been in love with a young musicologist for several years, but he'd broken off the relationship, a loss that left a watermark of sadness occasionally visible throughout her life. Her friend Ruth told her about the aspiring young writer coming to the party, and while the two spoke little that first evening, my mother recalls noticing him noticing her. A few days later, he wrote and asked her out, inviting her to the theater to see *Arsenic and Old Lace.* During the ensuing months, they talked, bicycled in Brooklyn, took in a Dodgers double-header, and strolled around Coney Island together. She visited and drank tea with him in his rooming house; they began meeting each other's friends. He conducted his life from a single room, but it was large and airy and in an attractive house. She recalls him as a polite tenant liked by his landladies.

The twenty-five-year-old Ann deChiara was a very pretty woman: five foot three, thin, full-chested, with fair skin, brown eyes, and shiny brown hair that waved slightly below her ears. She had delicate fingers and lovely legs, dressed simply — mostly in blouses and skirts — and wore lipstick but no other makeup. In certain photos, she resembles the young Greta Garbo. I can summon an image of her in Oregon, casting for just the right profile as she examined her features in the mirror, but her vanity was observed mostly in the breach: by the time I knew her, she expressed more negative ideas about her looks than positive ones and almost always disliked herself in photographs. My father commented repeatedly how she had declared herself too old for short pants at thirty. (A friend recently recalled how, many years ago, when Dad had said of Mom, "She was an Italian beauty," I, sitting nearby, had piped up irritably, "Was?") I picture her in the hot, dry Oregon summer wearing a tan, embroidered Guatemalan cotton skirt that fell below the knee, a light white cotton blouse, pale arms freckled, bare-legged, in sandals and silver earrings, her hair clipped back against the heat.

Bilingual in English and Italian, fluent in French, and plausible in Spanish, she had lived abroad twice — once in 1926, at age eight, for a year in Naples with her mother and grandmother, and again in 1937–1938, in Paris, during her junior year in college. Her stepfather, Gino, had come to America as a young man on the promise that he would be hired as an assistant conductor at the Metropolitan Opera. Whoever had offered the job reneged. Even so, there was a lot of music in their apartment. Ida sang lyric soprano, Gino played the piano, and friends joined them often for evenings of music. My mother soaked up the family opera knowledge, possessed a keen ear, and, often unable to afford a seat, regularly paid the small cost to stand through performances at the back of the Metropolitan Opera. Sometime around 1964, she took my brother and me there to hear *Fidelio*, my first opera. She wanted us to see the old Met before it closed for good.

I remember how easily my mother and her mother and stepfather talked about different singers, their merits and deficits. (My last memory of my grandmother is of her at age eighty-five in a California nursing home, rapidly dying of ALS, Lou Gehrig's disease. Her wheelchair is set before a television on which Pavarotti is singing *La Bohème*. A white shawl covers her much shrunken shoulders. Voice weakened by neurological devastation, she comments hoarsely to me on how fine a tenor he was before overuse harmed his voice.)

I see Gino at his piano in California in the late 1950s, testing my pitch and my brother's, hoping, in my case fruitlessly since I had Dad's absence of ear, for a trainable voice in the next generation. Enrico Caruso had ridden with the family to my mother's christening, and early in their California days, Gino had served as assistant to the baritone Andres de Segurola. There was a tradition to uphold.

Sometimes when my mother was young, she liked to go dancing. On visits to her mother and stepfather in Hollywood during the 1940s, she enjoyed playing gin rummy and canasta, driving to Laguna Beach, watching movies, and occasionally visiting nightclubs. Once or twice, she and her mother went out to a nightspot to watch for movie stars. More than my father, my mother appreciated leisure for its own sake and took pleasure in spending relaxed time with friends and family.

An intellectual Italian family friend had become an avuncular presence for the fatherless young woman during her teenage years, and the relationship had deepened her interest in ideas; she read steadily. In 1946, together with her friend Bernadette Inkeles, she took W. H. Auden's course on Shakespeare at the New School in New York. When it came time to discuss *The Merry Wives of*

Windsor, Auden opined that the play's sole worth was as a source for Verdi's *Falstaff.* Then, phonograph at hand, he announced that the class would listen to the opera. A bunch of students, irritated that there would be no lecture, huffed and marched out; Bernadette and my mother happily stayed. (She sometimes quoted an Audenism uttered during the course: "You bury the hatchet, but you always know where you put it.")

She remarked to me once that she was happy to have saved much of Proust until she was fifty; time and middle age had given her a greater appreciation of him. At seventy-five or so, she noted one day, upon closing *The Golden Bowl,* that she'd finally finished reading all of Henry James's novels. She reread Jane Austen regularly.

More liberal than her family, my mother was a New Deal Democrat who believed that FDR's social programs had been enlightened. She supported Adlai Stevenson, despised Joe McCarthy, quickly embraced the civil rights movement, and opposed the Vietnam War. I remember her, along with my father and brother, going to a local Corvallis hotel one afternoon in 1960 to hear JFK speak. When my mother had first applied to college, at Duke, she had been turned down, while other, less qualified students she knew had been admitted. She'd always wondered whether the era's anti-Italian sentiment had led to her rejection. Her response was to oppose all kinds of discrimination.

She read newspapers, watched the news on television, and kept abreast of current events. Throughout her life, she enjoyed mulling the day's political happenings with friends over a late-afternoon glass of vermouth. When the subject was contentious, she'd brace her view by citing someone else who shared it. "So-and-so and I agree," she would say, as if her own insights were never quite adequate to carry the day.

My mother was honest and had a critical mind and a sharp, intuitive intelligence. She had no particular ambition or single sustaining craft. Her lifework was caring for herself, my father, and my brother and me. I suspect, having grown up in a turbulent household, she wanted stability. She also came directly out of a Neapolitan professional family where men and women assumed distinctly different roles.

My mother rigorously downplayed her own abilities, almost everything about herself, and it took me a while to appreciate the figure my father must have seen. Several years after he died, she and I were sorting through some books as she readied their Vermont house for sale. I came upon a well-worn 1930s copy of Henry Adams's *Mont-Saint-Michel and Chartres*. "I didn't know Dad read this," I said, ready to be impressed by a piece of his intellectual life that had slipped by me. "That's my copy," she offhandedly replied.

One time in Vermont, she attended a party with Stanley Edgar Hyman, the polymath literary critic and intellectual whose pontifications ruled the Bennington College community when we first arrived in the early 1960s. She had been auditing his class on myth and ritual. He complimented her about some idea she'd expressed, and then, when she demurred, he lectured her on the need sometimes simply to say thank you. Protesting her adequacy was a core reflex, even as she was often outspoken. Another evening during the Bennington years, she told the art critic Clement Greenberg that for all her efforts, she could not always make sense of contemporary art. "Keep looking," he commanded.

I EARLY OBSERVED my parents' shared belief that my mother's labors were necessary but inconsequent, while my father's work mattered. He wrote; she typed his drafts, occasionally commenting on what she read, telling him what she thought was better or worse. When we lived in Corvallis, he liked a small half glass of beer before dinner to settle his stomach and whet his appetite; he liked dinner served on time. She made sure the cans of beer were in the refrigerator, the meal *à l'heure*. Dad was not openly domineering in his requests, but he assumed a prerogative. He was extremely time-conscious and methodical, continually attempting to organize her according to his scheduling ideas. She was more meandering and resisted his efforts to engineer her into the sharp-cut channels of his wishes.

A year into their courtship, in 1943, Dad spent the summer writing at Brant Lake, in rural New York. He had chronic stomach trouble and missed the comfort of Social Teas, a brand of crackers not available at the local grocery. Could she mail them to him? Apparently, much to his frustration, she posted them erratically, prompting this response. "Baby, send me a box of crackers once a week. Send me a box when you get this letter, and then send me a box next week on the same day and so on without my having to tell you. Will you please?"[1]

Once they were married, he readily gave her money as she designated family needs, but it was his to manage. So, too, his dependence on her was mostly denied and hidden, lived out between them in their mutual recognition of hers on him. She seemed in principle to agree with their division of labor and assignment of worth.

Neither of them cared a lot about money — more as they had some, but never obsessively. They actively valued intangibles more — art, music, literature, social justice. They favored the artist/academic's slightly bohemian life. Although my mother took pleasure in occasional shopping, appreciated well-crafted objects, and enjoyed particular bits of jewelry, she and my father were never primarily focused on possessions. In part, of course, they invested in the intellectual and creative because it was years before they could afford the rest, and doing so also helped bridge their backgrounds. But their values ran deeper. I'm not sure I ever heard either of them seriously covet anything beyond his means. She never pushed him to earn more. They genuinely favored substance over style, the inner life over outer show. They shared a strong humanism and admired integrity and moral courage. It seemed completely right to them that Eleanor Roosevelt should resign from the Daughters of the American Revolution when it barred the great contralto Marian Anderson from singing in its hall, and that Pablo Casals refused to perform publicly on the cello as long as Franco ruled Spain. They were generous even with their limited money and expressed sincere concern for other people — victims of McCarthyism, Spanish refugees, African Americans in the segregated South. As soon as my father could, he sent small bits of help to Ida and Gino, to civil rights groups such as the Student Nonviolent Coordinating Committee (SNCC), and to an array of social causes. He opened savings accounts early for my brother and me, and I remember how he showed me the markings in my bankbook of his tiny, regular contributions to meet my future college needs. By the time we lived in Vermont, he had me tallying monthly household expenses with him, tapping in numbers and rapidly pulling the handle on his sturdy mechanical adding machine so that the white paper strip of dollars spent spat jerkily out of the top.

Later in life, Dad took satisfaction in the money that came to him from his book sales and movie deals. It let him cut back on teaching, divide his life between Vermont and Manhattan, live one winter and part of another in London, educate his children at private secondary schools and universities, and eventually buy two small etchings by Rembrandt. Yet it's equally true that he forsook any number of opportunities to make more money. After *The*

Fixer, the Franklin Mint offered him $75,000, quite a fortune in 1967, to sign twenty-five thousand copies of their special edition of the book. He demurred; he didn't want to participate in creating fetishized objects. He joked sometimes, half proudly, half ruefully, about how Philip Roth took the deal and built a swimming pool.

His eventual bit of wealth signaled to him that he'd succeeded on his own terms. The achievement gave him moments of substantial satisfaction. I can't say it ever made him deeply content, but I don't know that he was capable of more than tourist status in that territory. He could relish a good movie or play and was easily delighted by art exhibits, concerts, and animated dinners with their many friends. His letters home from Yaddo, the New York artists' colony he first visited in 1958, tell of raucous games of charades, rounds of bad croquet, and hands of poker. (He played poker throughout the time he lived in Vermont.) One evening, he and a couple of others slipped out to watch a local boxing match, and another day they bet on the horses at Saratoga. People there saw him as entertaining, lifting the mood at the dinner table with amusing stories and ready jokes.

Yet at home in the family, he rarely seemed to relax fully into what little leisure he granted himself. He wrote to his friend Rosemarie Beck, "I have never really learned to be at leisure. I'm not satisfied, most of the time, unless my leisure is 'producing' for me, e.g., reading."[2] When my mother pried him away for a vacation, he immediately hunted down some quiet place to write each morning. He often grew impatient for home and his own desk. He mostly stole his pleasures, by which I mean he allowed himself bursts of delight but nothing that accrued. They and his accomplishments bought him meager respite from a relentless wish to write the next better thing, from his guilt and sadness, his continual, murmuring self-criticism. He had too many nerve endings. And while the excess helped generate his art, it often made everyday life uncomfortable. He told me once about Proust's cork-lined room. Perhaps he longed for its insulation, for the self-protective prerogative of the truly eccentric.

BETWEEN FEBRUARY 1942, when my parents met, and November 1945, when they married, their courtship had ups and downs, with each of them more or less certain about the relationship at different moments during the three years. Much has been written about "writers' wives," with Vera Nabokov held up as the gold standard. The notion feels a little tired, but as I understand the template, it describes a woman who sees her husband as an exceptional creative talent, someone who must be protected from the everyday tasks that fall to the rest of us and completely supported in his pursuit of genius. My mother discharged many such duties. Yet unlike some who admired this schema, my father never assumed that he could simply write. He knew he needed to make a living, to support his family. But he didn't know how he'd do it. His early letters to my mother are filled with continuing money and work worries. Can he find sustaining employment? Can he find a woman who will understand his commitment to writing? And, of course, the deeper underlying question: Will he ever realize his talent? He was just beginning to publish book reviews and a few stories in small magazines.

IN MAY 1942, three months after they met, he penned Ann deChiara a charming, unsigned note:

> May 28, 1942
> What does it mean when, increasingly, you find yourself thinking about one girl; when you read, and the words are woven into thoughts of her; when you work, and her image, like light falling upon darkness floats into your mind; when you rest, and her presence is with you?

What does it mean when, in memory, you hold her beautiful body in your arms and rekiss kisses: when you constantly hear her voice, see her face, remember her laughter, tell her loveliness and take quiet pride in her wisdom —

What does it mean?

Brooklyn, New York

Around the same time, he wrote semicomically to her about his job dilemma and lack of prospects:

So far I have been offered — with various degrees of promise — the following jobs:

A. One plumber's asst. in Floyd Bennett Field.
B. One brush maker, asst. and general factotum to boss Sobelman.
C. One job to teach summer school in private school.
D. One post-office clerk's job.
E. Add to those the fact that I can continue to be an unemployed writer, and you see, my dear, what diversity I possess. How can you help but like me?
F. Oh, I forgot — my camp counselor's job.
G. Also you might add that this summer I should be an unemployed evening school teacher.[3]

In November 1942, he pulled back from the relationship. He had become uneasy, and he told her that he felt so upset at the prospect of causing her pain that he'd even seen a psychiatrist. (During the years I knew him, in spite of his fascination with the literature, he mostly believed that seeing psychiatrists was a good idea for *others* — his brother, mother-in-law, children, wife, lover. Later in life, though, after his heart surgery and stroke, when he was deeply depressed by his loss of words, he made some more visits of his own.) Dad felt disadvantaged by his sense that he'd seen little of the world and lacked the money to buy even the smallest things. (Several of his letters from this period recount borrowing from friends and Eugene bits of cash to tide him over between jobs.) It's hard to say how much of his hesitation was from particular reservations about this girlfriend as he got to know her better and how much from a more general angst. "Lust" may have been one part of the "wander lust" he cites in the following passage. Also in play must have been his intense fear of replicating his family life. He continued to feel deeply oppressed by the narrowness of Max's existence — the way the grocer never left the store and his apparent lack of curiosity. He felt terrified about somehow losing — forsaking, giving over — the lone exit visa he possessed from that fate: his hope of becoming a major writer.

> The first thing is that I feel miserable for having hurt you . . . For some reason I can't explain well, I want to be free. It's got something to do with my writing. I've seen so little, done so little. I want to do and see; I want to get the urge out of my system before I think of settling down. I'd hate to be in the position of breaking up a marriage to satisfy this sort of wander lust. Better that it comes now. Better that I rid myself of this urge now in my youth.[4]

In his story "The Lady of the Lake," published in 1958, right after our year in Italy, the protagonist, Harry Levin, travels to Italy and, "tired of the past, tired of the limitations it had imposed upon him," changes his name to Freeman. "Freeman still hoped for what he hadn't, what few got in the world and many dared not think of; to wit, love, adventure, freedom. Alas, the words by now sounded slightly comical."[5] The Henry Jamesian story includes a fantasy exploration of the same fears, urges, and conflicted hungers that had made Dad hesitate a decade and a half earlier. Rowing upon a lake to a forbidden island, Freeman glimpses there a beautiful young woman named Isabella. He falls in love with her and pursues her. Believing her to be a highborn Italian, he lies and hides his Jewish identity. But it turns out, despite her initial deception, that she also is Jewish and impoverished, a tattooed survivor of Auschwitz. Freeman ultimately loses her because she will not marry outside her faith. Isabella is chimerical, lovely, and receptive, but without substance or personality — little more, really, than a juvenile fantasy. Still, she embodies the writer's continued longing for something better, a freer existence, a more perfect woman, together with his lifelong question: How imprisoned is he by his past? By himself? I wonder if she also carries some of his discoveries about the limits of the cultural transcendence a mixed marriage could achieve: his recognition, as his commitment to an Italian lapsed Catholic progressed, he became middle-aged, and his children grew up with no introduction to his religion, that he was more irrevocably Jewish than he had once grasped.

THE COURTSHIP RESUMED. The couple felt deeply for each other, and the relationship held. By the summer of 1943, they were back together, if still out of sync: she was again ready to marry, he still was not. He had started a novel and wanted it further along. He wrote:

July 23, 1943

You brought up marriage in your last letter, dear, and there are a few things I want to say about it.

My own idea is to get married when I am far into the book so that I know, no matter what new changes I am undergoing, I shall not give it up.

I am trying to find myself as an artist, dear, yet at the same time I'm cognizant of your needs. I'll say what I said before, we'll be married, at the latest, by next June.

He apparently thought it a good idea to ask her to read the early chapters of his novel soon after putting her off. Was he aware of what he was inviting? How rejected and angry she would be feeling as she turned the pages? Apparently not. Her telephone remarks, followed by a seven-page letter of criticism, devastated him. She attacked where he was most vulnerable, and he struck back.

August 14, 1943

Dear Baby,

If there is one thing that I have learned from sad and bitter experience, it is that a writer should ask for no opinions until he has completed his first drafts of his entire novel. For the second time my morale has been smashed, and I'm trying to put together the pieces so that I can go on without trying to recast my idea still another time. I tell myself that it took Scribners a year to edit and revise Thomas Wolfe's typescript of *Look Homeward Angel*. I know another case where a successful novel received more than one hundred pages of publisher's criticism and suggestions for revision, before it was published and well-reviewed. I tell myself that your opinion is only one and that you've been wrong before, and that you've been too close to it to get perspective, and too ignorant of my intentions to know what I'm trying to do . . .

Eventually, in Oregon, he burned the manuscript of this first unpublished novel, *The Light Sleeper*. Although I never heard him talk about the book or his experience, I imagine that his short story "The Girl of My Dreams" captures his defeated grief. It begins, "After Mitka had burned the manuscript of his heartbroken novel in the blackened bottom of Mrs. Lutz's rusty trash can in her back yard . . ."[6]

THEY WEATHERED THE CRISIS and continued to court. Two months later, he wrote:

Dear Snookie Pie,

After considering whether to get you a birthday card, I have decided not to because none can convey my feeling toward you. I wish that I had saved some money to buy you a gift of some kind. You are a loyal, sweet, lovable woman, always a giver, and my impulse is to give to you in return. May your twenty sixth year bring you the happiness that you want and deserve, darling, and may it set you on the road to fulfillment.[7]

Growing up, his own birthdays had gone uncelebrated, and he never became adept at giving birthday, or the even more alien Christmas, gifts to my mother, although we observed Christmas each year and even trekked once with friends into the Oregon woods to cut our own tree. Often, later, he would either offer her money to buy herself something or have her pick out a piece of jewelry, and they'd go together to purchase it. As he aged, he asked for large parties for significant birthdays — sixty, sixty-five, seventy. She arranged them, and it was assumed between them that he would not reciprocate.

HIS LETTERS, intermittent since they lived within easy phone and visiting distance, are sprinkled with requests for her to type manuscripts or mail copies of his published magazine stories for him. However conflictually, he was also feeling his way into becoming the husband of a writer's wife.

If you do think you can type a chapter now and then, I'd like you to do it within a week after I send them. It makes me feel bad when you leave them lying around untyped.[8]

Thanks for the criticisms. Most of them were good. You may do this with every chapter I send you if you care to. Even when you are typing, and something strikes you as being off, make a note of it, and, if necessary, I'll change it in the typescripts.[9]

Send out *Threshold* [a small magazine that had published a short story of his] to the following people . . .[10]

Early in 1945, he was ready to marry her, but she no longer felt so certain. She may have become genuinely less clear about loving him, or she may have felt irked by how he had long stalled. Rather than withdrawing before her reluctance, he mobilized. In response to her telling him that her love had lessened, he instructed her, albeit ruefully, about the ways her resistance was misguided. She needed a focus, and he was to be it.

January 24, 1945

Dear Annie,

I want you to be true to yourself, but remember that there are times when we lack a full knowledge of what we are. Then, maybe someone else — a lover perhaps — can point more surely to the direction of truth.

I have told you what you are suffering from: dissipation of love energy; lack of a focus for life. To a large extent, that is my fault. I have been most prodigal of your love. Now I am on my hands and knees, trying to collect the substance I wasted. I'm suffering for my blindness, and I should like to spare you the same suffering in the future.

You mustn't think that your love for me is gone. If you think so, you do not understand yourself.

But, truth is my master, and though my heart wants you with a single purpose, I must repeat again what marriage to me will mean for you. Though I love you and shall love you more, most of my strength will be devoted to realizing myself as an artist. I will need your help to overcome weaknesses in health, finances and steadfastness. You will be called on for all the love, patience, courage, understanding — and paradoxically — selflessness that you are capable of bestowing.

They were married in early November 1945 — he was thirty-one, she had just turned twenty-eight — by Algernon Black at the

New York Society for Ethical Culture, with her grandmother Josephine Ettari and his friend Allan Rothenberg present as witnesses. They were not members of the congregation but felt sympathy with the society's commitment to social justice and activism. Ida, who was fond of Dad, had already moved with Gino to California, and the remaining family members were hostile. Neither Max Malamud nor her father, Albert deChiara, received them in his home until more than two years later, some months after my brother was born. Eventually, Max tried to explain to my mother that his feelings were not personal: his formative encounters with Christians had occurred during pogroms. Her own father's reservations were more simply bigoted, based on anti-Semitism and social class. The deChiaras and Ettaris were professionals — businessmen, teachers, doctors, military men; the Malamuds were poor Jews in trade. He likely thought that she could do better.

However cautious my father felt about making the decision to marry, however difficult they could be with each other, however much their love seemed prey to quick disappointment and mutual wounding, marriage and then fatherhood catalyzed and steadied him. Their early married life gave them pleasure. Finally making the leap emboldened Dad, rather like Levin with Pauline at the end of *A New Life*. Having someone to look after was good for him, and his luck improved.

Over the years, on several occasions, I suggested to my mother that she was important to my father's success. I contended that they ran a mom-and-pop operation, where she supplied plenty of the labor that made the enterprise go. More than that, her particular sensibility, her belief in him, and her support of his daily routines were crucial. She always demurred, saying, "Your father would have written no matter what — with me, with someone else, alone." I suspect her opinion and mine both hold pieces of truth. But in the most concrete and immediate sense, in the late 1940s, it was she who suggested that he look for college teaching jobs, a shift crucial to his career. She grasped better than he that a demanding high school life would kill his writing. However tough the schedule at Oregon State, it gave him a full-time job at a college, where the day, unlike at a high school, included unscheduled hours and flexibility. Although the constraints of his low rank and the mediocre department frustrated him, he partly escaped them by offering an evening course in creative writing. And simply being in an academic job positioned him so that as his literary reputation grew, he could leave for a better school.

MY MOTHER, father, and brother arrived in Corvallis in 1949. My mother had typed and mailed two hundred letters to schools around the country, hoping to find someone willing to hire a man without a doctorate. Oregon State College, a modest agricultural school, decided it could let Dad teach English composition but not literature. A college in New Mexico made a similar offer. That was it. My mother favored Oregon for its proximity to her mother. My father knew no one in either place. For a promise of $3,400 dollars a year, the Malamuds departed their Greenwich Village apartment — a space so cramped that a friend had once deemed it possible there to fry an egg on the stove while using the toilet — and headed west.

Chapter 4 ⤙

The Year I Was Born

Bern once accused me — in a friendly way — of having started the fiction that he had ordered you not to produce Janna on one of his writing days. I didn't start it and don't know who did . . . But like many an apocryphal tale, it had a certain truth in it: it said something about Bern's phenomenal self-discipline and his ability to do two jobs virtually at once. It was this quality of the story, I'm sure, which got it so much appreciated and so widely circulated.

— *Jim Groshong to Ann Malamud, October 31, 1998*

⤙ ⤙ PICTURING MY BIRTH YEAR in Oregon, if I thought about it at all, I used to imagine a young family in a quiet western town, living in a small rented house, short of money but otherwise pleasantly getting about their lives, my almost-thirty-eight-year-old father teaching and writing, my thirty-four-year-old mother home with my brother. Then I arrived one January day in the midst of a typically gray, rainy Oregon winter, the second living baby. (There had been a miscarriage during the four-plus years between my brother's birth and mine.) I thought of myself as a pleasant addition to lives that were otherwise calm. I was wrong. When I finally read folders of old letters — my father's correspondence with his father, then my father's and mother's letters — I discovered I had misimagined the situation. Yes, my parents were delighted to add a baby girl to the family. But, at least where my father's life was concerned, mine was a kind of shipboard birth — a pleasurable distraction on a heaving deck.

The autumn of 1951 through the late summer of 1952 were arguably the twelve most eventful months of my father's life. In November 1951, Eugene became psychotic and entered a hospital in Brooklyn. His deterioration is recounted in almost the only letters that survive between my grandfather and father. Because Dad looked after Eugene quietly and told me little, I have only lately understood how constant and painful a presence he was in my father's mind — although I caught a glimpse in the autumn of 1973. I was just out of college. My mother was briefly in Italy. Dad telephoned and told me calmly that Eugene had died. A day or so later, he called again, this time from a hospital bed in New York City: his first bad episode of angina. He urged me not to worry. I remember thinking then that his great effort to hold his grief within himself had taken a toll on his heart. (In the thirty-four years I knew him, I believe I saw him cry only once: in 1963, the evening of President Kennedy's assassination. I was eleven; we were living in Bennington. He came downstairs from his late-afternoon nap wearing a shirt and boxers, having uncharacteristically neglected to put on his pants before descending. Slightly dazed from sleep and upset, he was hurrying to catch the Huntley-Brinkley news broadcast. The grim newscasters reiterated what viewers knew. Our black-and-white screen replayed the shooting, the frantic speeding-car aftermath, the hospital failure. Dad, overcome by grief, spread his hand across his forehead, lowered his head so that his fingers shielded his eyes, and sobbed, shuddering intensely for a moment before stopping himself.)

*　　*　　*

IN THE AUTUMN OF 1951, my father's worst fears about Eugene materialized. Having witnessed Bertha's course, neither he nor his father could muster much illusion. Their sense of déjà vu dread was immense. Yet this time, for Dad, the demons returned in the company of thrilling, opposite news. On January 7, 1952, twelve days before I was born, a telegram arrived.

WE LIKE THE NATURAL ENORMOUSLY AND WANT TO PUBLISH IT I AM CONTACTING DIARMUID RUSSELL AND WRITING YOU LATER THIS WEEK ABOUT SOME REVISIONS I HOPE YOU WILL CONSIDER BUT THIS IS JUST TO SAY HOW DELIGHTED WE ARE AND TO TENDER OUR BEST WISHES = =ROBERT GIROUX HARCOURT BRACE =

Diarmuid Russell was Dad's agent at Russell & Volkening until he retired in 1973. Robert Giroux would remain his editor for life — indeed, posthumously. In late June 1952, Dad traveled to New York for eight weeks, a trip planned since the autumn, when Max had proposed that Eugene might improve if he saw his brother. By the time Dad actually boarded the train east, the original purpose had shrunk to half the mission. However apprehensive he was about his brother, he also was elated to be returning home to greet his first book off the press. He had by then spent almost two decades teaching himself to write fiction. While staying with his father and stepmother, he delivered copies of *The Natural* to friends and mailed them to a host of other writers, into whose ranks he headily found himself stepping.

I BELIEVE I MET EUGENE twice in my life. The first time was in 1957, when we returned to Oregon through New York after a year in Italy. Dad took us to the Brooklyn grocery to visit him and their stepmother, Liza Merov. I remember nothing about either of them.

I do recall excitedly peering down into the store's small, white, frost-encrusted freezer, choosing my own Popsicle from a bounty of open boxes. The second time was in the 1960s, after we'd moved back east. Eugene attended a book party for Dad in Manhattan at Roger and Dorothea Straus's. I have a vague sense of my father leading me through a crowded room to greet him, a slightly overweight, mild-looking man in a gray suit seated alone in a straight-backed chair. Eugene and I had a perfunctory correspondence throughout my growing up. He'd send me an occasional birthday card, and I'd write indifferent, bright thank-you notes. I knew him not at all.

When my father and mother were first getting to know each other in 1942, he wrote a little about Eugene to her: "Our mother died when he was twelve. We didn't tell him. Then we took him for a suit on the day of the funeral, and while they were shortening the cuffs, we went outside of the store, and it was raining, and I told him. Then he said he knew — he guessed it, and I wanted to cry — so heavy was the pity in my heart."[1] In an undated letter to my mother from the same era — Eugene was in the army and apparently stationed in New Orleans — Dad confided to her, "I got a very shocking letter from my brother yesterday, in which he exhorted me 'to understand,' in case he felt the necessity of doing 'something drastic.' I wrote to him at once, describing the suicide tendencies of young men of his age and condition, and pointing out that this was no solution."[2]

The rest of what I now know comes from a fifteen-page letter Dad wrote in late November or early December 1951 to the doctors looking after Eugene in the hospital.[3] Dad sought to provide useful background about his brother, to pass along information he imagined psychiatrists might want to know. It is a vivid and unusually frank recounting for him of his family's past:

Eugene Malamud was born on May 4, 1918 in Brooklyn, New York, the second son of Max and Bertha Malamud . . . [Max, growing up in Russia,] had had very little education, perhaps about the equivalent of a grammar school education. As a person he is a kindly man, tender, stubborn on occasions, good to his family though fundamentally unambitious. He is generally inclined to pessimism and in later years used to infuriate Bernard by his baseless pessimistic reactions to hopes and plans. In a way he is like a character from a Russian novel. Both boys remember being belittled by him often — in the sense of his making light of their accomplishments. No harm was meant by him — it was just his nature. He pooh-poohed anything they accomplished, though secretly he seemed pleased. It was almost as if his attitude were: how can anything that comes from me possibly achieve anything? Not so direct as that — but such an attitude seemed to underlie his deprecatory remarks . . . He had been very poor in Russia and apparently used to drudgery. His work in the grocery business was a continuation of that drudgery. He used to get up at 6 A.M. and work seven days a week, until about ten or eleven P.M., apparently the kind of life he was used to and the only kind he would respect. He is honest, sincere, "good," hardworking, a loving but unimaginative husband and father.

Bertha Malamud also came to America from Russia. She was a sensitive woman and romantic. Her education was also meagre though she was innately bright. After her marriage to Max her first child was stillborn. Apparently this had a physical as well as mental effect upon her. She had trouble with a leg for years afterwards, which the family attributed to either the birth of the first or second child. Bertha was a devoted mother to both of her later children, too devoted, in the sense that the children occupied almost all of her time. She had no desire to go out but stayed home every night of the year except for about a dozen days in as many years, when she went to a Jewish theatrical performance or, rarely, to a movie. She spoke often of her girlhood and of her mother and father. She seemed to know a better life.

With Max — probably his fault though I cannot say for sure —
there was no visiting of friends, no intercourse with other families
as a family. Bertha's brother puts the blame entirely upon Max for
their empty social lives. He asserts she had the capacity and imagination to live but that Max didn't. During our childhood I remember only once staying overnight at the home of friends in New
York City. These friends were always fellow countrymen or relatives — never "outsiders."

Both Max and Bertha limited their reading to one Jewish newspaper — the "Forward." There were no books or magazines in the
house, no music or pictures. Though our childhood was happy, because Max and Bertha were loving parents, it was meagre in terms
of family life and things cultural.

I recall that Bertha was considered and considered herself "fat."
She weighed over two hundred and hardly ever seemed to take the
trouble to "dress up," though she was a clean person — kept the
house and children clean. When the children were young, Bertha
stayed at home with them. Later she worked with Max in the store.
In the beginning this bothered her. She found it difficult to deal
with semi-strangers over the counter.

She and Max had many quarrels some severe, principally, as I remember it, over where he spat, and how he went around before the
children. Naturally, the children were frightened of these "fights."
Once Bertha asked Bernard if he would go with her if she left Max.
He wept, and she said, "No no, my child."

At about the time Eugene was ten or so she began to show signs
of schizophrenia. People were talking about her; a policeman followed her along the street. She peeked out of the window to see
who was in the street. She then gave up her few remaining old
friends. Max tried "talking" to her but things came to a head and
she attempted suicide by drinking a bottle of CR Disinfectant.
Later she was committed to Kings County Hospital, where she was
miserable. Though Max could ill afford it he had her sent to a private hospital in Queens. About six months (possibly a year and six

months) after her suicide [*sic*] she died here. Max's answers to questions about the cause of her death were always vague — a sickness of some kind.

On the whole, though, Eugene may be said to have had a happy childhood. However, he was overprotected and "over cared for." Bertha slept with him till he was five or six, possibly more. She dressed him every day till he was in grammar school, even helping him on and off with his overcoat. Nor could she bring herself to wean Eugene from his bottle until he was five or six, and already the victim of ridicule by neighbors and relatives who knew of the situation.

Almost from the beginning Eugene had difficulty in school. Bernard, who was bright and capable, aggressive and somewhat authoritarian, possibly because he was overpraised by his parents, made a name for himself in school, which his teachers tried to make Eugene live up to. Bernard was always the recipient of complaints about Eugene. From an early age he acted in loco parentis for Eugene. As a result, Eugene disliked and sometimes resisted school. Bernard had "power" over Eugene and frequently used his younger brother as an errand boy. When Eugene protested, he was hit by Bernard.

But Eugene was not entirely passive. He liked to get out and play ball. He had friends in school. He was perky, humorous and sweet.

The first strangeness Bernard noticed about his brother was during Eugene's early adolescence. He would sometimes look sidewise at the window as if he was afraid of something outside of it. After a while this symptom and fear seemed to go away.

Eugene continued to have trouble with his teachers in junior high school. Ultimately he transferred out of junior high to Erasmus Hall H.S. in Brooklyn, Bernard's school. Eugene did not do well in high school but he kept on at his brother's and father's insistence. He did leave day school but he finished his course in evening school. He was quite proud of his 85 in English and 85 in economics, possibly his highest marks . . . For good or ill, Bernard was always very much concerned about his brother, to whom he felt very close. Perhaps he was oversolicitous. He was the one who had broken the news to Eugene that their mother was dead and he always felt an aching pity for Eugene's situation.

During his high school years Eugene had no home life to speak of. For two years after Bertha's death . . . Max cooked and he and Bernard cleaned the house. Later he remarried, a woman not used to his sort of life. She was a "greenhorn," and did not know how to approach the children, nor they her. She devoted herself to the store. There was still no family life. However, it was her hardheadedness that pulled Max out of the economic rut he was in. Neither of the boys had any affection for their step-mother.

The depression was on in full force when Eugene got out of high school. He was "afraid" to go out to look for a job. The newspapers were full of stories about the unemployment that disheartened him. From this time on he began to develop a strong political sense and a belief in a better life for the "common man." Instead of looking for work (he had no desire for any higher education) he stayed at home all day. If his step-mother nagged, he walked out of the house. Upstairs he read the papers, listened to the radio, and when he grew tired of this, hung out with the boys on the corner, almost all of whom were unemployed too. Of course he had little money. Whenever he wanted a dime he asked his father, who usually doled it out. Eugene would derive a good deal of pleasure from going to a movie and then having a frankfurter and root beer afterward. The same sort of pleasure often sufficed him in later years.

He began giving up his friends as they got jobs and drifted off to work. Eugene continued to stay home. He was beginning to have a reputation as a recluse. Friends continued to look him up and occasionally he went to parties with them. He seemed to have no interest in girls. Both he and Bernard were very much embarrassed once when Bernard, by accident, came upon Eugene, masturbating. Bernard was disturbed by his brother's hermit's life and probably nagged the boy. He had no realization till years later that Eugene needed psychiatric treatment.

One cold day Eugene and a few other neighborhood boys joined the CCC [Civilian Conservation Corps]. They were sent out to Idaho. Eugene's first time away from home, to work on the land. Though Eugene was lonely and dissatisfied, he got along well with the other fellows and worked hard to make an adjustment to this new life. He always had courage, something Bernard always respected him for . . . Bernard's fatherly feeling to his brother was extremely strong . . . Possibly Eugene responded with a son's love.

Back from the CCC's Eugene again immured himself in his room after a few half-hearted attempts to look for a job. He was almost glad, after two or three years — perhaps more — to be drafted in the U.S. Army in 1942, at the age of twenty-four. He had not yet worked a single day in his life for an employer, and he was deeply ashamed of it.

In the army he found life more difficult than it was in the CCC's. The discipline sometimes bothered him, though he never actively rebelled against it. He had trouble with two or three of the sergeants over him. He hated the tedium. He found it extremely difficult to do such a comparatively simple thing as roll a pack. He had a friend or two in his outfit but generally he was a lone wolf and probably considered a little strange. He read a lot and wrote many letters. Now he began to correspond with women relatives. His letters were superior: he was an acute observer and he described what he saw vividly. He was much praised for his letters.

Once when Eugene was home on leave Bernard introduced him to a young nurse. They liked each other and went out — his first dates — a few times. Apparently they "necked" once and Eugene described it excitedly in a letter to Bernard. During the war the nurse broke it off. Eugene was bitterly disturbed by the "Dear John" letter. He had corresponded much with the nurse but she intended to marry someone else.

Eugene saw action in the Pacific — at Hollandia, Biak, New

Guinea, the Philippines. He entered Japan with the army of occupation. Later he was honorably discharged as a private first class.

When he came home he was dearly welcomed by his father, stepmother and brother. For a time he was afraid of what it would be like looking for a job. He began to fall back into his solitary life. Bernard had left the house in 1941 to live by himself and he was now married and living in N.Y.C. He got Eugene an appointment for a job with a friend, but Eugene never showed up. That was one of the patterns of his life — Bernard digging up job opportunities and Eugene never taking them.

Finally Eugene found himself a job, as a checker and stock clerk at Namm's, in Brooklyn. He was happy about this, Bernard too.

For the first time in his life Eugene had a decent amount of money to spend on himself. He made friends in the store and visited bars with the boys, played softball with them and talked union politics. He was soon made assistant shop steward, and later became one of the union representatives who bargained with management. His attitude to his employers grew truculent. He honestly felt they were unjust to their employees. Once or twice, now, he went out with girls from the store — usually timid or unhappy girls.

About once a week, sometimes oftener, he visited Bernard and his wife. Bernard's wife liked and respected Eugene. He liked her. When their son was born Eugene was delighted. He enjoyed the child from its infancy. Though he found it difficult to shop for gifts (Gifts were never exchanged or ever given on birthday's in Max's house) he did manage to buy the baby a toy bus that the baby enjoyed very much. Eugene liked to play with the baby.

Bernard had by this time become familiar with the writing of Freud [crossed out: Fromm, Horney, Harry Stack Sullivan] and others, and he now urged Eugene to undergo psychoanalysis. With Eugene's permission (after Eugene had read a few books on analysis) he wrote to Karen Horney for the name of an analyst. She suggested a man who was too busy to take Eugene, but he suggested another analyst, a Dr. Ernst Jolowicz, a German refugee, apparently over sixty . . . Eugene began to visit him once weekly. He did not like the psychoanalytic sessions but believed they were doing him good. This was probably in 1948, two years or so after he had got out of the army . . .

Then, Bernard, for professional reasons, moved away to Oregon. After that Eugene entered another period of difficulty. At work — he wrote Bernard — he felt he was disliked first for his union activities, then as a person. He wrote that he was suspected of homosexuality by people at work and by some in the neighborhood.

The letter then recounts in detail how Dr. Jolowicz suffered several strokes. The treatment would be interrupted and then resumed. Eugene became more depressed. Dr. Jolowicz saw him as "a very serious case." There is a hint that the psychiatrist tried to reframe Eugene's possibly homosexual feelings:

> [Eugene] once explained his sexual difficulties as derived from directing his libido to his father and brother. Sometimes he felt hope for himself; most often he said he was doomed — there was no way out for him.
>
> About a year after Bernard and his family left for Oregon, Eugene's letters became bleak . . . He felt that people, especially those in the neighborhood, talked about him. His moods were black — he got little relief from them.

He stopped reading, the letter said, started getting headaches, suffered severely from insomnia, and became more paranoid.

> Trivial incidents were magnified by him: recently he bumped his head in a bus; he felt the driver had arranged that because he didn't like the way Eugene had dropped his nickel into the turnstile slot . . . He often said he would be better off dead.
>
> One night, November 3, 1951, he came home from a visit to Dr.

Jolowicz, talking to himself. Max was frightened, called the family doctor who called Jolowicz. Apparently they decided upon committal.

From Coney Island Hospital Eugene sent Bernard a letter via Max. He had told Max he wanted to see his brother . . . He wrote of being used for "sexual purposes." He was afraid that he was going to die like his mother.

MY FATHER'S LETTER is gripping, sad, and vivid. The careful formality of the third-person voice at once distances the material and allows intimate disclosure. One feels the writer's own hunger for solace. Bernard, the brother/son, is speaking with the fantasy psychiatrists, pouring out heartache, grief, guilt, and family gripes. He's also weighing how damaging he's been. "She had trouble with a leg for years afterwards, which the family attributed to either the birth of the first or second child." Unstated: He was the second child. Did his birth harm her? At moments, forcing himself to tell what haunts him, he shifts to the passive voice: "When Eugene protested, he was hit by Bernard."

He describes Bertha's schizophrenia appearing when Eugene was ten, so he would have been at least thirteen. I am surprised by the late date he offers for its onset. Bertha had a serious depression after her first son was stillborn and another after Eugene was born. From Dad's comments, I had always thought that her insanity emerged then. I have gathered that at the least, she became withdrawn and half ill for a long time after Eugene's birth. It is unclear for how many years she endured a long, slow deterioration before becoming overwhelmed by her schizophrenia and/or psychotic depression, but I believe it must have been a quietly ongoing or intermittent process through much of my father's childhood. I may be wrong, or this letter may minimize the length of her illness. The letter neglects to mention Eugene's earlier suicidal feelings and his first mental breakdown and army hospitalization for "combat fatigue."

ONLY ONE LETTER EXISTS from Max to Dad before Eugene became ill. It's undated but likely written within a year or two of Dad's moving to Oregon. Although Max had been in America for more than forty years and had attended night school, his written English was meager. His thick-handed struggle to write and his illiteracy surprised me, as did his cranky loneliness. He was angry at Dad for leaving, critical of him — or perhaps protectively worried — for aspiring to own a house. There's a hint that Dad may have asked to borrow against Max's life insurance for a down payment, perhaps a source of irritation. Max may have signed his name "Sam" in reference to Dad's storekeeper character in his early story "The Grocery Store."[4]

Dear Bernie

I read your letter don't Bother Yourself With a 1 family house Figur it out, the interest Of the house, insurance liabety heat, repair you will See that the rent Will be bigger than you are Paying Now — for Your Apt. A 1 family house Is good for a rich man. the 2nd thin You are Not Sure Yet If Oregon Will be your home for ever. You better Come home And I will help you to buy a hous You will be Able to live in the Flatbush Section Just as good As in Corvallis. I think you did a foolish thing by moving Away from us. If you can get A Job in Bklyn as a regular Teacher you will be better off Any time any body who moves Away from N.Y. State is Sorry. The policy I have for you and Eugene was due last Year You Can't have the money Now. You will be able to collect that money *only* after my death!

Leza Went to chicago this week Sche will be there 2 week I'm

glad she went She is a very sick Person. if you Want to write a letter
to me you can Send it in my name. With Love to you, Ann, and
Baby Paul. Your father "Sam"

However abandoned Max felt himself, the unbearable reality,
clear in Max's later correspondence, is that Eugene, who after
many years of struggle had ventured out into the world and was
working, fell apart when Dad moved away. Bernard seems to have
been his brother's most sustaining love after Bertha died. Though
odd from childhood, troubled, and fragile, Eugene kept trying to
force himself out of his sheltering bedroom. Dad kept encouraging him. (The act of encouraging others to "live" fully, probably
directed first at himself and his brother, became a fundamental part
of my father. I benefited from it. Students often appreciated it.)
The few postwar years when Dad and Mom, then Paul, lived
within easy visiting distance were the ones during which Eugene
was most able to work and make friends. After Dad left, "Euge"
became combative, paranoid, and reclusive. Max may have particularly begrudged his older son Oregon because he recognized how
much his presence in New York had steadied his brother.

A second specter shading the correspondence is that Max and
Liza stopped talking to Dad for several years after he married. My
mother thinks Max may have sat shiva for his "dead" son, but it is
only a half recollection. Reconciliation came when Paul was born
in late 1947. Max and Liza visited the new baby and brought as a
peace offering a handsome set of silver-plated flatware. I know
nothing about Liza. The one story my mother recalled is that in
Russia, she had been relatively well-off, married with children, and
that something terrible had happened to her. She thought that perhaps Liza's husband and sons had been murdered in a pogrom.

*   *   *

THE FATHER-TO-SON account of Eugene's illness begins thus:

November 5, 1951

My Dear son Bernie

I'm Very Very saury to tell you that Eugene Sickness Went from bad to Worse! Since you left from New York he was talken to himself all that time. October 30, 1951 he came home from Dr. Jolowicz and he stard to talk foolish things. So I Called Dr. Bker and Becker Called Jolowicz and We Decited that the best Place for him will be the Hospital it took Dr Beckr One hour to Call all the Vetrans Hospitals and all of them answerd that they have No Emty beds for him So we were forced to call Kings County Hospital and they Sent for him that was Saturday Nov 3, 6. P.M. I Went With him and when I was talken to the Hopital Dr. I told him that I wald like that Kings County should send him to a Vatrans Hospital So he told me when I can See a Certain Man about this and he will Send him to a vatrans Hospital. Yesterday I was to see Eugene he is a quit Patient and he asked for you and he told me I schal brang him Cigaretts tomorrow I will see him again let us hope for the best your father With a broken heart.

Kings County Hospital was the one to which Bertha had first been taken.

A few days later, Max wrote again, telling Dad that Eugene looked the same and forwarding a letter Eugene had written to my father. Here is the letter my father wrote back, saved by Max.

November 13, 1951

Dear Pa,

Thank you for sending me Eugene's letter. I found it very moving. It kept me in tears all day. The letter would seem to indicate that he is in the beginning stages of schizophrenia. The only good thing about the whole business is that nowadays they can help people at that stage of the illness.

I know that Eugene has to be moved from Coney Island hospital but I would like you to do all you can to get him into a veteran's hospital rather than a state institution. I have the feeling that he will get better treatment among the veterans. Ask Doctor Becker about this. I am not clear from your letter exactly where Eugene is going in Kings Park. Is it a state unit, or a veteran's unit?

Don't forget to send me Dr. Becker's address, and if you have it, Dr. Jolowicz's. I have written to the superintendant of the Coney Island Hospital for any information he can give me.

I know this is a terrible blow to you and Liza, as it is to me — but we must be patient and hope for the best. He can be helped. Keep in touch with me and see that Euge has writing paper and stamps in case he has the impulse to write to me. When you see him, don't fail to mention that I would like to hear from him, and take any letter he happens to have written. Treat him like a grown-up when you see him and always tell him you have confidence he will be well soon. Tell him we love him.

Give him the letter I enclose, and let me know when his address is changed. Try to see him often but don't wear yourself out. With love, Bernie

Nov 15, 1951

Dear Bernie

I Just Came from Eugene I See him 3 times a week he looks All right Sometimes Well I talk to him I feel like to Sy to him Nunula Dress Yourself and I will take You home. You Can't depant on them they change theyre Minds to Quak. he Schould Me A paper that he has to be on the 2nd floor in the Same building they will talk to him there when they will Send him to Kings Park that is a State Hospital Last Friday I was over to see the main office of the Vaterans. I told them My Bad luck Story they Maid out papers for me and they told me that it might take weeks or Months Even years until they Will have a Place for him in the Vaterans Hospital I want You to know that Eugen is Now in Kings County Hospital Not in Coney Island Hospital he is their for obseration and from their they will Send him to a State Hospital Bernie let me know if you Understand my writing if not I will have Somebody to write the letters for Me. I Asked Eugene how he spels psychiatrist and he speled that for me

I don't think that he Will be all right Soon it takes time it took Eugene 4–5 years first He Blush, then he stard to talk To himself he Wasn't Sick for Weeks but it took him Years until he Came to that Stage he is now. this is a terrible Sickness I am more then good to him I talk to him like a good father can talk to a child I kiss him and I Bring to him Fruit and cigarettes. As is vey zi mir was ich obe therlebt az a grosen nonglick! [Woe to me; what I have lived through is a great misfortune.][5] With love to you your father + Liza P.S. I give to Eugene all the letters you write to him.

In another undated letter, Max reported:

yeastrday Eugen looks good. But he feels the Same. he is not interested in Books or papers he has to much time to thing. he told me that Everybody Deserted him and he asked me wich Neborghrs Complained About him I told him he Schould Worry everybody likes him. than He start to Cry and when he Stoped Crying he told me that he feels Better . . . I left the house 730 A.M. and I Came back 6 P.M. I asked Eugene if he Wants Leza to Come to See him he told me that his Place is not for liza. I gave him your letter he wred and he din't say any thing. He told me Nextime I shall bring him toth Paist and his toth brush and he told me that he likes Kings County Hospital Better I asked him why? and he Said Because its Near home. Don't Send him Anything. I Will Send him Everything he needs. Next Sunday I Will See him again. Love to you all Your Father

November 28, 1951

Dear Pop,

I would like your opinion as to how much good I can do for Euge if I come East for Christmas. There are two things that are bothering me. I have only two weeks off for Christmas and I would have to spend one of them traveling. That means I could see Euge only once or twice. I am very anxious to see him, but I'm doubtful about how much I can help in one short week. The second thing is that Ann is in her eighth month of pregnancy and I am afraid to leave her alone here without anybody to take care of her, in case she should need it. Both she and Paul have had three colds apiece in the last six weeks and I have had my hands full taking care of them. I thought for a while that we could get Ann's mother to come here, but she is too sick and there is no longer that possibility. However I will do my best to come if you think it will help. Why not ask the psychiatrist? (incidentally, get me his name — I want to write to him. And I am taking care of Eugene's life history that they want.)

If I don't come for Christmas, I can certainly come in June, and then I can stay in New York for from six weeks to two months and see Eugene frequently. I don't know how much good it will do but I want very much to see him often and give him the feeling that I care a lot about how he feels.

I think it will be all right for Liza to visit Euge. He ought to have more than just one person visiting him. However, is [if] she becomes depressed as a result of her visit, there is no point to it.

Write me an airmail as to whether you think I ought to come even if only for a week.

I will write a letter to Euge directly to the hospital. Next time you see him ask him if he wants to write me a few words. Tell him that you will send them to me. I would like to hear from him, if possible. My best to you, Bernie

When Dad describes how my grandmother Ida is too sick to come to Corvallis (from California) to look after her pregnant daughter, he is referring to Ida's mental state. She suffered throughout her life from serious bouts of anxiety and depression that periodically incapacitated her. Dad, at once needed as husband, father, brother, and son, must have felt besieged. He often coped with his own life by taking care of others, offering the support he thought people ought to have and feeling comforted by giving. But this approach had its limits, among them his primary loyalty to writing, and he must have felt torn when demands arose at once from so many quarters.

During this year, his blood pressure rose, and he gained weight. His checkups with doctors concerning his heart and other bodily conditions were among the few open solicitations of care he allowed himself. On October 5, 1951, he wrote:

> Dear Pop and Liza, . . . Yes, I did have a rise in blood pressure about a month ago. It shot up to about 160, which is high for a person of my age. The doctor gave me some pills and it went down to 130. He was worried because he thought the pressure could hurt my heart. However, I think I was working too hard all summer — trying to finish a book before school reopened. I didn't but am almost through. Since school opened I have been taking it easy and I'm pretty sure the pressure is down. I'll know next week when I see the doctor. I don't think there's anything to worry about . . . Ann is fine. She is pregnant and we are expecting another baby sometime in January. We'd like a girl but we both think we'll have another boy. Anyway, we'll take what we can get . . . Paul is also in good shape. He has grown tall during the last year — he will be four two weeks from today . . . I wish you could see him. He is a healthy little boy with an animated face. He's bright, especially in his use of language. He has a very fine memory — for stories and poems and likes music . . . Bernie

Max responded to Dad's November 28 letter promptly.

> Dec 3, 1951
>
> Dear Bernie
>
> I was to See Eugene Yesterday He was very Sick he Refused to take any thing I brought for him Even cigarets he Refused. So I gave him 2 Dollars and he Said that he will buy Cigarets by the

Pedler when he Comes to Hospital Bad feelings Bothers him that he cries all the time when I See Him I thing it will be Better for us when you will Come in June I don't think if you Will Make Better for him by Coming Christmas time to See him if he Wold be Interested in You he wold asked me for you or he would ask me if I get letters from you it looks that that he is verry Sick. So don't Bother Your Self. your family Comes first. And You schould Positive Come to See him in June . . .

last Sunday I Saw Eugen Dr. And I told him Everything he was interested to know About Eugene Life Story. With love to you, Anna and Paul. Your, father. Best Wishes from liza to you and family. The old Mr Merow Died lest Sunday.

I find all the letters sad, but the next one, written the same day Harcourt Brace telegraphed Dad accepting his novel, though bland on the surface and mundanely told, is, to me, the most wrenching.

Jan 7 1952

Dear Bernie

I Saw Eugene Sunday he told me that he received writing paper and a Pen from you. But he trough Every thing out The window. Wen I Went home he saw me Standing Waiting Outside for Taxes he said To me through the Window Pop look here Maybe you Will find the Pen. I was looking But I Coulnt find her. don't Send him anything except Something to read I give him Everything he Needs. lest Week I Sent You his new Address and the Tax Papers don't forget Don't send to Eugene Raiser blats or a knife. he is Not allowed to have Such thing You have to be very Carefull With Such Patients You Can't Trust them

With Love to you all. Pop.

There is something unbearable about Max's account of Eugene's crazy/angry gesture — his throwing the pen his brother had sent him out the window, then his wish to undo it — and Max's futile search. Nothing reveals more plainly Eugene's helplessness, anger, and illness, as well as his grief about Dad's departure. Max's own despair also is unsettling. His experiencing of the illness as a personal betrayal led him to turn Eugene from a son into one of those patients "you can't trust" with razor blades or a knife. Yet he was also trying to teach Dad, to prepare him for what had happened to his brother. The pen carries connotations of Dad's writing, Max's illiteracy, Eugene's inevitable recognition that his older brother had escaped and he had not. But it was also a purchase made, a gift given and rejected, within a financially strapped family. Eugene calling to Max through the hospital window evoked for me my father's last view of his mother through another hospital window.

TWO DAYS LATER, Max wrote to Dad, who was helping him with his taxes, and confirmed some poor earnings. As a postscript, he added, "I Send You a lettr Yesterdy Abut Eugene Today Jan 9th 1905 I Came to America 47 Years Ago." The day before I was born, Max secretly sent my parents $200, a huge gift, so that they could buy a washing machine for what he assumed would be their second son. In the accompanying letter, he asked Dad to signal him discreetly that the money had arrived. He didn't want Liza to know: "Jan 18 1952 Dear Bernie I am Sending to you 200 00 Dollars for the boy when he will Arrive. I am going this Sunday To See Eugene. When you Wride a letter to Me Say Something I schol understand that you Received the 200 00 Dollars. Pop."

Eugene stayed in the hospital until July 1952. On March 14, 1952, Max wrote:

> Dear Bernie Last Sunday my sister her Son in Law and I Went to See Eugene He was very glad to See us He looks and he talks the same. We Received Your Jannas Photograph Sche is a very nice baby Liza and your Aunt Bertha Said that she is going to be Miss

America when Sche grews up. We also received Your and Pauls Picture you are telling us that You Solt the Novel but you don't tell us how Much Money Your are Getting. the Main Thing You din't tell Me. I am up Stairs Now I have a Cold I will be all right in a few More days. With love to you and family Your Father

I suspect the "cold" was in fact the heart attack he'd had and was hiding from his older son. Hearts are a family liability, and Max didn't tell Dad about his attack until the following summer. (June 24, 1952, a letter from my father to my mother: "New York is unchanged — the weather is mild and comfortable. Frankly the home depressed me a bit: too many memories. Moreover my father informed me that he had suffered a heart attack a few months ago. He is better now — he says. You can imagine how I felt.") Watching Eugene become ill must have triggered Max's memories of Bertha's disease and death. Struggling to visit his sick son, managing the hospital stay and paperwork in a still foreign language, and dealing with his ongoing difficulties with the store and with Liza overwhelmed him. In the mid-1970s, quietly working a little on his family history, Dad quoted Dr. Becker, an old family friend whom Max had helped put through medical school. Becker had looked after Eugene and had taken care of Max during his final illness. Dad later wrote, "He said my father wanted to die."[6]

I HAVE ALWAYS BELIEVED that Dad had to leave Brooklyn and his family before he could write freely. What I didn't understand until I read these letters was the price he paid. Neither his father nor his brother really survived his departure. He was the capable person among them. Max's final heart attack did not occur until March 1954, and Eugene lived on for another twenty years before dying of a heart attack at age fifty-five. His existence was minimal, his sense of despair huge. He sometimes wished to end his life. My father knew this, and it haunted him. When Dad spoke briefly about Eugene at his brother's tiny funeral, he said, "He was a wounded man trying to keep going. He did so for many years. He had very little, perhaps some small pleasure, but he had courage. He wanted to live; he wanted to be well. He wanted a better life. Rest in peace, my dear brother."[7]

IN MID-JUNE 1952, Dad rode the train east for an eight-week stay in Brooklyn to see Eugene, Max, and Liza. Mom traveled south with us to Los Angeles to visit her mother and stepfather. I was five months old; Paul would turn five in October. Ida's aged mother, my mother's fond "Nonni," Josephine (Ponzi) Ettari, had been living with them and had died only a week or so earlier. Gino and Ida, then in their fifties, together with Gino's nephews, had started a frozen pizza factory, said to have been the first in the country. He was working hard, and Ida would join him some days. Gino, often unlucky, was eventually cheated out of his share of ownership. He then gave voice lessons and scrambled to earn a living. On visits to their various homes in Hollywood and Los Angeles, we would have to make ourselves scarce when his students came and went. I recall my grandmother occupying me all one afternoon by baking macaroons together in the kitchen, doors closed. She taught me how to drip in drops of red, yellow, and blue food coloring to dye batches variously.

Gino was trim, suntanned, almost dapper, with very straight posture and a full head of gray-white hair. He spoke with a heavy Italian accent. He would leave half-sucked licorice cough drops stuck to the piano between lessons. He was gruff, argumentative, and said to be difficult. But he was devoted to my grandmother, who could be a handful. He and I got along. We'd walk his dogs and brush their fur together, or water his vegetable garden, or carefully pick a ripe lemon from a tree. He ate *verdura* (cooked greens) each day at lunch, drinking the water they'd been cooked in before sprinkling them with lemon juice.

Gino and Ida had moved west in 1943 and there largely survived by buying houses, fixing them up, and reselling them at a profit in the early Los Angeles/Hollywood real estate bubble. She was warm-hearted, generous, and, when well, a vivacious, charismatic woman. "She will give you her shirt," one of her brothers observed about her, "but demands yours in return." She couldn't tolerate regular work or much stress. She had something of the diva about her, loved having people around, and entertained many houseguests. (I recall as a child being taken along on visits to their compatriot friends. Italians found the Southern California climate and landscape simpatico with their Mediterranean roots, and many had settled there, replanting familiar crops. On outings into the countryside, we would pass vast fields of artichokes, olive groves, almond orchards, orange and lemon trees, and roadside stands where you could buy produce freshly picked. Almost inconceivable now, Los Angeles and the nearby countryside in the 1950s often smelled of gardenia and orange blossoms.) In her late seventies, widowed, my grandmother lived for a while in a grand hotel in Naples, partly supported by my father, who refused her wish to live with us. There, in spite of her age and excess poundage, a much younger widower courted her, and a hotel bellboy, who was an amateur filmmaker, featured her in several of his films.

Ida, along with her two older brothers, Hector and Oscar, had come to America from Naples as a six-year-old. When she was still a teenager, she married Albert deChiara, another Neapolitan immigrant. My mother, an only child born to a twenty-year-old girl whose husband soon departed, was extremely close to her mother. They were mother and daughter, but the relatively small age difference gave them some qualities of sisters, particularly since they lived in an extended Italian family in New Rochelle, New York, headed by my great-grandfather and great-grandmother. Francesco Ettari, the family patriarch, had been a principal at a lyceum in Naples. He was an educated, upright man, apparently not gifted in political compromise, who had defied the wrong politicians and after losing a court case had fled quickly to avoid jail. Sensing his imminent conviction, the family legend went, he'd sent word to his wife to pack his bag and meet him shipside. There, only a step ahead of the law, he had boarded a boat bound for America. Whatever the facts, his sudden departure caused some kind of nervous breakdown in his wife, Josephine, who was left behind with the three little children, and who, very close to her own family, wanted not at all to immigrate to America. Even so, she followed him some months later. Francesco eventually taught Italian as an adjunct professor at City College. He was my mother's substitute father until he died from a surgical complication when she was not quite eight.

The mother-daughter relationship was often tempestuous and damaging, but never distant. One of my parents' bonds was the symmetries of their difficult pasts. As a three-year-old, my mother more than once had to coax the hysterical, despondent Ida out of committing suicide. They'd be alone. Ida would be crying frantically on the bed, threatening to kill herself. Her daughter would have to offer her cause to continue. Behind each story is another story: Ida's own mother had, for a while when Ida was seven or eight, regularly dropped her off to visit with an Italian family friend in New Rochelle, who was said to have been fond of the child and who took an apparently avuncular interest. In the privacy of his office, he had molested her, his secret assaults no doubt contributing to her later debilitating periods of despair and otherwise mystifying histrionic behavior.

*   *   *

IDA AND GINO were the only relatives I knew well and loved while I was growing up. "Granny," as we called her, had time and patience for my brother and me. She recited Italian jingles as she bounced us on her lap, played games, and sewed clothing for my dolls. She was a good sport, and my friends were as eager for her visits as I. She cooked marvelous meals. My mother, brother, and I made regular trips to California, often riding the Southern Pacific train from Oregon overnight. Sometimes Ida and Gino would drive north, or Ida would bus to Corvallis. Five foot three, neatly dressed within her modest means, she weighed at least 170, often ten or twenty pounds more. (When David and I visited her in Naples in 1975, she spoke daily of her current weight in *chili*, or kilos, and invited us to supervise her eating, a spectacularly bad idea we mostly ducked. The waiters at the hotel were so fond of her that even when she ordered modestly, they delivered her extra treats — *arancini*, fried mozzarella, *calamari frite* — to make sure she tasted all the day's specialties.) I remember her gingerly exiting one long, overnight Greyhound ride in her tailored rayon dress and strapped, open-toed, high-heeled pumps. Perfumed, hugging and kissing us effusively, she paused to complain bemusedly to my mother about how badly the trip had swollen her ankles and feet. Unlike my mother, my grandmother used powder and rouge and regularly set in rollers her permanent-curled hair. When we visited, she'd let me loose among her bottles of cologne. I'd squeeze their atomizers and inhale the haze of sweet droplets. Paul and I got in slight trouble once when we discovered how well these bottles doubled as squirt guns.

Dad was fond of Ida and appreciated her acceptance of him at a time when others in both families had been so hostile. He often spent time on the telephone soothing her, and when she visited us in Oregon or Vermont, he took her out for drives in the country, patiently hearing out her troubles, attempting to settle and encourage her. He used to play cards with her and Gino in the evening sometimes. I recall her once in Vermont appearing at the living room door when the rest of us were scattered about the room, books in laps, and announcing with stentorian disapproval, "All anyone in this house ever does is read!" But her sweetness and her willingness to accommodate, to go along and have fun, were equally a part of her character.

DURING THE SUMMER of 1952, my mother and father wrote to each other several times a week. (My father began the exchange by instructing my mother how to time her letters so as not to cross with his.) Much of their correspondence sets his New York adventurer's thrill against her more constricted life with us. She was carless in Los Angeles and dependent on Gino or his nephews to take her out. She had little money and two small children. Ida, when not producing pizzas, often played with us, so the single parent got some respite, but the correspondence depicts a large difference between her day-counting efforts to tolerate Dad's absence and his liberated wanderings and animated literary encounters. The publication of *The Natural*, the long-awaited and dreamed-of event, was happening. He was eating out nightly with all their old friends, attending Brooklyn Dodgers games, lunching with his publishers. He was also back in his family and trying to comprehend Eugene's situation. But what could have been singularly difficult was mitigated by the joy of the coming book. She was looking after us, sometimes taking us to the beach with her mother's friends, once in a while joining Gino and Ida's evening card games, reading, and occasionally managing to talk one of the nephews into driving her to the movies. Ida and Gino owned a newfangled television (no signal yet broadcast to Corvallis); Mom was skeptical but watched an occasional show.

June 26, 1952

Dear Ann,

I saw Euge yesterday. He spoke to me for the better part of three hours — told me everything he went through, and from what he said and how he looks, I gather he is not as well as I thought — though certainly improving. He is not deluded about present time, but he is about the past. It's almost as if his memory has solidified around these delusions and he finds them difficult to give up. He was quite shaken when I pointed out that one thing he persisted on saying was real, could not possibly be. Oh, Jesus, he said, then I must really be nuts. I'll never get out of here. Despite this, I got the feeling that he wanted to *connect* with reality and so I left not at all depressed. If there were only some psychotherapy around, I am sure he would make better progress.

A great heat mushroomed out the day after my arrival. Yesterday was 97°, a record for June 25. Today was 97° or better, but I did not mind it in the least because of the interesting experiences I was having. This morning I spent an hour with [Diarmuid] Russell, learning about movie possibilities, reprints, etc. . . . We had a cordial, enjoyable conversation. He tells me Mike [Seide?] is two-thirds finished with his book. JF Powers is in Ireland. He is writing a novel about a prison. Russell is sore at [Robert] Giroux for handling him the way he did in reference to my book. Apparently he doesn't talk to him and does all business with Harcourt through Eugene Reynal, the vice-president. I think Giroux does alienate people. Russell says he sometimes doesn't answer Eudora Welty's letters, which disturbs her. Odd man.

I met Giroux at 3:30. He is young, prematurely grey, nice, and he gave me the impression of being a bit distracted; hence he did not project warmth. But he was very nice to me: Gave me six books to read; invited me to lunch for next week; had me meet Reynal, Lindley and another editor, who all said nice things about the book, which is now at the bindery. The editors were splendid — middle-

aged, reserved men, all nice, all warm. I can't tell you how friendly
their reception was. Lindley told me he envisioned a good press for
the book. Harry Sylvester is doing the review for the N.Y. Times.
He's reading from the page proofs. The book will be ready next
week. You will be surprised who read and like the MS. — Kather-
ine Ann[e] Porter and Alfred Kazin. Those words at the end of
that letter full of suggestions — remember? — saying that mine was
the first advance in the baseball novel since Ring Lardner — those
words were written by Kazin and will be published in a full page ad-
vertisement in Publishers Weekly.

Giroux showed me the book jacket: it's a very nice job in green
and bold black. In the center a powerful, black, almost hawk-nosed
Roy, with a bat on his shoulders — an abstract, as I wanted it.
Around him, well composed, an interesting group of Daumier life
figures — fans and other characters in the book. On top, my name;
on the book "The Natural." A strong imposing cover, in good
taste.

Prior to going to Harcourt, I met Robt Warshow and Clement
Greenberg at Commentary. They too are delighted with my work
— were most cordial, told me they thought most highly of my writing. Warshow said he thought Mike Seide and I were doing original
worthwhile work. Warshow wants me to have lunch with him.
Greenberg, who I took to at once, a sweet, enthusiastic unassuming
man (he lived 4 blocks from my house as a kid + went to Erasmus
Hall) is arranging an evening at his house so that I can meet the PR
[Partisan Review] crowd. He said my PR story was superb.

Had anyone before (or since) labeled Clement Greenberg, the
brilliant kingmaker art critic, "a sweet . . . unassuming man"? I met
him several times as a teenager in the mid-1960s, when he used to
visit the painter Kenneth Noland regularly in Shaftsbury, Vermont.
Noland's daughter, Lyn, and I were good friends. My image of
Greenberg is of a large, powerful man demanding the center of
whatever space he inhabited. I see him in bathing trunks, sunning

in a chair beside Noland's swimming pool, his chest and belly half covered by a white terry cloth robe. He was by then almost completely bald, and the top of his head gleamed. He had a sharp, prominent nose and intense eyes, and seemed utterly sure of himself — apparently a partial truth. Noland was making big bucks and spending hard. He and his wife, Stephanie, each owned a Lincoln Continental. I recall Greenberg emphatically telling all within hearing, voice edged, how when he and Noland had traveled to New York City together, he'd instructed Noland to drive the Lincoln right past his father's home so he could flaunt their collective success, show his doubting father how well he was doing. He may have been more diffident in his youth, or Dad may simply have felt so happy that afternoon that the whole world seemed benign.

Robert Giroux, who entered Dad's life that June day, is arguably the great American literary editor of the twentieth century. I met him a number of times at public events but never knew him. His quiet style was opposite Greenberg's boisterous, opinionated roar. But his genius for seeing talent was certainly equal to the art critic's. Giroux possessed a singularly honed sense of serious literature, and his writers knew it. When in 1955 he moved from Harcourt Brace to Farrar, Straus, seventeen authors, including T. S. Eliot, Flannery O'Connor, John Berryman, and my father, moved with him. I have read that he was the editor who encouraged J. D. Salinger to write *The Catcher in the Rye*. Similarly, it was Giroux who published Robert Lowell's *For the Union Dead* and Thomas Merton's *The Seven Storey Mountain*, and who gathered all of Elizabeth Bishop's letters into *One Art*.[8]

Giroux was a scholar who worked in the publishing world in the days before trade editors had become primarily salespeople. (Besides the many introductions he wrote — for collections by my father, Bishop, O'Connor, Berryman, and others — he also wrote his own book about Shakespeare's sonnets.) Over the years, my father came to love and trust Giroux, and particularly appreciated how little he impinged on Dad's writing, how much he simply worked to comprehend and support the artist's effort. When Dad finished a book or story, he would send it to Giroux, or have his agent send it. Dad saw Giroux as his close, fundamental ally in the large literary world. While my father enjoyed Roger Straus and valued the publisher's braggadocio and gusto for books, it was Giroux whose counsel he sought on serious writing matters. In September 2004, at a reception after a memorial service for Straus, I talked with Giroux for a minute. Close to ninety, white hair thinning, supporting himself with a cane but still completely cogent, he carefully recalled, words distinct amid the people-jammed roar, how when Dad had finished writing *The Assistant,* Harcourt Brace had rejected it. It was Giroux who had grasped its worth and took it to Farrar, Straus, where it remains in print today, half a century later.

DAD ENDS the June 26, 1952, letter by mentioning friends he'd contacted, including Alex and Bernadette Inkeles: "I spoke to her. It was so sweet to hear her voice. I am really very fond of her.

"And to top a delightful day, I had bananas and sour cream for supper and here I am writing to you. Love to all. Give the enclosed ring or coin to Paul. I got it in Coney Island, where I went to cool off last night. Bern."

When Bernadette Inkeles died early in 2005, her death ended a friendship of almost seventy years with my mother. Bernadette and Alex met at the same time she met my mother — when they were all undergraduates at Cornell in the late 1930s. Alex had grown up in Brooklyn in a Polish Jewish family; Bernadette Kane's Irish-German Catholic family lived in Bronxville. Bernadette was an unusually generous person, intelligent, with a lovely sensibility and quiet talent. I remember learning not many years before she died how poems she wrote had won her admission — I

believe the same year Anne Sexton and Maxine Kumin attended —
to a poetry seminar with Robert Lowell. Alex, a sociologist, started
out as a Sovietologist. Much of his work was devoted to studying
the modernization of rural communities, but he found time to
write about diverse cross-cultural issues. He did stints as a professor first at Harvard and later at Stanford as a senior fellow at the
Hoover Institution.

The Inkeleses, often with their daughter, Ann, in tow, traveled
everywhere — Chile, India, Japan, and the Soviet Union, to name
only a few of the many places they visited. They sought to know
the world and had impressive stamina. I think of Bernadette as a
person who worried a fair amount, but she was also intrepid and a
good sport. Their house in Cambridge, Massachusetts, which we
rented for a year, was full of art objects carried home from Asia
and South America. They haunted museums. In the summer of
1965, when we lived in France and Spain together, we made visits
to many, including the Matisse chapel in St. Paul de Vence and the
various Gaudí buildings in Barcelona. (In the unfinished Sagrada
Familia, Dad talked a Spanish stonemason into letting him work
one end of a big two-person saw so that he could help cut one of
the huge, soft stones with which they were building the cathedral.
He wanted to know what the effort felt like — possibly particularly
for his stories about his artist character Arthur Fidelman.)

Alex and Bernadette shared many interests with my parents:
ideas, art, theater, literature, travel, food, mutual friends, and the
understanding that they were citizens of a larger world. Alex particularly was an important figure in my childhood. He had a tur-
bine mind, with endless facts at his fingertips, and he professed
opinions on all subjects. He stood out to me as unusually com-
petent, and I early on appreciated his authoritative approach to
knowledge. He liked to have it, and he liked to use it. When, in the
late 1940s, no one was sure how to think about the postwar Soviet

Union under Stalin, Alex decided to go to Russia and survey the population. The result, in 1950, was *Public Opinion in Soviet Russian,* a classic study that launched his career. Visitors to the Soviet Union in those days were followed by spies. Tailed by an obvious one for several days, Alex stopped suddenly, turned around, surprising his pursuer, and said, "Hi, I'm Alex Inkeles — I assume you know that. But what's your name?" His approach to academic questions was often original and a little brash, and I enjoyed it. I think my sense of him was further polished by the fact that my mother and father tended to defer to him about many worldly matters. "Let's ask Alex" was a phrase regularly on their lips. Looking back, I am struck by how much time the two couples spent together. They managed to meet up frequently — whether on travels or on visits to each other's homes.

THOUGH FAR AWAY, and clearly relishing his time alone, Dad continued to take a close, instructing interest in our family life that summer of 1952. My mother had longed for a loving father, and I think Dad's paternalistic style often went down fairly well with her because of the absence it filled.

June 28, 1952

Dear Ann,

I'm glad little Jan is better. You did right in immediately going to the doctor. That's what I want you to do always and immediately. Be sure you sterilize all her stuff. As for the crib, money is no object. If you haven't got one her size already, rent one at once. I enclose $30 for you. When you get down to $10, let me know . . . Please keep Paul away from the gangster movies — I insist on that. If necessary, disconnect the plug of the set if he has access to it while you're busy. I want him to see only children's programs . . . He may also see a science subject if not too frightening. Please be careful about this . . .

Liza and Pop are very good to me — oversolicitous as a matter of fact. There is too much of the usual Jewish "Eat, eat, do me a favor." And Pop is a nag: "When are you going to take a shower — it's so hot." "That's not the way to shave with an electric razor. Let me show you how." — all day long. I have no doubt that I get my own nagging qualities from him. But they are both good: offer me all sorts of money and services. Liza uncomplainingly does most of the work in the store — even getting up every morning at six to open the place. She reminds me of Zenobia in *Ethan Frome*, at the beginning incapacitated; at the end, when Ethan and Mattie are crippled, taking over competently. Anything the writer imagines can be duplicated in life.

Dad mentions his uncle Casile's heart attack and his visit to him: "With all he was amused about my experience in the publishing world. He has, from the time I was fifteen, predicted fame and fortune for me, and he thinks that his prediction is coming true. He was also calm when discussing the Jewish theatre with me. He and Anna said nice things about you — your appearance and intelligence — and they wish to be remembered to you."

He describes how he went to the theater and saw *I Am a Camera*. The play inspired seedling thoughts anticipating *The Assistant*.

After seeing the play I decided that I will write one sometime, based on my store-life short stories. I have an idea about a grocery couple and their son, a boy in college who doesn't know what to do with his life.

Tomorrow I am seeing Eugene. Monday night I'm going to a night game at Ebbets Field with Bill Borst, the Harcourt book salesman, who read my novel and wrote me a very nice letter about it. Thursday afternoon I am going to Ebbets Field again to watch the Dodgers play the Giants, a spectacle I could hardly miss. Tuesday is lunch with Giroux, instead of Wednesday, because of Euge. I shall also see about four or five more people, when I decide whom.

So far I have done no writing and very little reading. I hope, after next week, that I can start a story, though, frankly, the prospects are not good.

The common ground of my parents' marriage reveals itself in the diversity of his subjects. He discusses a friend's art exhibit: "I saw Ben-Zion's show at the Jewish Museum, today. In a way its very impressive: the first-rate compositions and brush work. The color is startling, quite different from what he has been doing up to now, and really the weak point, it seems to me, of some of the pictures. As a matter of fact I thought they were dramatically more effective as etchings."[9]

He tells my mother about other friends: "I heard from Miriam Lang. Apparently some N.Y. columnist wrote that I had a book coming out and Miriam picked it up. Her father died of cancer in March. Poor Doris had her spine fractured in an automobile accident . . . Neither Dorothy or Bud [Evslin] liked The Natural."[10]

He wants her to read pieces that have excited him: "Lillian Hellman finished her piece in the New Yorker on 'The Red Badge.' Since they sent this issue of the mag to Corvallis, it should reach you (I got another copy out of them) but if not, let me know, and I'll send this to you."[11]

He keeps at family finances: "I've taken care of the bills you sent me. Please send out the bank statement as soon as you get it."[12]

He speaks frankly about some of his feelings: "Now that I have been gone two weeks I find myself beginning to miss you and the children. Not any great loneliness, because I am kept very busy (absolutely no time for writing), but I do wish I could see you all and hug each of you."[13] And later: "Saw Norman Peach the other night. We walked along the lake — around it — in Prospect Park and then crossed the Parade Grounds. I remembered kissing you there in the dark and it really gave me a thrill."[14]

He thinks about his children and gives permission for purchases: "Paul may have the rubber raft if Granny wants to get it. I think the sprinklers are good enough. Thank him for his nice letter."[15] "How is Paul's cold? I'd not have unpacked the wading pool at that late hour."[16]

On visiting with the Inkeleses and watching how they parented their daughter, he writes: "They do not shout at her or nag her, and quite frankly, observing them, I felt guilty about our handling of Paul. I vowed I would improve on my handling of him, and I know you feel the same. I am dead serious about that. I will make a greater effort to control anger and impatience and I only hope we can check or assist one another when we have to."[17]

Responding to her description of an earthquake in Los Angeles and its aftermath, he says: "The earthquake was nightmarish. You did all right with Paul but I wish you had kept him away from television and radio reports. There is no reason for compounding his anxiety . . . I'd have gone out of my way to give him a pieceful [*sic*], playful day without subjecting him to the talk that multiplies anxiety. I'm sorry you were frightened. I can well understand why."[18]

He fills her in on Eugene, noting that Dr. Jolowicz "advises taking Euge out [of the hospital] but doesn't offer too much hope of further improvement."[19] "Eugene is home. He is both good and bad. The story is too long and complicated to tell by mail."[20] "The situation with Eugene is mauvaise. Prognosis poor though spontaneous cure is possible . . . Details when I see you. Sad."[21]

They have their tensions. He becomes irritated by her longing openly for his return: "As I told you, I do not know whether I shall stay on an extra week or not: It depends on if and when Eugene is released."[22] He responds to jabs she's made about the weight he's gained: "I have given up the thought of dieting till we get back to Corvallis. There is simply too much social opposition to it; however don't get scared: it has high priority in my mind."[23] He complains when she doesn't write: "Tomorrow will be five days if I do not get [a letter], and I've had only three (if I get one tomorrow) in 10 days. Describe Janna as she is now, and Paul, at length when you write again."[24] He anticipates her resistance to the consequences of his book buying: "I have sent out to my office three 35 pound boxes of books. We will need a new bookcase — without complaints, please."[25] And he grouses a little about having to visit her dear family friends the Lanfranchis: "They are nice-hearted old girls, but I tell you frankly next time I come to N.Y. Nobody gets any advance notice. There were just too many people to see."[26]

MY MOTHER was my father's first audience for all that was happening around the publication of his book. Regarding book publicity, he proudly describes how he drew the line: "But I did have to refuse to pose for a picture of myself reading the baseball encyclopedia." Mostly, he just enjoys sharing his excitement: "Bob is sending copies out, in the firm's name, to Lewis Mumford, Ernest Hemingway, Jean Stafford, Charlie Chaplin and to several other writers in the hope that they will comment . . . [Giroux] wants me to try for a Guggenheim."[27]

Then, on the big day, July 4, 1952, he writes: "I have a copy of The Natural in my possession. Bob Giroux sent it special delivery and I got it today. Very thoughtful of him, especially since I said he needn't bother about sending me one. He enclosed a card: Dear Bernard — Congratulations! And signed it Very very nice."

A few days later, he describes another "moment of arrival," his first formal photo. The photographer

took about 30 candid shots of me and guarantees at least two good ones. After Harcourt takes its choice, he is going to send me the

proofs so I can have one or two made for future use. He showed
me pictures he had taken of Eudora Welty, Jean Stafford, Lionel
Trilling, A. J. Liebling and others. Now I join the sacred company
. . . I understand Eugene Reynal, the vice-president praised me to
the sky at the salesmen's meeting. Said they had been watching me
for a long time. I was a writer of genuine literary merit.[28]

Finally, a few weeks later, he recounts meeting "Saul Bellow, a
really wonderful, really superior person. We chatted for two hours,
including time spent in his car, as he drove me from Queens, where
he lives, to Manhattan. He said so many nice things about my book
and stories that I was infinitely elated."[29]

Although the enthusiastic responses to *The Natural* far outnum-
bered the criticisms, Dad also recounts how the New York literary
world did not welcome the book unreservedly.

> July 26, 1952
> I had lunch with Robert Warshow, the Commentary editor. He
> too [along with Bud Evslin] thinks *The Natural* is "unsuccessful."
> He said it was a better first novel than Saul Bellow's first, and it
> certainly deserved to be printed, but it was thin in plot, character-
> ization ("lacking in invention") and in symbolism. (He saw the
> cracked bat coming a mile away.) He thinks the book is a let down
> (You stubbed your toe) from the short stories, one of his favorites
> of which is "The Prison." He read the book through in pretty
> nearly one sitting but wasn't much moved by it and didn't care
> whether the Knights won or lost. Roy, he called "catatonic." He
> said Clement Greenberg felt "much the same" as he did. Yet he is
> going to have a review of the book "because you're a good writer"
> and Wm. Phillips, one of the Partisan Review editors, and a re-
> viewer of stature, is going to do it.
> Since hearing him and Bud on the subject of the book I've sort
> of felt that one has to have the humor to come along with me in my

jest or get absolutely nothing from the book. I know well that the book is no masterpiece but it is clever entertainment and says something to perhaps simple people. Love, Bern

INTERWOVEN WITH THE NEWS on Eugene, his book, and mutual friends, Dad offers a single, more intimate and immediate glimpse of his family in a letter he wrote to my mother a day or two after his uncle Casile died suddenly. In his letter of June 28, he identifies Casile Fidelman as the family member who, when my father was fifteen, first predicted his literary success. The reference suggests his uncle as the person with whom he discussed the arts, certainly playwriting. Since Dad was fifteen the year his mother died, it seems that Casile may have offered writing and creative achievement as a partial antidote for the loss. I suspect that Dad named his artist protagonist in *Pictures of Fidelman* Arthur Fidelman as an evocation of his uncle and a nod to him.

July 15, 1952

Dear Ann,

A while ago I came from a funeral. Casile died in Jeanie's house Sunday night. I did not know till this morning. After I awoke my father came up and said, today we must go to a funeral. I said, whose. He said, Casile is dead. He died of a heart attack. My father cried.

The service was short — in at one P.M., out at one fifteen. Jeanie [Casile's daughter, my father's first cousin] was grief-stricken but controlled. As they were praying at the grave she rested her cheek on the coffin, as if it were against his face, and said papa papa papa over and over again. Gently, she said, when they were lowering the casket into the grave, gently, gently, gently.

A friend of mother's was there. She is the sister of Isidore Cashier, the actor, who, you will remember, died on the day of Jeanie's wedding. This particular plot in the cemetery is for Jewish theatrical personnel, so they were all there . . .

She went with my father and me down a ways to hunt for my mother's grave. We didn't know the exact plot and for a while I was worried because it meant so much to my father to see it. I wanted so much to find it and then I did. My father came over and he wept and asked my mother to take care of Eugene. Then Jeanie said in Yiddish, Bertha take care of us. My father was surprised when I showed him on the stone that mama was only forty-one when she died.

BERNARD MALAMUD, published novelist, left New York City at the end of the first week in August. He had much to think about. The three-day train ride, the continent clacking by his window, provided him time to digest impressions, to contemplate his new identity. Fittingly, *The Natural* begins with a haunting description of the protagonist's own cross-country journey.

Roy Hobbs pawed at the glass before thinking to prick a match with his thumbnail and hold the spurting flame in his cupped palm close to the lower berth window, but by then he had figured it was a tunnel they were passing through and was no longer surprised at the bright sight of himself holding a yellow light over his head, peering back in. As the train yanked its long tail out of the thundering tunnel, the kneeling reflection dissolved and he felt a splurge of freedom at the view of the moon-hazed Western hills bulked against night broken by sprays of summer lightning, although the season was early spring. Lying back, elbowed up on his long side, sleepless still despite the lulling train, he watched the land flowing and waited with suppressed expectancy for a sight of the Mississippi, a thousand miles away.[30]

Although he may have been writing lightly when he told his wife, "Now I join the sacred company," my father was stating his deepest feeling. Whatever hunger for faith existed within him, he had transformed it into a belief in the sanctity of literature. Nothing mattered more to him than joining the community of recognized, serious writers. And in Manhattan, the buzz about *The Natural* — the lunches with editors and salespeople, the photo session, the early reviews — informed him that he had stepped across that threshold. Twenty years of lonely practice preceded the moment. His had been a long apprenticeship through many a night tunnel. Finally, he'd found the baseball story, a good choice both for a Jew intent on becoming an American and for a Brooklyn boy and Dodgers fan who'd never been physically graceful, yet who understood viscerally the mix of aspiration and frustration that could propel a writer, an athlete, a game, a book. More than that, Hobbs's opening gesture of lighting a match evokes my father's journal entry of "looking at Mama with a match." In *The Natural,* the long since wounded son found a disguised way to write about his grief. He deposited his great, aching hurt into the tale. He had made it funny, mythic, American, almost bearable — but not quite. When a publisher bought the novel, when admired writers praised it, their acts elevated its creator from the farm league into the majors. He returned to Manhattan amazed to find he had been given a uniform, chosen to play on the team whose banners had long decorated his wall.

THE SUMMER HAD also been about Eugene and my father's "aching pity" for him. He had visited many times with his ill brother, consulted doctors about his care, stayed east longer to bring him home from the hospital. He had seen that Eugene was desperately sick and would never return to full health. I wonder if he would have traded his literary success for Eugene's health. It's a preposterous question, but I raise it to touch again the guilt that underlay some of his best writing, that lit his moral quandaries. He had once had an argument with his Bennington College colleague Stanley Edgar Hyman about whether one should sacrifice a baby's life to save a Shakespeare play, or vice versa. After reading the letters recounting his father's and brother's anger at him for leaving them, and the deterioration of their health in the wake of his departure, I understand something more of the question's meaning to him even if, realistically, Eugene would likely have become ill even if Dad had stayed in Brooklyn.

ON MONDAY, August 11, my mother took a train north from Los Angeles, and they met in San Francisco to enjoy a week alone together. Ida and Gino looked after Paul and me. Everyone then reassembled and headed north again to Corvallis, to begin the family's fourth Oregon autumn.

Chapter 5 ⤙

Corvallis

⤙ ⤙ SOMETIMES, IN THE LATE summer afternoons, the curved brass handle on the front door of our house on Thirty-first Street would become so hot that I could not grab it properly to thumb down the latch. I was six and already had the run of our yard, our block, and my grade school playground across the street. I'd use my shirt to mitt the metal, or knock or ring until someone came. I recall the intense, west-leaning sun angling onto me as I waited, the absorbed heat radiating back from the dark green–painted wood.

The front door opened directly into a narrow living room, with a couch on its far side — which was not far — my father's reading chair beside it, both inexpensive, brown and black woven fabrics, Danish modern pieces. Nelson Sandgren's watercolor of an Oregon coast landscape hung over the couch. Sandgren taught painting at the college. An etching, *Abraham Sacrificing Isaac*, by New York friend Ben-Zion, dominated the space to the left of the hall entrance. On the near wall, a low brick and board bookshelf stood beneath a window, and a fireplace occupied the right end of the room.

Turn left from the front door, take two steps, and you were in the corner dining room. My mother had found and stripped a substantial round, claw-footed oak table that, together with four chairs and a bookcase, filled the space. From the dining room, you entered the kitchen. I believe it was painted yellow and had a linoleum floor and counters, and a view of our pear tree out a back window. A short hall ran behind the living room, past the staircase and the bathroom, to my parents' tiny bedroom. Upstairs were the two little eaved rooms Paul and I occupied.

When my father was out, I could make noise. But if I knew he had returned and retreated into his bedroom for a nap, I would gently pat the warm door instead of pounding. The day's teaching or writing tired him enough that he usually rested before his evening of reading. We were not to wake him. Since the house was small and the one bathroom and one telephone only feet from his bedroom, the assignment was large and success not guaranteed. We would tiptoe and whisper, lunge to catch the phone on the first ring, and answer it in barely audible voices. Occasionally, we'd bungle our duty and make some loud noise that roused him grumpy. Without giving it much thought, I mostly cut my paths according to his habits. Parental needs are native terrain, formally mapped only in retrospect.

I REALIZE NOW that Dad saw Corvallis as an exile's way station. Almost as soon as he arrived, he began looking for grants, fellowships, and other positions that might allow him to leave. It has taken me time to grasp his view because the rest of us, certainly I, held the place so oppositely. I knew it as home and found sustaining pleasure in its physical beauty and fellowship. Reconstructing a chronology, I finally put together his restlessness. He spent the summers of 1952, 1954, and 1958 alone back east. For a year, the autumn of 1956 to the summer of 1957, we lived in Italy. Tucking me in one night in 1959, he warned me that we would move in two years. (Meant well, the news settled on me ominously.) Although he had grown fond of many people and close to a good handful, he claimed barely to look back when we departed in 1961.

Like his protagonist Levin in *A New Life*, Bernard Malamud had arrived in Oregon shadowed by self-doubt. Dad also worried about supporting a wife and son. Unlike Levin, my father carried substantial talent and endurance, as well as, to borrow again from the Keats sonnet, "a teeming brain" he hoped to glean. The college initially disappointed, even shocked, him, its cheerful blandness causing him to bridle. I suspect he may have shared Levin's urge: "Levin saw himself fleeing with both heavy bags when he learned the next morning that Cascadia College wasn't a liberal arts college."[1] Early in *A New Life*, Pauline, speaking apologetically about her husband, Levin's new colleague, Gerald Gilley, captures the arriving Malamud's view of the faculty's mediocrity and its absence of scholarly intent: "He's done a few textbook reviews here and there, but not much else. Gerald is an active type, too much so to write with patience. And there's no doubt he's lost some of his interest in literature. Nature here can be such an esthetic satisfaction that one slights others."[2] Harder still, Dad found himself at the bottom of the school's pecking order, instructing students in grammar, his desire to teach literature initially blocked by his lack of a Ph.D. He found it irritating to be outranked by men who he felt appreciated books less than he, and who seemed without the intellectual curiosity he prized.

But Corvallis — a steady paycheck, a rented house, new colleagues, college teaching, a predictable routine, and small-town family life, with the attendant duties of leaf raking and Cub Scout potlucks — offered my father much more than Levin would have predicted. The experience steadied and centered him. Whatever his quarrels with the place, he also responded pleasurably. He found the landscape beautiful, enjoyed frequent good times with friends, and liked himself as a family man. So, too, the community's relative isolation and privacy, together with his slight alienation, assisted him in coming into his own. He was the town's serious writer, and while the singular status made him lonely, it also sheltered him, defined him, and freed him from constant competitive scrutiny — from having to attend at close hand to more accomplished rivals or to the whole fractious New York literary scene.

While temporarily transplanted into the valley's fertile soil, he became a published fiction writer. In a proud 1951 catch-up letter to Miriam Milman Lang, he wrote, "Oregon is a wonderful place to live . . . Since we left New York I have begun to sell my stories. Five pieces have been printed and another will be this year. Also possibly an article requested by the American Mercury. Since last summer I have been at work on a novel which ought to be ready by this winter. Houghton Mifflin has optioned it but I am not sure that they will take it up . . . The idea is to get the thing done, so I am spending the summer in my office."[3] Along with *The Natural*, while in Oregon he also wrote *The Assistant*, published in 1957, which won the Rosenthal Award of the National Institute of Arts and Letters; most of the stories in *The Magic Barrel*, which in 1959 won the National Book Award; *A New Life;* and many of the stories in *Idiots First*, including several that would become the core of *Pictures of Fidelman*.

BERNADETTE INKELES wrote to me after Dad died how when he arrived in Corvallis, he described with delight the way people planted flowers in the narrow patches of dirt that ran between the sidewalks and the curbs in front of their houses.[4] It was perhaps his first taste of the homesteader's pride that characterized the place. The tiny town was barely a hundred years old. Its natural beauty went way beyond anything he might have seen before: rhododendrons; azaleas; and plum, apple, pear, and cherry trees in yards everywhere in bloom in the spring. A short drive took him to old-growth forests and rushing streams. The young highways on which he traveled were edged with wildflowers: vetches, foxgloves, cornflowers, so many daisies in June that some fields seemed snowcovered. Even though as a small boy during a polio epidemic, he'd been sent with his mother for several weeks into the New York State countryside, and he'd later spent weeks of two summers as a waiter in adult camps in New Hampshire and Vermont, he wasn't any kind of outdoorsman. What little he knew of nature and wilderness had come to him courtesy of city parks or writers such as Melville and Wordsworth.

Set on the Willamette River, Corvallis circa 1950 had a population of around sixteen thousand residents, including six thousand students.[5] The broad, flat valley was bracketed by mountains, the Cascade Range on one side and the Coast Ranges on the other, with the Pacific Ocean just beyond. The town itself was mostly level, edged with gentle green hills that burned brown in summer. Climb any rise when the clouds lifted, and you could glimpse snow-covered peaks in the distance: Mount Hood, Mount Jefferson, the Three Sisters. Marys Peak, where we picnicked, was our small local mountain.

The nineteenth-century settlers, mostly white Protestants, had wedged their shoulders against the wilderness and survived, sometimes prospered, by harvesting its bounty. They felled huge trees; netted masses of silver salmon; hunted Pacific seals for fur and bears and deer for meat; raised dairy cattle, sheep, and chickens; speculated on land or plowed and seeded diverse crops into the valley's unusually fertile soil. Vast rolling fields of red-green wheat turning gold in the heat, silverish rye, backed by tall, dark green Douglas fir trees provided the emblematic landscape of the Willamette Valley. Grapevines were taking root when we left in 1961, but the wines that now make the region famous did not yet exist. Instead, sawmills burned everywhere outside of town, and with them mountains of orange sawdust produced a sweet, wet scent of freshly cut wood mixed with the deeper smokiness of the huge, beehive-shaped furnaces. Diesel trucks — gigantic logs, piled high upon their beds, chained down in pyramidic stacks — barreled along roads too narrow to hold them. As kids, we would repeat stories we'd heard about chains breaking and logs crashing through the windshields of unlucky cars caught behind them. Assorted factories dotted the landscape, some for milling wheat and one in Corvallis for canning vegetables.

Later, in high school and college, I wrote term papers about the meaning to America of the loss of the frontier. Partly, of course, I was settling my own grief and grievance about my premature uprooting. But more than that, I was describing something our family had witnessed. Living in the Pacific Northwest, we had inhaled a final whiff of lower-forty-eight American frontier life. Harding School, the grade school Paul and I attended, made a very big deal of the state centennial in 1959, and we all enthusiastically rehearsed "our" anthem to perform for parents: "Land of the empire state builders, land of the golden west. Conquered and held by free men, fairest and the best." Since it was the anticommunist 1950s and church and state mingled unself-consciously, we also sang a reverential praise song for Oregon that began, "Oh the place where I worship is the wide open spaces, built by the hand of the lord." And we enacted our own Wild West. In Corvallis, my brother, like all the guys, eventually owned a BB gun, which, through trickle-down family economics, yielded me much-coveted access to his toy six-shooters. My friend Janie wore a leather cowgirl skirt and vest with fringe and a single gun in a holster. We considered ourselves expert on bullet trajectories.

LATE AFTERNOON would find my mother in the kitchen. The daily housework belonged to her domain: cooking, dishwashing, cleaning (eventually with help), laundry, ironing, and grocery shopping. She, like my father, favored a clean, uncluttered house, everything straightened and in its place. She did not cook before she married but quickly found pleasure in it. She had absorbed generations of Mediterranean food knowledge, and we ate well, aided by the Oregon wealth of seasonal fruits and vegetables. If I came in hungry after an afternoon of play, she'd sometimes spoon simmering tomato sauce onto a piece of bread for me, as her grandmother and mother had done for her. A summer Sunday family outing often included a stop at a farm stand for fresh corn. My father and I enjoyed the local Dairy Queen soft ice cream, so the pursuit of a nickel cone offered a ready after-dinner mission. If illness kept my mother from the kitchen, Dad would take my brother and me for hotdogs or burgers there, or to the Sunnybrook diner. Indeed, the occasional pan-fried hamburger, dabbed with mustard but a little too dry, was all I ever remember him cooking, and only if my mother was out or ill.

When my grandmother visited in the spring, we would sometimes walk or drive to vacant lots to scoop up wild mustard and dandelion greens, which she would carefully wash, then stew up in a little olive oil and garlic. As often as we could during her stays, we'd put Granny up to making gnocchi. I recall the small kitchen counter and table spread with floured dishtowels, each covered with crowded rows of the delicate potato pasta. Production took the afternoon. She'd wrap one of my mother's aprons around her ample waist and position herself firmly before the counter or stove. First, she boiled, peeled, and fork-mashed the big potatoes, chosen for age so they'd be starchy. Then she added just enough flour to make the mass hold together as she gently hand-rolled it into fat, off-white coils, cutting from them several hundred bite-size pieces. Sweeping her thumb along the top of each with delicate pressure, she'd slowly shape a sea of chubby shells. When the moment was right — the table set, my father up from his nap, and all else at the ready — she'd poach the gnocchi ever so briefly and deliver them in a tomato sauce that she or my mother had cooked up, or sometimes simply with butter and Parmesan cheese. My mother, brother, and I might help, but Granny was in command.

Dad sometimes groused to me about my mother's unwillingness to cook the Jewish foods he'd eaten as a boy. He mentioned matzo ball soup, maybe gefilte fish from scratch. I'm not sure his nostalgia was for actual family dishes. No one had cooked much in his boyhood home, and they'd often grabbed dinner — graham crackers dipped in milk, or potatoes with milk — between grocery customers. More simply, I think, Dad was expressing a slight, chronic alienation, a desire for an evocation of neighborhood. He liked to confide in each of us about the others, I suppose to heighten our allegiance to him, certainly to blow off steam. In truth, he mostly enjoyed what his wife set before him, even ate Italian or French food in restaurants when he could. He accepted that she brooked little supervision in the kitchen. The stove was her territory. He appreciated her ability, particularly later in Vermont, Cambridge, and New York, when they hosted frequent dinners for friends and colleagues — evenings increasingly, as time went by, sprinkled with other accomplished writers, academics, and artists. She became adept at entertaining several times a week and brought to it a gracious authority she rarely allowed herself in other realms.

THE WHOLE OF DOWNTOWN 1950s Corvallis spanned a few blocks square. My mother would buy the weekly groceries at

Safeway, entering beside a pile of big, pastel-colored salt blocks stacked ready for purchase by farmers for their cows. I favored the candy store across the street, unusual in that era for being air-conditioned. On hot summer days, it would vent a cold bliss of sweet chocolate air onto the sidewalk. There was a small department store for clothing and shoes, a J.C. Penney, a sporting goods store, a stationery/book store, hardware stores and lumberyards, two or three movie theaters, a handful of bars, and a motel or two. A railroad track ran through town, and inevitably, driving to and fro on errands, we were forced to wait for the long freight trains to pass. My brother and I would count their cars — sometimes more than a hundred — of grain, produce, logs, milk, and god-knows-what in tank cars labeled CHEMICAL.

My mother occasionally used to take me around with her to a dingy warehouse near the river, where workers candled eggs and she'd buy us, for twenty-five cents a box, dozens of the bargain cracked ones or those with two yolks, which couldn't be shipped to stores. She and friends would scout local yards for fallen apples and pick them up to cook into sauce or pies. I remember going along once to gather someone's plums. The first fifty cents I ever earned was paid me for harvesting strawberries from our friends the Hansons' field one hot June day. I was seven or eight, and it took me hours, even with my mother's help, to fill twelve pints. Paul and some other boys crawled into a nearby hen house and broke the torrid monotony by pelting one another with very rotten eggs.

THE OREGON STATE CAMPUS where Dad taught and wrote started on the western side of town, its perimeter touching residential streets, and then spread out into the rural countryside. Not only did the generous grassy acreage — kept green all summer by sprinklers chirping out large, circling spasms of water — accommodate classroom buildings, dormitories, a football stadium and a gym, and plenty of sororities and fraternities, but there were also plantings for the forestry department, animal grazing fields, and many barns housing the sheep and cattle that students studied. Dad and the English department, second-class citizens on the practical, husbandry-focused campus, worked in an army Quonset hut, whose rounded tin roof sat on low wooden walls. His office there was an easy walk from our home. Some Saturdays, I am told, my mother would push a stroller with Paul or me to Dad's office window and pass a sandwich through so he could write without interruption. I remember that later visits held the prospect of a new, unbroken piece of chalk, with which I scribbled on his classroom board. Writing now, I can smell the pleasant, musty dead air of the place.

Colleagues marveled at his diligence. In a school where faculty-room gossip over coffee was a social obligation, he often passed; where doors were open, he kept his closed. His friend Chester Garrison recalled:

On Monday, Wednesday, Friday, he taught and had office hours. On Tuesday, Thursday, and Saturday, he reached his office at 9 A.M. and began to write. He sat on an upright wooden chair drawn up to a small table or desk . . . He has said that from three-hours' work, he was lucky to get one page done. Members of the staff on either side of him had to accustom themselves to hearing through the thin walls his voice notably raised as he tested out phrasing and dialogue to get them right. The neighbors knew that any interference would not be appreciated. From time to time they even listened and tried to make out what Bern could be up to. Also, he kept his door shut tight — probably locked — and his response to a persistent knocker (raider in his opinion) was through a partially opened door. I think I remember that for a necessary communication, I once yelled through the door.[6]

During the last two years we lived in Corvallis, Dad had a Ford Foundation Fellowship and so was able to write *A New Life* and not teach. In 1960, answering a question from his friend Rosemarie Beck, he described his day. I was struck reading the letter how firmly he left out mention of any social pleasures and wondered whether he was partly overstating his solitary routine to her. The description seems exact for a day but not a complete depiction of his life.

You want to know what I do. In the morning half a mile to work: at one I go [to] the college for the mail, then walk home. I eat lunch and look at the paper. At two I walk to work. At about four-thirty I quit. I do an errand or two and walk back home. I read the mail and if I'm tired I go sleep. All winter I wasn't tired, and now that spring has come I am. We eat: I listen to a record or two; I sit in my chair and read. Sometimes I help Paul with his algebra, or Janna needs salve on her eyelids, or this night wants me to put her to bed. Ann and I talk as I read the local newspaper, then the Herald Trib; then a magazine. Then I turn to books. I usually read about an hour and a half of fiction and about an hour and a half of non-fiction, possibly something I need for my novel. Sometimes I read poetry. Last week I read the whole of Roethke's Words for the Wind; the last part is marvelous, the spirit tormented into light. This week I'm reading Within a Budding Grove. Between eleven-thirty and twelve I throw out Pinky and put Cokey [our two cats] in the cellar. Fix the alarm and put it in Paul's room, check Janna, who usually falls asleep with Cokey in her arms, both sleeping; then I set out a few things for the morning, because I like to get up with Paul to be up early. The sound of his getting out of bed awakens me. I dress and make his breakfast; after he goes I have mine. I feed the cats, Cokey running upstairs to wake Janna. Everyone's awake; I go to work.[7]

*   *   *

BERNARD MALAMUD was a driven city boy, an indoor urban man, and Oregon was agrarian. None of the culture he sought — foreign films, classical music, museums, bookstores, public lectures, intense literary discussions — was available in Corvallis. Yet the post–World War II economic boom, the returning GIs with school money, and the resulting expansion of the college had drawn a good handful of new, better-educated faculty: some easterners, some older ex-soldiers rendered more sophisticated by their time abroad. Among them he found companions and gradually became part of a circle of good friends. Eventually, he helped start a foreign film program and an in-house liberal arts lecture series in which faculty members spoke publicly about their work. Other friends founded a readers' theater and organized a classical concert series. When I was seven or eight, we drove to Portland to see an exhibition of paintings by van Gogh; the following summer we traveled to Ashland to watch Shakespeare plays. For his forty-sixth birthday, in April 1960, a year before we left to live in Vermont, my brother bought Dad a hunting cap, and I bought him a fishing rod and tackle box, knowing he'd never use them. He wrote to Rosemarie Beck, "Janna gave me a fishing rod (her dearest wish is for me to take her fishing)."[8] We teased him for living indoors, for always writing; by then we grasped how out of place he was.

Apart from my father, no one in Corvallis seemed in a hurry. Improving a home or buying land and building a house, often performing difficult labors alone, was the chief pastime of some of dad's colleagues. Kids in school told stories of fathers hospitalized with internal poison oak after accidentally inhaling its oils while burning underbrush to clear new lots. Friends must have wondered how Dad could have devoted himself so to writing when there was plaster to spread, roofing to nail, decks to stain, and gardens to turn. I had something approaching such a conversation with Chester Garrison one afternoon when I returned with my own family for a visit in 1987. Chester tended to speak in a wry, understated way. I'm not sure what words he used, but he allowed that he had gradually, somewhat surprising himself, come to experience his hand-built home, the refinishing of furniture, gardening, his family, and his teaching life as the fully realized, gratifying alternative to Dad's literary ambition.

Chester, my father's closest friend and a scholar of Elizabethan drama, was also a transplant. Tall, on the thin side, understated, smart, observant, and droll, he took in the world around him clearly but tended, unlike my family, to stay calm. He was the person my mother called for rescue when she ran out of gas or, when Dad was away, for mini house crises: a half-drowned mouse stuck in a drain, for example. He'd grown up in New Jersey, gone to Dartmouth College, and then gone off to the war — with shrapnel to show for it — first parachuting into Sicily, then onto Anzio beach. Later, he'd earned a Ph.D. in English at Columbia and rambled west, stopping to teach in the Midwest before landing in Oregon. His wife, Louise, was good friends with my mother, and their oldest son, Peter, and I frequently played together. Often in the evening after dinner, Chester would drop by our house for a visit, bringing his large poodle, Toba, with him. He would cheerily greet my mother and brother, laughingly rub his nose against mine, and then sit on the couch, light his pipe, and chat with Dad about department matters, books, news from back east, and local gossip. The oversize, curly-haired dog would sit on his lap, legs splayed skyward, held firmly to keep him from chasing our cats. I believe it was Chester who would bring the *New York Times Book Review* to Dad a week or so late. Several faculty members shared the subscription, and each reader would make a check mark beside his initials before passing it on to the next.

*   *   *

MY FATHER'S URGENCY to realize his talent led us to move often. I count nine houses plus one apartment in two countries and three states that we occupied before I left for college at seventeen. But the small white cape with the dark green door at 445 North Thirty-first Street in Corvallis was, for me, the family home — the soil into which I set my taproot, the inner lining of my mind. The smell of the laurel shrub on a rainy day; the intimacy of tiny, white, bee-ridden clover flowering throughout the grass; the way the water puddled and rushed drowned earthworms into the street gutter after a rain; the raw walnuts and acorns scattered or mashed onto the sidewalk; myself in pajamas in the early morning balancing on first my mother's, then my father's blanket-covered knees, and giggling as they collapsed them suddenly and I tumbled off. These impressions get overlaid or joined, but never replaced. And, of course, their disproportionate significance to me is me. When the wind blew from nearby Albany, the air would arrive loaded down with the paper mill's cloyingly sweet sulfuric stink. But more often it was perfumed with thick spring grass, flowering shrubs, rain-wet sidewalks, cedar sawdust, and, in early summer, the scent of rosebushes blooming in almost every yard. Needless to say, there were bad times: family tensions; a knee bloody, full of gravel, after a bike skid; a panicked ten minutes locked by bigger kids in the college sheep barns; tales of a neighbor girl's huge, overall-wearing father whacking her with the broad side of a knife.

Yet, after all these years, the word *Corvallis* still gives off a particular radiance, lives singularly for me much the way the ancient Greeks declared Delphi to be the world's *omphalos,* or "navel." If you think simply about each person's first impressions, his or her earliest memories of the physical world, as a measure of what American immigration and mobility have meant, you would have to imagine my father's parents carrying the primary landscapes of a different Russian Jewish shtetl outside Kamyanets-Podilskyy, while my mother's parents' minds would presumably have been built around Naples and its bay, and the densely populated Mediterranean city's deteriorated Baroque beauty. My father would recall Brooklyn — small apartments above the family groceries, his streets and neighborhoods, the seasonal changes of urban trees that he notes in his journals. My mother, who grew up in the still half-rural New Rochelle, recorded her Italian grandfather's devotion to his flower gardens, her grandmother's elaborate cooking, herself, an only child, dressed up by her mother or grandmother and proudly paraded before guests.

What *did* my father hear as a young boy about his parents' Ukrainian Jewish lives? Had they each left behind villages of kin, generations of local graves? To know so little has shifted from indifference to hardened emptiness, thanks to the quick, brittle edge made by letting myself wonder. After the nuclear explosion at Chernobyl, I put aside thoughts of visiting the area from which the Malamuds and Fidelmans came, for I believed, misconstruing geography slightly, that its soil had become radioactive — as if pogroms, Nazis, and Stalin hadn't burned it enough. Meanwhile, one day some years back, I tried on a dress in a shop in Naples and suddenly realized that it fit me as no American clothing ever had. The knowledge unsettled me, made me feel as if I belonged somewhere, that my body inscribed me as part of a tribe. The Italian tribe, the Russian Jewish tribe, who could say? This possibility in turn raised the question of whether I might ever have felt deeply at home, native in my body, community, religion, or land. For better or worse, and in common with so many Americans, it is simply not a feeling that I know. Meanwhile, self-appointed ethnologists usually tag me as a New York Jew. I've never lived anywhere near the city and remain largely clueless about Jewish ritual, but they have a point.

My father's yearnings were different: he didn't like where he seemed to belong; he grew up hoping he could move into the new nation, away from his airless immigrant home, his family and cultural past. As much as anything, Corvallis showed him the limits of that fantasy, gave more information to him about who he wasn't, and with it greater voltage and definition for his fictions. Oregon, together with his marriage to a Gentile, revealed him to himself as more of a Jew than he'd previously grasped, or at least had to think about. The bland, friendly, Protestant place made him miss the combative, critical, Greenwich Village intellectual life, the arts scene, the political meetings, the private exchanges that by the next month would become public broadsides in *Commentary* and *Partisan Review*. When I attempt to encapsulate the meaning to his art of his encounter with the American West, I get an image of the Chagall murals in the Metropolitan Opera House in New York City. My father's sensibility has a kinship with Chagall's. Like the painter born a generation earlier, the writer also, at a greater remove, carried tales of the shtetl, had familiarity with Yiddish folk literature, found freedom in fables, and could capture in a short story a seemingly naive moral complexity in which studiedly simple words evoked deep feeling. Dad never particularly talked about or sought out Chagall's work — the comparison is mine — and much of his best writing is fine exactly because it is not lyrical, folkish, or otherworldly. Nevertheless, I choose the analogy here as metaphor to give a snapshot of a Russian Jewish American man who arrived in a small western town where, against its particular backdrop, he viewed himself anew.

Then, too, there was the historic moment. After World War II and the discoveries of its genocides, American Jews became creatures of interest. They were neither exactly exotic nor yet fully embraced and integrated. But rather than simply despised, they unexpectedly found themselves to be the recipients of both guilt and sympathy, subjects of significant curiosity. Seizing the day, they elbowed their way into the postwar world. My father, Saul Bellow, Alfred Kazin, Clement Greenberg, Lionel Trilling, and Irving Howe, to name a handful among many, were original, opinionated men born at the right time. Coming back to Corvallis from Italy in 1957, when I was five, we stopped in New York and went one day — perhaps to Long Island — for lunch with the Trillings. I imagine Dad, receiving the invitation, felt anointed. There was an apple tree outside the house, and their son, James, Paul, and I got into an apple fight. I winged one that struck young Trilling's back, and he turned and shot another hard into my eye, breaking my glasses on its way. It hurt sharply at the time but years later became a source of amusement; I'd privately summon the moment when strangers expressed envy about my childhood witness of the literary life.

Dad liked himself as father to a young family. Spring and summer evenings, he would occasionally go with us to the school playground across the street from our house and toss a baseball for my brother to bat, then for me. My mother did the lion's share of kid duty, but Dad would show up at significant performances. He might play checkers and gin rummy with us if we were ill or persuasively bored. When I was six or seven, my mother surprised me with a perfect, blue, twenty-inch English bicycle. For the next several days after work, Dad held the tan leather bicycle seat and walked, then ran, beside me as I learned to ride. I remember family Sunday afternoons at Kiger Island, a tiny pebbly beach on the then filthy Willamette River, my father showing us how to skip stones, teaching my brother how to row a boat on nearby Colorado Lake. On Friday or Saturday nights in the winter, the whole family would watch the Oregon State Beavers play basketball in the big college gymnasium. I'd gather with the other girls at the locker room entrance, autograph book in hand, yipping to the team "stars" for their signatures. Dad often found the games exciting and enjoyed being a shouting member of the local crowd. I can see him in our living room, kneeling, ear against the brown Zenith radio, agitated, muttering encouragement, intently following Sugar Ray Robinson's middleweight title boxing match.

My father's biggest Oregon domestic coup was buying our house. My mother, more familiar with homes and real estate from her family, urged him on. He paid $12,750 in 1955 or 1956. However much more he would later make, I'm not sure anything rivaled the distance the purchase signified he'd traveled from a young man who could not afford slippers to one who owned a place on the block. A year or two after I was born, he bought a used car, a pale green Plymouth. When I was maybe three years old, he taught my mother to drive it. He'd take us all over to a paved lot in the tiny next town, Philomath, where the motor vehicle registry ran its driving tests, and arrange orange cones so she could practice parallel parking. In 1959 he purchased a small black-and-white television, in 1960 a hi-fi and a set of 33s of Pablo Casals playing Bach cello suites.

ON SOME LEVEL, my father was deeply amused by what Oregon asked of him, and in many ways the labors grounded him. He dutifully pushed the heavy, wooden-handled lawn mower across our small front lawn. On autumn weekends, he would rake and then, in the gutter, take a match to the gathered leaves. Our small corner house lot had six trees, including a pear tree that ripened more sweet, yellow Bartletts than we could pick. I recall a family friend, John Haislip, a poet, on a ladder, helping my mother and grandmother harvest them one late-summer afternoon. My father sometimes picked a few himself, or carried in fallen ones to ripen on the kitchen windowsill. The walnut tree, on the north side of the house, each autumn dropped a crop we gathered up. Dad would spread them on old window screens and dry them over our furnace in the basement. Sometimes the project usurped the Ping-Pong table. In adulthood, Ping-Pong was the closest he came to sport. He taught the game to my brother and me and would play with us some evenings after dinner.

Our living room bookcase of stacked bricks and boards was his effort. He also had painted several rooms. But mostly he lacked time and interest to work on the house or fixing things. Once when they got together at their friends the Erlichs' home in Seattle, or maybe later back east, he and Victor Erlich and Alex Inkeles formed a club called the League of Lopsided Men. They claimed ignorance of all home repairs: not one of them, it was said, could mount a can opener on a door frame — though I think they may have manfully exaggerated their ineptitude. My parents had met the Erlichs in Seattle in 1959 and had a lifelong friendship with them. The Erlichs also moved back east in the sixties when Victor took a professorship at Yale. His wife, Iza, trained and practiced as a psychoanalyst in New Haven. In August 1959, Dad wrote Rosemarie Beck, "We will be having houseguests, one of the families we met in Seattle, a professor of Slavic literature, his wife, and their two boys. They are Polish refugees and quite the most interesting people I've met in years. Despite all they've been through their humor is rich and neverending. I find myself being humorous for them, they are such appreciators."[9]

IN THE LATE SUMMER of 1956, we rented out our house in Corvallis and traveled to Italy. Dad had won a fellowship; *The Assistant* was about to come out. My mother wanted him to see her family homeland and to meet her kin. He was eager. We took a train back east and sailed on the *Staatendam* out of New York City via Genoa to Naples, where many members of my mother's family still lived. Then we went north to Rome. After some days in a hotel, they found a two-bedroom apartment near Piazza Bologna which they rented for nine months. I was four and a half. My parents enrolled Paul, just turning nine that autumn, in fourth grade at the American Overseas School with other American and English-speaking kids. (I remember hearing how one of his teachers wore a big ring with which she knuckled the heads of obstreperous kids. I used to fantasize on my way to sleep at night about going up to her and demanding that she desist. When I finally met her, brought along to a parents' night at school, I became particularly mute.) They sent me mornings to a nearby Italian Montessori kindergarten run by Ursuline nuns. I was the only American. I got along, picked up words, and figured out the basic rules. My parents insisted that I be excused from the religious instruction, but for years after, I kept on my bureau in Oregon a small, plastic, glow-in-the-dark statue of the Virgin Mary that they'd issued to me as part of their drill.

Each week, in a long windowless hall, the nuns lined up all the girls from all the grades — navy blue or gray pleated wool skirts and white blouses — to inspect if we were minimally clean. We stood with our backs against the hall wall and waited, hands stretched out in front of us, while two or three sisters started at one end of the line and scrutinized each of us. One by one, they checked our fingernails for dirt. Then they had us tip our heads to one side. They carefully brushed back strands of hair and peered into an ear. Then we tipped our heads to the other side. The formality was daunting. But worse, every so often, for reasons I could not anticipate no matter how hard I tried, they would surround a little girl, publicly lift her skirt, and, in front of all of us, right there in the hall, peer into her underpants. It was a horrifying prospect, and I waited grimly for my own mortification. After some months, I began to realize that something about my otherness —

my agnostic family, my American nationality — was powerful enough to spare me their probings. Perhaps, obvious to them but not me, it was my clean clothes and bathed body that set me apart.

My parents later claimed that my Italian quickly became fluent enough that my father asked me to interpret when strangers came to the door while my mother was out. I don't know. Now I realize that Dad likely, as a grade school boy, had performed the function for his mother. My own recollections include a more anxious absence of words. A war-widowed farmwoman named Gina — big, heavyset, dark hair in a bun — worked for us part-time. I can see her cooking soup in the apartment kitchen, and I recall her taking me to a nearby park, where together we gathered pignolia nuts beneath the umbrella pines. We patiently scoured the dirt and pine needles, and picked up each tiny, hard-cased, black and tan seed until, after maybe an hour, we had collected a hundred or so. Back home, Gina took a sturdy butcher knife and, with the leverage of her large arms against a cutting board, skillfully split each one to release its kernel whole.

The two of us managed simple Italian. I had a rhyming chant I used to sing to tease her while she worked: "Gina, pastina, ministrina, minestrone, macarone . . ." I must have decided that American ways were alien to her, for I remember whispering to my mother how Gina had licked the Scotch tape before binding it around a package. My mother queried her and reported back that she had simply been exhaling warm breath upon it to help it adhere. At some point during the year, when Gina learned that I yearned for a gold-handled, silver plastic sword I'd seen, she, so poor every lira mattered, bought it for me and arrived at our door with it hidden. Once inside before me, she reached into her closed umbrella and exultantly drew it forth.

One late-autumn afternoon, gray November or December, the early darkness encroaching, Gina took me out for a walk. We wan-

dered toward the edge of a cemetery where I knew, from overhearing my parents, her soldier husband was buried. I also knew
my father had visited the grave with her and comforted her while
she wept. Death and grief were new to me. Her loss seemed incon-
ceivably grim, huge like the sky. I wanted somehow to acknowledge it. Not just for her sake, but because my almost-five-year-old
mind was forming the new category of the serious. Probably, too,
I'd already begun modeling myself on my father. I pointed toward
the cemetery, as if to say, "He's there, isn't he?" She took my gesture to mean that I, too, wanted to visit the grave. No. The prospect terrified me. I dreaded opening up her sorrow, facing an in-
comprehensible, flooding intimacy. I panicked, Italian words fled,
and I fell quickly into a string of noes and a ferocious tugging on
her arm hoping to stall her immense forward motion. She kept on
toward the cemetery gate. I protested more strenuously until, both
of us embarrassed, she turned around and silently, awkwardly
walked me home.

MY FATHER WROTE each morning in the apartment. It had marble floors and inadequate heat, and he would often become chilled.
Partly for the pleasure of it and to assist my mother, and partly to
restore circulation by moving, he occasionally collected me at
school at noon. One day, walking home, we came upon a small
crowd of people and several policemen. A middle-aged woman in
a brown skirt had been hit by a tram. I remember her crushed
glasses on the cobblestones, the trolley tracks curving through the
piazza.

   In the afternoons, Dad explored the city, walking or taking
buses, often with my mother, to see neighborhoods, churches, and
monuments or to visit art museums and famous tourist sights. He
stood in John Keats's death room and at his grave. I remember running around Piazza Navona, visiting fountains at night, climbing

the Spanish Steps, riding a bicycle with training wheels in the
Borghese Gardens. We dined sometimes with my mother's aunts,
cousins, and old family friends; I can still taste the hard, white,
sugar-coated almonds that might end a Sunday meal. Friends from
the States came by, and my mother and father would go out with
them to cheap trattorias. Having Gina around and Dad not teaching freed them to spend more time together. Her fluency in the language allowed him access. He had bought a grammar book and
taught himself some Italian. The melodic voweled language appealed to his ear and amused him, and forever after he invented
Italian-sounding words. "Ann," he'd announce at dinner, "I'd like
a slice" — in his mock Italian, a "sleechay" — "of bread, please."
The country's impressions on him are everywhere in his stories,
particularly the Fidelman tales.

It was a different Italy then, poorer, much closer to the nineteenth century than the twenty-first, still caught in the war's aftermath. Widows and older women wore only black. Men with don-
key carts swept the streets. There were few cars yet, mostly buses,
bicycles, and Vespas. I liked accompanying my mother or Gina to
the outdoor markets, with their seasonally varied piles of artichokes, tomatoes, escarole, dried fava beans, eggplants, onions,
tangerines, and chestnuts. Sometimes I'd be allowed to choose a
treat of olives, nuts, cooked chickpeas, or candy, and I loved to
watch the stall keepers fashion cone-shaped containers from old
newspapers to neatly package our purchases. My bouts of illness
impeded my family's freedom somewhat, but eventually Dad and
Paul made it to Florence and Assisi. We all visited Venice, Austria,
and Switzerland. And in the summer, before returning home on
the *S.S. Constitution*, we traveled to Paris to meet up with the
Inkeleses for a week. My mother recalls that Dad had come to love
Rome so much that when he first saw Paris during a June heat
wave, he found it out of scale, gray, remote, and disappointing. I

got sick again in Paris, and my mother stayed with me and Paul one very hot night while Dad, the Inkeleses, and William Phillips went out to see a play of Eugene O'Neill's — possibly *Long Day's Journey into Night*. Phillips was the editor and cofounder with Philip Rahv of *Partisan Review*. Stifling in the theater, the group eventually decamped to a café for a drink. While they were there, Jean Paul Sartre walked in surrounded by an entourage of admirers. Phillips was apparently feuding with Sartre — possibly because of *Partisan Review*'s strong anti-Stalinist stance — for he turned his head hard toward the wall so as not to greet the celebrity existentialist. My guess is that Dad was most pleased to be present — and to witness the kind of literary drama that Oregon lacked.

IN JULY 1959, when I was seven, Dad wrote to Rosemarie Beck:

> Yesterday, while Ann was preparing dinner, I took Janna to the bank of a river she likes. She waded in the cold water, scooped up minnows with a strainer and learned how to skim flat rocks across the water. She is very intense about these things and makes it a point of honor to learn when she is learning . . . As I sat on a log by the river, watching her yesterday, it was as if I were reading a long poem, every line full of beauty. The lines were her movements and the changing expression of her face, even the way the wind blew her hair. Children are such aesthetic pleasures to watch.[10]

As a little girl, I presumed that he and I loved each other best, though I think he conveyed that sense generally to intimates. It's more accurate to say that we had a passionate bond, kept fertile as much by my idealization of him in his absence as by those moments when I'd catch his pleased attention. I took for granted that I should keep my requests for his time short. I also inherited some of his traits, and we comfortably, intuitively, understood much about each other. "You're so like your father," my mother repeatedly noted, often to my irritation. I felt she was depositing me, but she had a point.

Unsure what to do with their Jewish-Catholic split, my parents briefly, halfheartedly, sent my brother and me to a Unitarian Sunday school in Corvallis. I remember a neighbor picking us up one rainy Sunday, but not a word of instruction. The moral education Dad offered was constant: read, value art, seek education and experience, attend to others, shelter the vulnerable, and try to treat each person fairly. The underlying biggie was, "Work to overcome yourself." An uncanny part of reading his books is not simply their psychic familiarity but also a sense that the quasi-comic worldview, the admonition to "take pity," and the relentless press to grate away at one's own failings have so formed me that I encounter them less as art, more as birthplace. He forgot to mention the rest of the story: that his expectations for himself were impossible. Dad's later protagonists — Fidelman, Dubin — understand this dilemma with full irony.

NOT ONLY WAS MY MOTHER sociable, but my father's otherwise relentless need to work was genuinely balanced by his pleasure in people and his curiosity about their experiences. They made many good friends. The Garrisons. The Hansons, who ran the big chicken farm and entertained a lot. The Norrises — Faith, the one woman who taught in the English department and who coauthored a children's book with Dad. Tom, her husband, a chemist in the science department. Jack Decius, also a science professor, and his wife, Ann. The Hovlands — Warren, who taught religion and philosophy, and Sue, who helped found the Readers' Theater. The Krakauers — Lew, an Erasmus Hall graduate, now a doctor at the local clinic, and Carol, who later taught art to children. Nelson Sandgren, a painter, and his wife, Olive. Marian Lonseth, one of my mother's closest friends, and her husband,

Arvid, a mathematician. Lots of others. Many of them were new to Oregon, too; their young families and shared moment of arrival bound them to one another.

The town social life was busy and easygoing. Neighbors came over and drank a beer before sitting down to a casserole, a baked ham, or a beef, onion, and red wine stew my mother had prepared. Occasionally, my parents would dress up a little: Dad would wear a jacket, Mom would pull her hair back and clip it in a bun, trade her blouse and skirt for a dress and heels, which accented her pretty legs. My brother recalled once watching a bunch of dinner guests, deep into their own hilarity, use only the grip of chin against neck to pass a grapefruit around the table.

A frontier generosity still prevailed. When, in 1964, we returned in the summer for a visit, I woke up early the first morning in our rented house and opened the front door to find its stoop crowded with gifts: fresh eggs, cookies, preserves, casseroles, welcoming notes taped to the foil and wax paper.

One of my babysitters, Kathy, had a Hollywood father who made a fortune writing the popular *Gidget* books based on her sex life. The situation titillated Dad, who more than once described to dinner guests within my hearing how Kathy would come home from dates and tell her father all the hand-unhooking-bra-type details of her sexual intimacies. About the same time, he took to announcing to everyone how he'd laid down the law and forbidden me to marry until I was twenty-one. I am unsure why he got onto that riff, other than in response to watching too many "coeds" drop out of college and marry prematurely. He called me his Oregon girl, and I suppose he feared I might go native.

SOMETIMES DAD, pried from his desk by the rest of us, would drive the highway, curved tight as ribbon candy, over the Coast Ranges to the beach at Waldport or Newport for a picnic with friends. In the late 1950s, that stretch of coast was unspoiled. There were fishing towns, piers, motels, and cabins here and there, but there were also vast, empty, driftwood-scattered beaches. The Pacific roared in, its water too cold for swimming, but we waded and jumped waves happily. I have a vivid recollection of going to the beach with the Krakauers when I was maybe eight. Jon, several years younger, got stuck on a high, eroding sand cliff he'd climbed and cried out for help. His father stood below him and told him that he could figure his predicament out. As the rest of us watched, the frightened boy gradually edged his way to safety. Used to my family's quick physical protectiveness, I remember feeling amazed by the paternal refusal to rescue. I both longed to be taught such boldness and was relieved that I was a Malamud, not a Krakauer, and no similar high-stakes competence would be demanded of me. Neither of my parents possessed a whit of interest in athletically testing themselves or their children.

My favorite place in all of Oregon was Cascadia, a sweet-smelling, evergreen-filled state park two hours away from town. A mountain stream shot through it, rumbling along on its pebble bed. At least once a summer, Mom and some of her friends would pack picnic baskets and caravan up there. We kids would blow up air mattresses, throw ourselves onto the frigid water, ride and reride the short strip of rapids, while the moms, shirts or sweaters over bathing suits, chatted and sunned themselves on the rocks.

ALTHOUGH MOST OF my parents' socializing was local, my father also occasionally met other writers. In two letters to Rosemarie Beck about visits to the Erlichs in Seattle, he offered a portrait of Theodore Roethke.

On the day before Thanksgiving we drove with friends to Seattle to stay with other friends for the holiday. We had a nice visit; the kids got along well together; I worked during the day at a university office generously lent me; the turkey dinner was very good; we saw "Wild Strawberries," a Swedish movie which I very much recommend to you; and there was a party for us where I met Ted Roethke, the poet. I spent two hours with him. When he came in he found it difficult to look at me until our host put a drink in his hand. Then he began to loosen up. He noticed I was not drinking and asked me why I wasn't boozing it up; I apologized for not drinking and he somehow liked that. Then he talked about his madness, and I told him what I liked about his poetry. He is a great hulk of a man, enormously tall and enormously big, a huge girth, though it does not strike you as fat; part of the time as he talked he held with both hands the back of a chair. He told me about his parents, their greenhouse — I asked him from his poems whether he had been close to flowers — and financial ruin. "Money, money, money," is a line in one of his poems. He drank and drank and we talked and I felt we were strangers because he was killing himself and I would have no part of it, and his wife (he had taught her in Bennington and years later run into her on Fifth Avenue and that was the fateful thing) was a truly beautiful woman, and for five years after their marriage she had kept him out of the madhouse. When he left I was a little depressed for the terrible loss.[11]

Roethke moves me. He is a giant of a man struck by lightning. His back is a yard broad; he must weigh about 250, and he's about fifty-two. He walks with a sort of limp. His talent is prodigious but he is overwhelmed by fear of madness and death. He drinks an awful lot. And talks about the booby hatch — his words. He is married to an absolutely beautiful woman, about twenty years younger than he. She tries to cut down his drinking. Such beauty, talent and sickness saddened me when I met them last Thanksgiving. For Christmas I sent him a dozen carnations: "To a good man and wonderful poet." He said nothing about them until we met after my reading. Then he thanked me. The next night he brought over a poem printed on parchment and autographed affectionately. I'm very proud of it. We talked for a while at the second party. He said it took a battery of psychiatrists to keep him alive, so strong was death in him. He wants to be — expects to be a great poet. I said he would be. This came out amid silences. The next day we went to see him in a huge house overlooking Lake Washington. He sat in a chair with the lightning that had hit him. His eyes looked elsewhere. I talked aimlessly. Then he got some poems out and shoved them to us. We read translations of his work in French. Then we heard him read on some Library of Congress records. He drove us home: I said goodbye but he didn't look as I said it.[12]

On October 26, 1960, Dad wrote to Rosemarie Beck about meeting Philip Roth and C. P. Snow:

In the past week I met two writers, C. P. Snow and Philip Roth; they were both in Oregon, Snow at the University of Oregon, forty miles away, and Roth at the house of a mutual friend, twenty miles from Corvallis. Sir Charles is a heavy, baggy man, good-humored, a public sort of person, perhaps still a little on the make, but simple and kind. A few minutes after we met he was telling me in public how good I was. He was "Sir Charles" and I was "My dear Bernard" (burnid). Before his lecture he told the audience that one of the reasons he had wanted to come to Oregon was that it was "the adopted home of that beautiful writer, etc." I was touched. I doubt that half the audience knew who I was. Roth is about twenty-eight, handsome, bright, witty with a bite. I met him a half hour before his lecture at a school of education where our mutual friend teaches, and he was a bit stiff but after the lecture he was very entertaining. He has an enormously fine critical sense — plows at once to a writer's strength and weakness. I found myself listening to a criticism of my work among Salinger, Bellow, Mailer, Gold, Ellison — and almost all of us were accused of, to some degree, getting lost in the self instead of writing about the world. My books were "universal" and I was in love with "humanity in general." By quoting an incident or two, including one from the Natural, he gave the impression, as some critics do, that I was essentially a fantasist, something like that. I let it go. He was strained when talking about me as I faced him in the audience, but when I told him later that I liked the lecture he seemed to be relieved. I later asked him, when we were leaving, where the Assistant fit in, and he thought that was universal too. I said "universal in Brooklyn" and he was a little puzzled. He asked me whether I didn't like what he had said, but I said I had already told him I did; besides, in the lecture he had also said I was one of the best writing today so I "forgave" him. I am a little surprised at those who circumscribe a writer in their minds because he will use more than one means to depict reality. *The Natural* has elements of fantasy, true, but it tells a moral tale, and morality is social. You can't be moral alone in the universe.[13]

MUCH ABOUT CORVALLIS life suited my mother. Her friends were always proposing outings or dropping by or phoning for long talks. She'd drive us to the town swimming pool or to friends' houses; Paul to Cub Scouts, art classes, and cello lessons; me to Brownies and ballet. She liked reading and hunting for old furniture to refinish. She baked often — bread, cookies, cakes. She sometimes volunteered for the local Democratic Party and for the League of Women Voters. One winter she took a painting class and completed a self-portrait in oils. She read aloud a lot when we were little, and her multivoiced rendition of *Winnie-the-Pooh* delighted her and us; I giggled over Piglet's and Roo's squeaky concerns. After we bought a television in 1959, she, my brother, and I would watch *The Phil Silvers Show* ("Sergeant Bilko") and laugh ourselves silly. If she was restless for the East, it didn't show. She occasionally had thoughts of moving to California, which was less rainy and where she would be closer to her mother.

All the same, my mother kept much of herself for herself. Indeed, as a girl I thought of her as quietly unhappy, strained, often too alone, and from early on I attempted to take care of her. I have memories of finding her crying, miserable after a fight with my brother or father, and of attempting to comfort her. She may have needed more of my father than he offered, or a different kind of husband. Or maybe hers weren't discontents a spouse could fix. I feigned strength, inflated myself to try to tower protectively over her, to stand guard. I sought intuitively to replace the father who had abandoned her, the grandfather who had died, the husband who seemed often to go missing. My stance and efforts were figments of my imagination, but they compelled me, defined my view of the family and my particular way of approaching her.

OUR FAMILY LIFE was often strained. My mother and father could get under each other's skin. Not horrendously, not yelling nightly at meals the way her family sometimes had. But there was plenty of irritableness and raised voices. He brooked little challenge, and she, while desiring his paternal care and in some ways inviting his control, also found it oppressive, sometimes humiliating, and would needle or provoke him. My mother disliked any vulnerability she sensed in men. It made her feel anxious and unsafe, and she tended to attack.

She and my brother could find little peace; their tensions often filled me with apprehension. I remember one day making matters particularly worse. Paul, probably nine, playing with a ball in the living room, a forbidden activity, broke the neck of a small brown, black, and white vase my mother had brought back from Italy. I came upon him, pale, standing on a chair, gently balancing it back together. He urged me not to tell. I told. She attacked him verbally. I had enjoyed tattling but quickly became her shameful accomplice, frozen with horror at what I had unleashed, filled with pity for him.

When home, Dad would often settle us, although his own temper could flare. One weekend or summer afternoon when my mother was out, my father was reading in the living room. I was six or seven. Paul and I had been fooling around, interrupting and teasing Dad. I think we probably wanted him to stop reading and do something with us. He didn't want to. We found a piece of string and tied him in his chair. He didn't notice that I'd also tied his shoes together. So when finally, irritated, he stood up to pursue us, he stumbled, and became furious. I raced off and locked myself in the bathroom. Paul stationed himself outside the door and begged me to let him in so he could hide, too. Not knowing that Dad was standing silently beside him, I opened the door to offer Paul refuge. Dad burst in, grabbed me hard, pulled down my pants, and, as I shrieked and begged him to stop, repeatedly slapped me. Not with full strength, but inescapably, to humiliate as well as sting. He laughed as he hit, taking control and yet excited and out of control. His behavior must have frightened him, for he never hit me again.

THE LARGER, shared, tacit family understanding was that women were less than men, labile, damaging. He repeatedly and powerfully conveyed that female aggression was not simply unpleasant; it was uniquely destructive. I have spent a lifetime trying to make sense of his view.

There's no doubt my father hungered to have me adore him most. And I favored him. More covertly, I took daily from my mother but left her love for me less acknowledged. In that sense, I think, I imitated Dad. He preferred always to feel like the one giving. Still, when I look back over the time in Oregon, I think it's right to say that in spite of discord and devaluing, my parents cared about each other and were solidly married. Each one also understood, somewhere beyond words, battles, and disappointments, that the other had already lost too much, should not have to lose a spouse.

Solidly married may not have meant completely monogamous. During the summer of 1958, when I was six, Dad traveled back east and spent a month at Yaddo, a writers' colony in Saratoga Springs, New York. There he met and became lifelong friends with the painter Rosemarie Beck. They maintained an extensive correspondence. He wanted a relationship in which he could talk art, reflect on his work, and report on its progress. I'd be surprised if they were not briefly lovers — Yaddo provided easy opportunity. I don't know for sure. A decade later, the summer I was sixteen, she came to Vermont and stayed several weeks, painting my portrait and my brother's. I suspect that she was broke and Dad wanted to help her. I disliked sitting for her, experienced her as too familiar in some way, difficult to finger.

Dad wrote his first letter to me while he was at Yaddo. My mother, brother, and I had gone to California to stay with Ida and Gino.

Hi Sweet heart:

I enjoyed talking to you on the phone. You talk nicely on the telephone. And I like your cards and letters. However, you are always giving me the same news. You always say, "I am having lots of fun." That's good, but what kind of fun? What do you do? Who are you playing with nowadays? Do you play with Granny too? And Gramps? If so, what do you do? If the words are hard to write, get Mommy to spell them out for you. I like to know what my girl is doing.

I live in a great big house with lots of other writers. There are also painters and composers. Composers are people who write music . . . One of the painters is painting a portrait of me . . . I'll be home in less than a month. Will you and Mommy and Paulie meet me in Portland?

Lots of love. Daddy[14]

Some years later, in 1975, when he was sixty-one, Dad wrote to me: "I am comparatively contented without making too much of it. More and more I feel that friendship is the key to a happy life at my age, possibly as well at any other. I have some good friends and wish I could see them more often. I sometimes wish I could be idle with friends for long periods of time, though given who I am and those I know and like best I doubt that they or I would let it happen."[15] Rosemarie Beck may have been a summer's lover. More clearly, she was a sustaining epistolary friend to him during the years in Oregon, a person from his homeland who could understand his ambition and his sense of exile.

Dad used to joke that his middle name should have been Ulysses, so that his initials would spell "BUM." Yet the wily, wandering warrior no doubt appealed to him beyond this alphabetic, Joycean incarnation, for his great capacity to temporarily go native anywhere, to outwit Cyclops and Siren alike, and to maintain hope far from home. Then finally, returning to his palace — lord disguised as bum — he would string his great bow and massacre the usurpers of his rightful station. *A New Life,* a quasi-comic send-up of a small-town college, published upon Dad's departure from Oregon in 1961, fired a full quiver at his more provincial colleagues and the small-minded administrators, the anti-intellectuals and sympathizers with McCarthyism, who he felt had, among other failings, undervalued and underestimated him. In 1959, he wrote to Rosemarie Beck, with perhaps a soupçon of self-dramatization, "I've gone through misery here, for the purpose of keeping myself writing. That's what I did and that's why I survived."[16]

*   *   *

THE LARGE YELLOW Mayflower moving truck picked up our furniture and boxes a day before we left by train to return east in June 1961. My mother had packed up everything we were taking. Our two cats moved to someone's house, ready to be caged and flown back to us after we arrived. My parents had been lovingly feted at a round of parties. Friends dropped by to pick up furniture and possessions we were abandoning, to offer last farewells. The house and car had been sold, as well as the big, claw-footed oak table. Our friends the Hovlands took us in for our final Oregon night and drove us early the next morning to the neighboring town to catch the train for Chicago and then Boston. I was nine and a half and had just finished fourth grade. We were on our way to a rented house in Belmont, Massachusetts. Dad had a summer appointment at Harvard to teach creative writing. In early September, we'd head north to his new professorship at Bennington College in Vermont.

I remember, a week or so earlier, carefully sorting through my books, choosing the difficult science and history ones to transport, the younger fun ones to give away. I had privately decided I would relinquish childhood. Lacking language for my loss, unwilling to display it, I clamped my jaw shut. The final day, my mother asked me to deliver my blue bicycle to the Garrisons, who'd bought it. I was a little girl wearing a T-shirt and shorts, flip-flops, energetic but not graceful, with pink-framed glasses over my blue eyes and a barrette pinned on each side of my thick, light brown hair to keep it from falling into my face. I slowly pedaled the several blocks. Then I stopped in the middle of a sidewalk, wept without wanting to, leaned over and — with a nine-year-old's solemnity, struggling, I suppose, to create some ritual of departure — carefully kissed a spot on the handlebars, and whispered goodbye. I knocked on the Garrisons' front door, handed the bicycle over to Louise when she answered, and walked home.

A few days before departing, Dad wrote to Rosemarie Beck, "I have no complicated emotions on leaving the West for the time being; that may be due to the fact that I shall someday come back to the West, or it may [be] due to the fact that I have no complicated emotions over places. I don't know why that is no longer in me; all places are one except when I am abroad; all places are places to work. Maybe that's the reason."[17] As his writer protagonist Harry Lesser put it some years later in *The Tenants,* "Home is where my book is."[18]

Chapter 6 ⊷

Bennington and Its College

⊷ ⊷ IF YOU DROVE west out of Belmont for a couple of hours on Route 2, across Massachusetts to Williamstown, picked up Route 7 north, and approached Bennington from the south as we did in late August 1961 — suitcases and two caged cats crowded into our pale green Rambler station wagon — you would wind through maple and birch woods, hilly old fields of rutted farmland edged with stone walls, and the occasional apple orchard. And close by Bennington, just a few miles before you hit the straggle of houses and businesses that anticipate and then intersect Main Street, you would glimpse a small cemetery up on a rise. It's been almost two decades since I've traveled that route, so I don't know how developed it's become or what's still visible. But that cemetery was there forty years ago, because my brother spotted it as we nervously — carsick cats ratcheting up the mood — edged toward our new home. Dad driving, Mom holding the map in her lap, the two of them tracking a route through Bennington to our little white farmhouse up on the hillock at the far edge of North Bennington. Paul glimpsed the cemetery and managed, like a lightning rod perfectly placed on one of the big slate-roofed barns we kept passing, to draw the jagged anger flash of both parents at once. "Look," he joked, pointing out his back window, up at the grave-covered knoll, "there's Bennington now." Set on hair trigger, they were down his throat. He'd spoken the collective unspeakable: Where the hell were we?

Vermont made a bad impression. After Oregon, I found its landscape gnarled, convoluted. The lush woods and wildlands seemed crowded, overgrown, and mosquito-ridden, its vaunted Green Mountains worn dentures beside Oregon's pristine Cascade Range. After a while, I began to grasp the perfect beauty and, looking back, can summon November air frosting into winter, the last yellow leaves on white birches in late autumn, but I never successfully rerooted. I made friends and had some good times, got immersed in an intense intellectual community and the raucous chaos that went with it, but for half a decade my roots grew hard upon themselves, potbound. My father's experience was different. He found the college intellectually stimulating, and within months of arriving, he met a student with whom he would fall in love.

THE SMALL WHITE FARMHOUSE we had rented came with a working hay barn. The owner of our place, "old" Miss Anderson, lived in a bigger white house next door, but otherwise the property was surrounded by hay fields and forest. We were maybe three quarters of a mile out of North Bennington's town center, with its three stores: Powers' Market, a small, well-stocked, friendly grocery; Nadeau's, where you could buy or service a lawn mower or snowplow; and Percy's, a run-down, dark, single room that sold a handful of magazines and comics, claimed a taxi service, and smelled like boiled cabbage and unattended cat. Percy also kept a very old hearse on hand to transport the occasional coffin. The Rainbarrel, a French restaurant in a gray clapboard house, sat on the corner, and catty-corner from it was a two-room brick public library. Up the road about a block were a bank and a bar; down the other way, on the Walloomsac River, was a small factory. If you walked the pitching, marble-slab sidewalk or drove maybe a third of a mile past the one-truck firehouse up a long street of older houses, straight to the top of a steep hill, you'd come to the college's north gate. The town of Bennington was several miles farther along.

The North Bennington public school, where kindergarten through high school filled one aged, two-story brick building, flummoxed me. Whereas kids in Oregon — many of whose dads worked at the university — were mostly scrubbed, middle-class Protestants, those in North Bennington were mainly from big French Canadian or Irish Catholic families. The more affluent had parents who owned small businesses, but a good number were factory or farm poor, worn down, hard, and hostile. In seventh grade, my English teacher, Mrs. Woodcock, lost her patience with me for protesting after a boy read aloud his excited account of blasting a snowy owl at close range with his shotgun and watching its bloody parts splatter. No doubt I was being irritating, while she was relieved he had done the assignment. The word *ecology* had yet to cross anybody's lips. But I wasn't ready for the rural harshness the place took for granted. (I remember, during one of those first years, overhearing our friend Pat Beck tell my mother how a bunch of guys at the local factory had turned a powerful air hose, used for stripping bark off trees, onto the genitals of a "retarded" man who worked there. Every place has its cruelty, and partly I noticed it because I was older. Yet we'd also shifted worlds.)

Each grade contained one or two "faculty brats," instantly pegged for not attending Mass on Sunday. Everyone knew that the college was a "commie" place, and more than a few people were certain its denizens worshiped the devil. I was entering fifth grade, when girls began forming cliques and shaping their nails on one another's flesh. One spring day, two of them — Christine and Pat, who already wore makeup and stockings and smoked cigarettes, because they'd "stayed back" a few times — followed me and another girl home, taunting, shoving, pinching, and calling us "pinko" and other diminutives. Within a couple of years of arriving, I had gotten the hang of the method, and I remember, with a friend, hurting her younger brother for fun. Meanwhile, Paul had to make his way into tenth grade, where my chief memory is of my parents' horror after they learned that his text in English class was to be monthly copies of the *Reader's Digest*. (Four years later my ninth-grade English class spent the first half of the year on Longfellow's *Evangeline*, a curriculum that I imagine had not been tweaked for a century. I rather enjoyed it.)

WHEREAS PEOPLE IN OREGON, as in much of the West, put out the welcome mat for newcomers, Vermonters generally wanted nothing to do with you unless your family had arrived before the American Revolution. The migration of whole-grain cityfolk up into the rural state hadn't occurred yet, starting later in the sixties, and, with a handful of artisan exceptions — a potter, a jeweler — the town of Bennington lacked even the slight cosmopolitan inclination of Burlington, where the bigger university attracted a mix of types. Vermont, Dad used to point out, had more cows than people. Natives were polite but deeply reserved and wary. (Some years later, our city-born friend Peter Maller banged up his car and took it to a local garage. "Where'd it happen?" the mechanic asked. "Over on the dirt road at the intersection by that old Vermonter's place. You know, Fred's house," Peter answered. Fred was maybe eighty-five, and his family had owned the property since the previous century. "He's no Vermonter," the mechanic shot back, dead serious. "They moved here from Texas when he was seven.")

In 1961, Bennington College had around 350 female students housed on as many acres, and the faculty community was small, eccentric, and, from an Oregon nine-year-old's initial perspective, weird as hell. To frame it more positively: the college had terrific avant-garde credentials. Started as an experimental/alternative school in the early 1930s — for a few years, students and faculty farmed and grew some of their own food — it featured tiny seminars taught by professors; a very intimate advising system, in which each girl had her own hour of faculty "counseling" each week; and a bunch of active, working artists. There was a three-month "nonresident" term in the winter, when the students left campus to pursue jobs or projects — "Learning by doing" was the school's motto — and the faculty, pursuing their own art and studies, traveled from Vermont's hard-frozen ground to warmer climes. (Parents with school-age children had to stay put. Some campus families developed a car-pooling system: kids would get driven the mile or so to school only when the mercury fell below ten degrees. Among ourselves, we called it "snot-freezing" cold.)

BENNINGTON EXHILARATED DAD. At forty-seven, he found himself back east, less than four hours from New York City, an established novelist in a college that valued his craft, free to teach more or less what he pleased and to devote six months a year solely to writing. I believe the full course load was two classes a term. He mostly taught seminars in creative writing and literature. He wrote to Rosemarie Beck:

> I've been teaching for a week and if I must teach it may just as well be here. The girls are very bright, very perspicacious about literature; it's something to hear them analyze a story. They increase my own understanding, which is what good students should do. The counseling is what wears me down a little. I have ten girls to coun-

sel with once a week for an hour a week; but the college is very liberal about what one does in counseling and I may run a fiction tutorial for four in one hour, which should make the job easier.[1]

A New Life was hitting the bookstores just as we unpacked in Bennington in 1961. The reviews were largely excellent, although Dad was disappointed when the sales did not go as high as he'd hoped. He thought he'd start a play next, pull together a collection of stories, write more about his artist character Fidelman, and then begin another novel. After working on the play during the winter of 1961–1962 and finishing a first act, he abandoned it, having found the medium too sparse and constricted. He wrote to his student lover-to-be, "I have completed an outline of three acts, a frustrating experience for more than one reason that daily puts me out of sorts and makes me question everything I ever did, an experience that repeats itself no matter how much one has written before . . . I feel lost almost without the advantages of a narrative technique to develop character and the thickness of time."[2] A month later, he added, "I can't get over the loss of narrative and thought and the limitations of dialog."[3] He returned to writing stories, and in 1963 Farrar, Straus brought out a second volume, *Idiots First*, in which the extant, rather stiff scene from the play is published under the title "Suppose a Wedding."

Dad discovered Flannery O'Connor's work around this time. He admired her writing and used many of her stories in what must have been a class on the short story. (Tillie Olsen, whose work he also taught, stayed with us once for a night or so when she gave a reading at the school, half a decade before feminism discovered her. She wrote my parents a thank-you note in minuscule, dollhouse handwriting, the smallest I've ever seen.) Some years later, Dad started reading Virginia Woolf and taught her books. (In 1972 he wrote to me a bit on Woolf that I'm sure he found charming but that set my twenty-year-old's teeth on edge: "I'm reading 'To the Lighthouse' which unfortunately has escaped me until now; but how beautiful it is, how moving — perhaps more so than it would ordinarily be, because I love Virginia Woolf. I wish I could have held her in my arms and kissed her."[4])

He loved Chekhov, Eudora Welty, and Hemingway, and now he could teach them. Being respected and being able to choose his material felt to him like a great leap forward. By his second year, he had negotiated a contract that required him to teach only one term per year, and as fame accrued, he whittled his obligation further to one course per year. He chose to continue some teaching because he found the classroom exchanges vitalizing. He maintained undiminished gratitude for his own teachers and wanted to give as good as he'd gotten. I'm not sure what he thought about the sexual possibilities he clearly felt. Did he acknowledge them to himself as part of the draw? Or were they, as for his protagonist Cronin in the story "A Choice of Profession," primarily something to be resisted? "Though Cronin wasn't planning to become involved with a student, he had at times considered taking up with one but resisted it on principle. He wanted to be protected in love by certain rules, but loving a student meant no rules to begin with."[5]

DAD'S COLLEAGUES were fellow literary travelers, artists, and intellectuals. Although Theodore Roethke, W. H. Auden, Erich Fromm, and Martha Graham had come and gone, and the literary intellectual Kenneth Burke had just retired, the campus was still chock-a-block with creative people: dancers, choreographers, poets, sculptors, painters, theater directors, musicians, and composers ruled the roost. Among the many who spent time in the place during the years Dad taught there were poets Ben Belitt, Stephen Sandy, and Howard Nemerov; literary critic Stanley Edgar Hyman (married to the writer Shirley Jackson); literary theorists Barbara

Herrnstein Smith and Camille Paglia; painters Jules Olitski, Paul Feeley, and Pat Longo; sculptors David Smith, Tony Smith, and Isaac Witkin; art critics Lawrence Alloway and Gene Baro; composers Henry Brandt, Lionel Novak, and Louis Calabro; and novelists John Gardner, Alan Cheuse, and Nicholas Delbanco. Others living in the environs or cycling through as visiting firemen included painter Kenneth Noland, composer Marc Blitzstein, British sculptor Anthony Caro, and the ubiquitous Clement Greenberg. (I think it was sixth grade that was redeemed for me by the arrival of Caro's son, Tim, who had a pudding-bowl haircut and a London accent. Beatlemania was just frothing forth, and it must have panicked the lad to find every girl in the class swooning each time he uttered a Brit-inflected sentence, all of us giving chase, made mad by Anglo-pheromones. I failed to win his romantic interest, but my heart beat hard for a season.)

The summer I was sixteen, I spent a week auditing an alumni course on contemporary painting taught by Robert Motherwell, whose ex-wife Helen Frankenthaler was a famous alum and someone my father later befriended. My first taste of *foie gras* was delivered indirectly by Leonard Bernstein the year Marc Blitzstein was in residence. Bernstein's wife, Felicia, and Mike Nichols had driven up from the city to visit Blitzstein and serendipitously fell into helping him judge the local high school one-act play contest that evening. They all dropped by our house in the late afternoon. I recall that they brought a bottle of champagne and, probably warned by Blitzstein about the meager local rations, a can of jellied beef consommé with which to surround the goose liver.

I also remember the exoticism of my first taste of Brie in Bennington. You couldn't yet buy the cheese there, but John McCullough, our local "millionaire," threw a big party one New Year's Eve (probably in 1964) in the huge Victorian, onetime governor's mansion he had inherited. He stunned his guests by laying out huge white wheels of ripe Brie imported from France via New York City. That night was also the only time I ever saw Dad tipsy. Victor and Iza Erlich, who had recently moved east, were staying with us and accompanied us to the party. Dad joked to Iza about the masturbatory possibilities for a boy she knew who fondly kept a pet boa constrictor. When he noticed me standing at his side, he was mortified. He did not want me to witness his casual sex talk and, like so many, worked to hold his sexual excitement compatibly with his more austere notions of paternal behavior.

EVEN MY FATHER must have felt a little culture shock when he first set foot on the Bennington campus. The edgy, outspoken, blue-jeaned, often braless (way before the undergarment had become a political trope), long-haired "Bennington girls" (an epithet already with plenty of outré connotation in places like *The New Yorker*) were a far cry from the prettified Oregon coeds still in their skirts or Bermuda shorts, Peter Pan collars, and Keds. Dad missed the more conventional feminine display. His first weekly seminar in creative writing went so well that the students begged him to add an additional evening time. He agreed, but only, he informed them, if they would shed their jeans and don dresses. And in 1962 they did. I remember he came home on the first of these nights chuckling mightily. One student, I believe it was Betty Aberlin, arrived in class in a full-length evening gown and cowboy boots. Midway through, she reached into her décolletage and pulled out a banana, which she casually peeled and ate as the group parleyed and the instructor gaped.

That first winter, in January 1962, we moved from one returning professor's house to that of another departing on sabbatical, and found ourselves living on campus in "the Orchard," a group of eight small, mostly red faculty houses set in an old apple orchard. Beginning to settle in, my parents threw a party. Stanley

Hyman and Shirley Jackson, Howard and Peggy Nemerov, and perhaps ten others were there. The next morning, I remember my mother and father clucking in dismay. They weren't in two-beer Oregon anymore. The Bennington drink was bourbon on ice, in big glasses, or occasionally Scotch, hold the water. They had served a bottle of each, but I recall Dad, wide-eyed, observing to my mother, "Next time we have to buy more. Hyman and Nemerov can drink a fifth apiece."

HYMAN AND JACKSON lived with their four children in a massive, somewhat dilapidated, gray, slate-roofed Victorian in North Bennington. Stanley was a collector of the first order, and to visit them was to enter room after room of floor-to-ceiling books — the number twenty-four thousand floats up. There wasn't a free wall anywhere. He also had a huge coin collection, with coins dating back to the Romans, and thousands of records, jazz and blues being his special interest. He had been a staff writer for *The New Yorker,* and I remember hearing that he had worked hard with Ralph Ellison to make the unwieldy manuscript of *Invisible Man* into a book. As well as teaching, he wrote book reviews for the *New Leader* and read constantly. Hyman was a physically unprepossessing man, fleshy, with thick black-rimmed glasses, dark somewhat balding hair, a brown-black beard, a big belly, and pale unhealthy skin that never saw the sun. The girls in his classes fawned over him. His mind was voracious, intimidating, amusing, his knowledge vast. In 1963, he published his ambitious work *The Tangled Bank,* on Freud, Frazer, Darwin, and Marx. He could expound on anything and took no prisoners.

He and Shirley had met as students at Syracuse University. Like him, she — remembered now primarily for her story "The Lottery" — was passionately devoted to writing. She was obese, with untended light brown hair (often unwashed and pulled back clumsily), winged glasses on a pudgy face, and intense eyes; her size made her formidable. Their son Barry was in my class. Sally was a couple of grades ahead, and Joanne, older still, soon became my camp counselor at an overnight camp near North Adams, Massachusetts. I never knew Laurie, their oldest son.

Stanley and Shirley invited us to Christmas dinner our first winter in town, and I remember Shirley as kindly and solicitous. She gave Paul and me each one of those Belgian chocolate balls in the shape of an orange — exotic, then, to me. She had a necklace of real birds' skulls, which she sometimes wore, and was deeply superstitious, skirting electrical outlets wherever she walked. She kept dolls with pins in them to help her manage enemies. Once, several years later, she telephoned Dad and asked him where his car was parked. He replied that it was in the driveway. "Bern," she said, "do me a favor and move it into the garage." "Okay, Shirley, but why?" "Well, earlier this week, my car caught on fire. And then Irving's car caught on fire. [Irving was a writer living locally.] And you know, Bern, they say, 'Never two without three.'" Out of kindness, Dad moved his car into the garage.

STANLEY DIDN'T DRIVE, and Shirley drove him everywhere — to and from the college, out to the local bistro, and on all of his errands. She daily retrieved his morning newspaper from Percy's. They owned a tiny car, I think a Morris Minor or a Deux Chevaux, and how they even got into and out of it is something of a mystery. Between them, the local gossip claimed, they weighed more than five hundred pounds — this at a time when fewer people were overweight. I later read a biography of Shirley that suggested pill as well as alcohol abuse, and a life that was further out of control than I saw. My own child's impression of her focused more on her strangeness and kindness. I recall after William Fels, the college president, died of cancer, around 1964, Shirley drove me and several other kids an hour or so to Putney to visit his teenage daughter, Anna, at boarding school, so she'd have hometown company on an occasion her own mother couldn't attend. Shirley brought brownies she had baked.

Early on in Bennington, when Dad and Mom were out to dinner one night with Stanley and Shirley, Dad introduced them to other friends as Mr. and Mrs. Jackson. His error mortified him. Few women in those days kept their own names. Apparently, he feared that he'd somehow humiliated the husband by giving his famous wife preference, and the next time he was in New York City, he bought Stanley several very good cigars to make up for the faux pas.

DAD LIKED TO CONVEY the flavor of the place by telling visitors a story about Stanley, who read a book a day, often very late into the night and often accompanied by a lot of bourbon. One night, or probably in the wee hours of the morning, Stanley dozed off and then awakened to find himself naked and cold, with no idea how or why he'd shed his clothes while reading. He reached to his desk, took one of the pieces of paper on which he'd been writing, covered his genitals with it, and fell back to sleep. I think Dad liked the strangeness of the image, the notion that written words warmed, as well as perhaps the slightly embarrassing exposure of the community's alpha male.

Shirley died in 1965 at age forty-eight. Stanley was taken under the intensely devoted romantic wing of Phoebe Pettingell, one of his Bennington students — twenty years old, like his daughter, Joanne, when they started dating. He remarried quickly and lived a few years longer, dying of a heart attack in 1970 at his beloved North Bennington restaurant, the Rainbarrel, where he more or less owned a table. He was fifty-one. The Midieres, a French Algerian family, ran the unlikely place, memorable not just for its fine

food but also for the mural the grandfather had painted of a Rabe-
laisian drunk, belly engorged, buttons popped off his vest, lying
passed out under the open spigot of a large wine barrel. For years,
the Midieres rose every morning at four or five to start preparing
the day's fruit tarts and chocolate mousse. I remember them stopping Dad and Mom as they left one evening a short while after
Stanley had died. Awkward, tripping over their words, they explained sincerely in thick-accented English that it hadn't been their
food that had killed the great man. When I think back on the onion
soup crusted with bubbling Gruyère, the crisp chicken amandine
arriving deep in melted butter, and the desserts made with egg
yolks and heavy cream, it's little wonder they fussed. Dad gently
reassured them that they had not been responsible for Stanley's
appetites.

HOWARD NEMEROV was my father's first friend at Bennington.
He would appear late Sunday mornings at the door of the North
Bennington farmhouse to take Dad for long winter walks on the
frozen, snowy roads around the McCullough estate across the
way. Writing to Rosemarie Beck at the end of 1961, Dad described Howard and ruminated about signing on permanently at
Bennington.

> They have offered me a job and I may take it on half time. I have
> asked until the middle of February to make up my mind. I would
> feel easier about a decision if the schools were good for the kids.
> And in a way this is a lonely place. People keep to themselves more
> than they do in the West. Yet I've never walked with anyone as
> much as I do with Howard Nemerov. He has his ashplant and I
> my daughter's birch stick and we walk and talk with miles, as
> much as one can talk with Howard. He is a sensitive, very intelli-
> gent man but tell him no intimate things and expect to be told none;
> and no great guffaws of laughter to set the birds flying over the

fields; though he will often point at one with his stick and name it for you.[6]

A week later, he wrote a letter to the student with whom he was falling in love (she was off campus for the school's nonresident term). Its description of walking with Howard is almost identical to what he wrote to Rosemarie. Maybe the poet was particularly on the writer's mind, but the younger woman may also have been taking the painter's place as confidant and muse.

> Winter has surprised me. Though we've yet to go below zero for an extended time, I don't find the cold as bothersome as I thought it would be, after several years in a tepid climate, the warm Japanese Current skirting the Pacific shore . . . But the true beauty of the winter is visual. We live on the campus now — moved on the first of January, and from my window in the morning my first sight is the vast white sweep of the hills and trees, and in the background the mountains. I walk to my office along the path by the pond, enjoying the sensation of being alone in the landscape, and remembering what it was like as a child to walk in snow to school; only then, in the city streets, there was an ambitious stamping of one's footmarks on the clean white snow, a symbolic conquering of space, and destruction of white experience. Now the emotion is in looking, in the poetry of white, with hills and the white rhythms that feed the hungry eye. And Nemerov and I, on Sunday mornings, have taken to walking with our sticks, he with his ashplant and I with my daughter's rough-hewn birch staff, discoursing about literature mostly as we plod the white roads around the McCullough estate, each calling attention to what the other sees, and Howard naming the birds.[7]

The two men would go out for a couple of hours at a time: Howard tall, crew-cut, bareheaded, a wool scarf around his neck. Dad shorter, solid in his winter jacket, balding head under a tweed cap. As they rambled, Howard filled Dad in about the college, the local luminaries, the way it all worked. They enjoyed each other's company and shared both larger literary interests and smaller amusements. In 1964, Dad wrote to Rosemarie Beck, "About a week ago Howard Nemerov and I drove down to Saratoga Springs to play the horses. I lost seven dollars and Howard twenty-one, which means he was three times more adventurous than I."[8]

Howard was a handsome man, tall, with very short, bristly, salt-and-pepper hair covering much of his head, dark circles under his deep-set eyes, and a low voice. He was often depressed or in his cups, but from any mood, once in company, he could summon a gentle smile. He always greeted me warmly and inquired wryly as to my doings. One day when he visited, I, having in seventh grade commenced my futile lifetime effort to learn French, was working on memorizing a list of nouns, including the one for grape-fruit, *pamplemousse.* He loved the sound, played with it fitfully as he conversed with Dad, and for several years afterward teasingly addressed me in person and in the occasional short note as "Dear Pamplemousse."

Six years younger than Dad and Harvard educated, Howard had joined the Canadian air force and flown in Europe during World War II. He had met his wife, Peggy, in England, married her in 1944, and published his first book of poems, *The Image and the Law,* in 1947. He also wrote novels. Eventually, he won a Pulitzer Prize and spent two years in the late 1980s as America's poet laureate before dying of cancer in 1991. I heard Peggy once say to Mom that Howard slept late, sometimes didn't get out of his pajamas all day, and would eat only scrambled eggs. She was not terribly happy in Bennington. When their first son, David, was already a teenager, they had two more sons. They left town for other academic climes a few years after we arrived.

Howard ended up briefly at Brandeis during the two years we lived in Cambridge, so we also saw him then. I remember one

semidisastrous dinner party when Dad, eager for a literary evening, invited Howard, Robert Lowell, and the John Keats biographer Aileen Ward to dinner at the house we were renting on Wil-
lard Street. Lowell was a little manic; I recall him admiring my red
knee socks more intently and repeatedly than they warranted. At
some point, he and Howard had an off-key exchange, and Howard
left with his pride wounded, apparently feeling he'd been treated
as the lesser poet. I read several books of his poems that same year
and had the hubris at age fifteen to write an English paper measuring him according to the standard Shelley had put forth in his defense of poetry. I memorized parts of his gorgeous poem "The
Blue Swallows" and still carry these lines from it: "O swallows,
swallows, poems are not / The point. Finding again the world, /
That is the point, where loveliness / Adorns intelligible things /
Because the mind's eye lit the sun."[9]

After Dad died and my mother moved back to Cambridge, she
and I attended a reading Howard gave at Harvard, in 1990 or 1991.
It was right before he died. I hadn't seen him for a very long time.
He read beautifully, and I found a number of his poems haunting;
their striking language just the right tone. When he finished, we
joined a line to greet him, and he kissed each of us, alcohol heavy
on his breath. He was far into his cancer and haggard. He seemed
vague and absent, the old warmth gone. It was a sad goodbye.

I UNWISELY OPINED to Dad one day when I was perhaps sixteen that Howard was smarter than he — indeed than any of us.
And he was. Elliptical, caustic, hilarious, with a lightning mind and
a thousand erudite references casually at the ready, the poet was
more brilliant than just about anyone I'd met. Dad bristled more
than I'd expected at my comment. No doubt I was oblivious to my
own aggression, but I think I had actually begun the conversation
with some term subtler than "smarter" and perhaps partly meant

that Howard's intellect was more scholarly. As much as anything, Dad took umbrage because of what he felt to be the limits of his talent and his mind. He envied the fluency of John Updike and his young Bennington colleague Nick Delbanco. His slow, laborious writing and rewriting, and his equally slow reading, wore on him. In a letter to Rosemarie Beck written in Corvallis as he was taking on a third draft of *A New Life*, he mentioned the genius of Picasso and Shakespeare and wistfully observed, "I'll bet none of the great ones ever labor. This comes to my thoughts because my own labors are unending." He knew that the only thing he could control was effort, so he demanded that his be unstinting. "If I tell you I am utterly tired," he added, "don't pity me."[10]

During the two years we lived in Cambridge in the mid-1960s, Dad had a professorial affiliation with Kirkland House, a residence for undergraduates at Harvard, and I remember him returning from one faculty lunch there stunned by his tablemates' erudition. A fellow diner had casually described the floor plan and contents of the Uffizi Gallery in Florence. "He knew each room, the individual paintings on the walls!" I suspect that his awe-filled comment also may have contained recognition of the kind of ease, the well-traveled erudition, that can come to someone who not only possesses a different type of mind but who has means, who doesn't have to do it all by himself. Cambridge was probably the first time Dad lunched regularly with the WASP intellectual establishment, many of whom came from old, wealthy New England families, whose grandfathers had stopped in to visit Carlyle in England before traveling on to Italy.

THE LITERARY CRITIC Granville Hicks and his wife, Dorothy, who lived forty-five minutes from Bennington across the New York State border, in a small rural village called Grafton, became close friends with my parents. In the autumn of 1961, Granville gave *A New Life* a positive review and then, learning that its author had moved nearby, wrote to propose a meeting. Thirteen years older than Dad, already sixty when they met, Granville was a smallish, thin, white-haired man with glasses, a reddened high-blood-pressure complexion, a cigarette in hand, and the habit of sitting like an impatient boy, with one leg pulled up, its ankle propped on his other knee. He had been born and spent his boyhood in New England, attending first Exeter and then Harvard. He had been friendly toward the Communist Party for a few years in the 1930s and worked as literary editor for the *New Masses*. He also wrote for the *Saturday Review* and the *New Leader*.

Their one daughter married, the couple lived alone in an old, low-ceilinged farmhouse. Dottie, who became an older sister to my mother, had grown up in Maine. Thin, also a smoker, she had cropped white hair and often wore a white blouse and a straight, midcalf-length wool skirt or slacks. She was plainspoken, smart, well-read, and extremely able. She tended a large garden and taught my mother about gardening. She also sewed, and I still own a braided rag rug she made for my parents' bedroom in Vermont. Their three grandsons, who visited sometimes, were age-mates of mine, and I occasionally went along on evenings to their house. I recall a New Year's Eve there, spent playing charades. I can't say I ever felt close to them, or even really knowledgeable about who they were. I was half out the door by the late sixties, as they increasingly spent time with my parents and eventually traveled to London with them.

My father and Granville talked about books, writers, and politics. I remember conversations about contemporary writers, the civil rights movement, and a fundraiser for the Student Nonviolent Coordinating Committee (SNCC) that they all attended together. Granville's opinions could be sharp. I believe I once made the mistake of enthusing about some play of George Bernard Shaw's and slightly raising his ire. A few years later, he told me in passing — though I am quite certain I had not broached the question — that I was an open book and advised me never to write fiction, because I was too straightforward for such an undertaking and had not lived enough to have anything to write about.

LIFE IN THE ORCHARD had its share of pleasures. Much of the college property had originally been one family's estate, and the grand Jennings mansion, atop a small hill overlooking lawns and fields, now served as the music building. The carriage barn had become a performance center for concerts and lectures. The whole campus was filled with places to explore and archaeological relics from different student eras to dig into. At some point, rows of evergreens had been planted to form an outdoor theater, with stage and wings. No one put on plays there, but as kids we spent hours fooling with the theatrical possibilities. In the nearby woods were several abandoned chicken coops. My friends and I spent days in those woods, hacking down saplings to build lean-tos, creating elaborate camps, and learning to smoke cigarettes. I remember a particularly happy early-summer evening when my friend Deb Scott, her sister, Cathy, and I chased the hay baler as it wound through the freshly cut fields below their house, a big hazy sun setting behind the green hills. We jumped onto and among the bales as the lumbering machine spit them out.

Down the path that connected the Orchard to the main campus, there was a pond where a bunch of us poled through the water on inner-tube-supported, scrap-wood rafts we'd hammer back together every spring (before the summer stagnancy dissuaded us). We always fell in and trailed home in wet-heavy, muddy clothes and squishy sneakers. In the winter, we skated. We would test the ice daily starting in early December, tossing rocks into the middle and stepping tentatively onto the mica-like edges ourselves. We were eager to have it freeze clear and smooth, unridged by wind, before the snow came. One year half a dozen of us rushed the season. We were skating just fine until one of the older boys jumped and broke the surface tension. An instant later, we all fell through in turn, like a Radio City Music Hall kick routine gone bad — plop, plop, plop. We were near the edge, and the frigid water came only up to our knees.

One June night, Orchard dogs treed our cat up a telephone pole, and he refused to come down. My father fed both cats each morning when he got up and put them to bed in the basement at night. Pinky's stranding became a family story. Here is my father's contemporary account, written to his student, with its humorous and seductive telling:

Last night our orange half-Persian Pinky was chased all the way up a telephone pole in front of G's house by three dogs — Ranger Durand, Cinder F., and Ginger Bastard. After the dogs left, Pinky wouldn't come down though we all coaxed. I said he'd come down in the dark or by morning, but Janna was disturbed and asked me how I'd like to be up there all night in the dark with three dogs chasing me; and I didn't like it. I'd been reading, and listening to Vivaldi and the Schubert Dichterliede [*sic*] sung by Lotte Lehman[n] (love makes her cry out), and when I was ready to go upstairs I thought of Pinky, got his dish and spoon and went out to see if he had come down. He hadn't. The moon had risen and there was Pinky in the moonlight sitting on the crossbar of the phone pole. Come down, Pinky, I said, come to your father. He answered me plaintively, please to come up and get him. I tapped the spoon against the dish and he rose and explored the crossbar but said he didn't think he could make it. We talked in the dark, Pinky saying he doubted he could. Then I saw it would be all talk as long as I stayed there, so I left. But on the lawn I tapped the spoon again against the dish, and from afar it awoke old longings in him and he dug his claws into the wood and gently lowered himself, tail first, down the pole. I called him a good boy and give him an extra ration of cat food in the kitchen and this morning he got an egg.[11]

I spent a lot of time roaming the campus among the students and befriended several, including one whose babysitter-love sustained me through those years. Early on, a friend and I conceived a plan of going door-to-door in the dormitories soliciting empty soda bottles, then worth two cents on deposit. The pesky enterprise quickly introduced us around. We'd turn the bottles in, trade our earnings for a thirty-five-cent cheeseburger or ten-cent ice cream at the school snack bar, and sit eating in the commons lounge, watching the older girls. I can still see Andrea Dworkin, maybe nineteen, wild curly hair uncombed, black T-shirt, dirty black jeans, perhaps a red plaid wool lumber jacket, fleshy, feet in flip-flops, looking terribly depressed, no doubt observing enough sexual politics going on to fuel her fury for a lifetime. She frightened me a little; even at a distance, I had a sense that no fence would hold her.

Sometimes we used to sneak in to watch dance and drama rehearsals. One afternoon during a dance class, a bat flew in, and a friend and I watched Bill Bales, the still lanky but aging dance instructor and choreographer, on a chair — girls gathered close to encourage him — wildly and futilely swiping a broom at the disoriented, fluttering creature. In the theater, we got to know the players and the plays, and before I was twelve, I'd seen the whole García Lorca trilogy — *The House of Bernarda Alba*, *Blood Wedding*, and *Yerma* — with Betty Aberlin and Reed Wolcott sharing leads. For lack of anything else to do, I took to attending the Saturday night foreign film series. If my parents didn't have guests, they would occasionally come. I watched many movies but can now summon only a few: *A Taste of Honey*, *The Cranes Are Flying*, *The*

Loneliness of the Long Distance Runner. The single projector had to be rewound between reels.

A SOURCE OF HAPPINESS for my parents back east was reconnecting with many friends. They made regular trips to New York City, where they visited Dad's P.S. 181 and Erasmus friends, as well as their circle from Brooklyn and Greenwich Village: Karl Schrag, his brother, Paul, and their wives, Ilse and Susie; Lillian and Ben-Zion; Mike and Catherine Seide; Ruth and Bernie Morris. On some weekends, they drove to Cambridge to see the Inkeleses or to New Haven to see the Erlichs. As Dad's fame put him more in demand as a reader, they visited different campuses and made friends as they traveled. I remember the academic year 1962–1963, when Marc Blitzstein was in residence at Bennington. Alfred Kazin and his wife, Ann, and daughter, Katie, came and stayed with us. The Kazins may have known Blitzstein already. They all dined with us, and by and by everyone started urging Marc to sing a few songs from *The Threepenny Opera*, the Bertolt Brecht–Kurt Weill classic that he had famously translated. Marc was reluctant, but the pressure built. He was a slim, small, balding man with a mustache, irascible and averse to being pushed. Finally, he called to me and Katie; took us into the little room off the kitchen where the upright piano, television, and ironing board elbowed for space; shut both doors; and intently, fiercely, pounded out and sang "Pirate Jenny" only to us. I revered the song, sung on the record by Kurt Weill's wife, Lotte Lenya, which spat out a bitter revenge fantasy of a black freighter slipping into port bringing death to all the streetwalker's enemies and johns. I had been listening to musicals since Oregon, but *Threepenny* revealed a sharper spectrum of feeling — sexual tensions resonant of the college scene. I felt rapturous hearing it so intimately, and pleased by the power reversal Blitzstein had accomplished. I remember looking around at one point and seeing the Kazins and my mother and father piled together, peering over one another into the room, listening through the narrow space they had boldly cracked between door and jamb.

Marc and Dad became friendly that year and decided to collaborate. Marc was in the midst of working on an opera about the controversial trial and execution of the Italian anarchists Sacco and Vanzetti, but he was having trouble with the piece and perhaps wanted distraction. He read through a number of Dad's books and chose the stories "Idiots First" and "The Magic Barrel" to turn into operettas, thinking the pair would add up to an evening of song. When he left Bennington at the end of the spring term, he began working on them and stayed in touch. The next winter, he traveled to Martinique for an extended visit. One day in January 1964, my father, shocked and miserable, came in from work. He sought out my mother: "Ann, Marc is dead. He was murdered." The ugly story stunned the community. I remember sotto voce exchanges between campus neighbors as the news spread. In the course of a night of heavy drinking, Marc had picked up and propositioned a couple of sailors, who, hinting at sex, had led him into a back alley, stripped him of wallet and clothes, beat him, and left him naked and bleeding. He'd died a day or two later in the local hospital. He was fifty-eight.[12]

His murder, along with his songs, my father's influence, and the whole Bennington scene, became a substantial underpinning of my sensibility. As I write, I see the Ben Shahn series on the Sacco and Vanzetti trial. I think of Walker Evans, James Agee, Archibald MacLeish, and Dorothea Lange, writers and artists whose work I came to know. Blitzstein's death became an emotional gateway for me into the whole world of politically aware art and social justice commentary. Coming close on the heels of the John F. Kennedy assassination and the first civil rights killings, its brutality eddied into the larger collective mood of civil drama and solemnity, of in-

nocence lost, which would soon become the Vietnam protests. I
think it also may have marked the beginning of a different kind of
conversation between my father and me. I became more cognizant
of his world, more interested in eliciting his opinions about news
stories, books, and events. I increasingly tested out perceptions,
and he was serious back to me, and patient. Whatever else happened between us, I met each day with the sense that he would
take my side on the street. A little later, in eighth grade, I behaved
badly in music class — disrupted the lesson, then talked back —
and rightly got into trouble with the teacher, Harold Rohinsky,
who threw me out for the day. Mr. Rohinsky was a good-humored
guy, a musician who also taught me clarinet, an urban man recently
arrived and completely out of place in the North Bennington
school. That night, I told my father what had happened. He allowed to me that Mr. Rohinsky had overreacted, probably because
he was new to teaching and not yet experienced in controlling his
class. In my private lesson the next day, as we talked over my exile,
I brattily repeated Dad's comment. Mr. Rohinsky grinned broadly
and said, "Your father really loves you."

IN JUNE 1964, we drove to New York City to attend a large memorial concert for Marc at Lincoln Center in which Leonard
Bernstein and Lillian Hellman participated. (Blitzstein had based
his opera *Regina* on Hellman's play *The Little Foxes.*) Also in June,
Reed Wolcott, who'd studied with Marc during his year on campus, staged parts of several of his operas, including *The Cradle
Will Rock* and *No for an Answer,* on campus. I recall vividly her
deep-voiced, anguished performance of his songs.

At the New York tribute, Bernstein had announced that he was
planning to finish and stage *Idiots First,* a project he never carried
out. At the end of the evening, after warmly greeting Dad in the
green room, Bernstein took him aside and invited him to bed that

night. Dad was agog and couldn't stop himself from reporting the sexual offer to my mother, and indirectly to me, as we rode in a taxi back to our hotel.

BERNSTEIN'S PROPOSITION fit perfectly within our Vermont life as it was developing. Indeed, the Orchard at Bennington now mostly stands in memory as the easiest way to describe the sexually insidious nature of the college community. A publicly unspoken aspect of the school was its decadence, particularly the way the older male faculty "fucked," to use the campus vernacular, their young female students. They apparently considered it their prerogative, part of the stipend. That my father fell in love and joined this camp is no doubt central to my observations, but the phenomenon was much bigger. He took the opportunity the environment offered. Sometimes, particularly later when the school became more coed, some male faculty fucked the boys, and some female faculty fucked the boys (and probably the girls, too).

"Fuck" was the chosen community word, ahead of much of the nation. I remember Dad coming home one night after a disturbing jazz concert in the spring of 1964 in which an African-American jazz musician played. He had been deeply angered by some exchange during the "Jazz Weekend" at the college and was reluctant to play his solo gig. When he did play, he kept repeating "fuck" under his breath as he pounded the piano keys. That was a big deal in 1964. The whispered gossip was that he had been seen drinking a lot of milk and thus, according to Dad's sources, might be strung out on "smack." I think I remember the moment because it was the first I'd heard about a real person using heroin, but also because there was something about the event in the midst of the civil rights era — very white, outré, elite school invites exotic black musicians to campus — that created an overexcited, obliviously racist en-

counter with the bad boy "other." I sensed the crazed, ricocheting
energy.

ONE GOOD FRIEND of my parents and longtime teacher in the
humanities division every so often took a boy student into his
home. These boys would serve him sexually, and he would tu-
tor them in a kind of Greek/Eastern philosophic mentorship. He
possessed a vast knowledge of philosophy and had an extraordinary aesthetic sense — in his house, cooking, and flower garden,
and perhaps in bed as well. The first female president of Bennington, Gail Parker, got herself drummed out of the job during the
1970s for her very public affair with a history teacher (not even a
student). Some male presidents also had affairs, but more discreetly. Parker's in-your-face gender reversal and the couple's bad
taste — stripping off sweaters in the class they co-taught to reveal
on each of them a scarlet *A* — must have felt way too mocking to
the board of trustees, who fired her. But the couple was merely
buffooning into high relief the school's ethos. However chilling
the male boy hunting or the bad girl shenanigans, they were all
kind of secondary to the patriarchal harem entitlement that ruled
the place.

The living arrangements in the Orchard demonstrate this more
quotidian carrying on. There were eight houses. In the first house,
at the far corner, the eighty-year-old past conductor of the Des-
soff Choirs lived with his fourth wife, a onetime student maybe
forty years younger than he, and their three young children. In the
next house, a psychology professor, wedded — apparently quietly
and monogamously — to an ex-student. In the third house, a charismatic music professor, married to his second wife, a onetime student, and carrying on an affair with a current student. This liaison
was so boldly open that many other husbands, including Dad,

pointed to it as a template for their own entitlement, an ideal living arrangement.

Next door to us resided another music teacher, who had married a younger student after his first wife had become mentally ill. Across a small orchard-cum-field lived Howard Nemerov, who stayed married to his wife, Peggy, but who years later brought a mistress to visit my parents in their apartment in New York. The pottery and ceramics professor in the house next to us, across the road, eventually left his wife for a young female teacher on the faculty. Finally, in the last house, lived Oliver Durand, our family doctor, and his wife, Dorothy, also a doctor, who ran the student health center. Oliver apparently left the students alone.

Another model to be envied was Pablo Casals. Several times each summer, we would drive forty-five minutes across the mountains to watch him conduct at the Marlboro Music Festival. I can still see the railing that had been built around the podium to keep him from falling off the stage. Aged, fragile, and transported by melody, he would sit waving his arms, humming, and noisily shushing any musician whom he found too loud. Dad would observe with delight and repeatedly recount to friends the devotion of Casals's much younger wife, ex-student Marta Montañez, who would slowly walk him onto the stage, supporting his weight on her arm.

I remember a spoof concert in the spring of 1965, when three senior girls, music majors, dressed as their male teachers, sat down to perform. The one imitating Lou Calabro was wearing his jean jacket, secretly borrowed from his wife. The one pretending to be Henry Brandt started to play his flute as the trio commenced. Finding its sound strangled, "he" took the flute apart and carefully pulled a silk stocking from its clogged chamber. More of the same ensued as the three mimed their way through the local, unspoken/unspeakable leitmotif. Within the decade, Calabro had left his wife, Tina, and their four children for a Bennington music student. Brandt, too, had left his wife for another woman, although I'm uncertain of her status.

THE OPEN SEXUALITY and partner swapping in part was a rejection of the hypocrisies of more conservative communities, where identical affairs and exploits were simply kept secret. At times, it represented creative excitement boiling over. Bennington, in its irreverence, was more interesting than Corvallis, more intellectually alive, and more stimulating. Everyone read and thought and talked. Passionately dedicated teachers taught well. Artists made important art; musicians composed; writers published. People chose to stay there because they wanted something different, something riskier and edgier. To come into their own, they needed an alternative to Main Street America. And if experiments sometimes brought pain, the tradeoff was worth the liberation, the self-realization, and the joie de vivre that preceded it.

Yet, the Bennington scene was a louche vision for a wide-eyed girl arriving on the cusp of adolescence. It provided lessons about adulthood that, however commonplace, proved less than salubrious for me as time passed. It taught that the impact of age and power differences on relationships should be denied and sexual damage should be silenced, the very notion ridiculed. Teachers sleeping with students was fine. Only petit-bourgeois straights grew queasy at unconventional pairings or proclivities. I remember Sally Hyman, having taken some part of my education upon herself when I was thirteen, carefully explaining to me a view she attributed to her father: No woman had ever been raped. However adamant, female protest was simply foreplay. Women wanted to be forced, and ultimately their excitement made them receptive no matter what their claim. Sally, out of place and desperately bored in the North Bennington school, taught me to recite all the kings of England and had me memorize every possible way to win the matchstick game played in the French film *Last Year at Marienbad*. Meanwhile, her mother, Shirley Jackson, together with other faculty wives, used to complain about how sexually aggressive the Bennington girls were, always slyly seducing their husbands. Their position anticipated something like Camille Paglia's later stance on female prowess and correctly stated a piece of erotic truth even as it omitted the larger reality.

During one of the several mid-1960s summers during which I hung out at Ken Noland's house in nearby Shaftsbury with his daughter, Lyn, it was rumored that he, his wife, Stephanie, and Clem Greenberg were all in an unusual form of analysis that promoted very free behavior. I have no idea how much truth was in the buzz, but I remember my mother mildly suggesting that perhaps I ought not to spend so much time up there. I bridled and appealed to my father, who backed me up. My mother had correctly sensed something about the "anything goes" ambiance. In practice, my own days and nights at the Nolands' were benign, and the images that return are pleasurable: listening with Lyn to the Beatles, the Stones, and Bob Dylan; fishing for trout in their newly dug, stocked pond; skinny-dipping late at night in the swimming pool; examining Ken's multicolored striped paintings in progress, the huge canvases taped to the studio floor. The rolls and rolls of masking tape, used to separate the different colors he laid down, made me wide-eyed. I felt close to Lyn and our bunch of friends in an intense teenage way. She would arrive from Washington, D.C., in late June and leave in August, causing unbearable partings but benefiting from the distance, which made her a little more sparkling and shiny than the rest of us, daily together, could be to each other.

I loved visiting the Nolands. Stephanie was friendly; Ken was excited by his new wealth and growing success and expansive in his spending. I had never before seen such open pleasure in having things. He was a forty-ish southern boy, soft-spoken, handsome, with a lick of hair that always fell mid-forehead. He wore glasses, Izodesque shirt, paint-covered jeans, and loafers without socks. He seemed to enjoy gathering people around him — the guest room was often full — and at dinnertime, if Stephanie had tired of cooking for the hoard, he would sweep everyone off to some local restaurant. Occasionally, deeper tensions bubbled over — a guest would leave in a huff, Lyn would describe a late-night fight — but it was screened from younger visitors. I found Ken affable, kindly, intense about his art. The farmhouse had once belonged to Robert Frost, and it must have felt city-clothes-itchy under the trendy leather Eames chair and zebra-skin rug with which they decorated the telephone nook. I remember one evening when my mother and father and I had been invited to dinner. Clem Greenberg was there, along with his wife, Jenny. When, late into the night, the discussion turned to Solzhenitsyn and Russian dissidents, I brashly jumped in, using a Wordsworth sonnet, about the freedom one finds within the prison of a chosen poetic form, to make the case that liberty exists in the mind. At seventeen, I was in over my head, but they were wine-mellow and indulgent.

THE BENNINGTON sexual environment provided a perfect reef on which to scrape the bottom off our Oregon family. My memory of those first years after our arrival is that something ineffable but sustaining ended. My brother, just fourteen and unhappy in the North Bennington school, stopped talking. This might not be absolutely true, but my recollection is that he withdrew hugely. After two years, my parents reluctantly sent him to the Cambridge School in Weston, Massachusetts, to board, and he seemed happier there. I was twelve when he left. My mother missed her Corvallis friends, no doubt worried about my father's emotional departure, and became depressed. By the summer of 1963, she was seeing a psychiatrist. I have read that Shirley Jackson saw the same psychiatrist — there was but one in town — after one of Stanley's student affairs, and I know that a family friend made visits to him after her husband started an affair. I now wonder if the good doctor didn't earn his living on cuckolded wives — a comic/sordid variant of Alice Toklas's Paris assignment to entertain the spouses while Gertrude Stein spoke meaningfully with Picasso and the other geniuses who dropped by their home.

My parents saw me as self-sufficient and somehow sensitive but indomitable, and once Paul left for school, they must have felt that their parenting era was mostly over. In a newsy letter to Dad when he was in Europe in 1963, my mother, having joined the Nemerovs and Durands for a cocktail one afternoon, recounted:

> Peggy's mother was there and paid me a compliment about Janna, and then Oliver, in one of his mellow moods as it was cocktail time, said he thought she was the best adjusted child he knew, that she has the "world in the palm of her hands," and etc, and Dorothy praised her too. I was most pleased, though I do think Janna is a bit more sensitive than most kids, so that in spite of her excellent balance, she is not quite that "square," if you want to put it that way; she isn't quite the cover of the Sat. Eve Post (as it was! not as it is). But she's great![13]

My mother was defending me according to local rules: in Bennington there was nothing worse than being seen as square, wholesome, and Rockwellesque.

In 1964, Dad wrote to Rosemarie Beck, "Yesterday the ice on the pond had melted. It was loose and sinking but [Janna] walked across it in red boots and no sweater. I remonstrated when I heard about it. 'Ah, come on Dad, let me show you how I did it.'"[14] Three years later, he wrote to Beck again, "Janna, as usual, flourishes.

She considers herself plain and is beautiful but how can I tell her when she thinks me prejudiced."[15] In truth, the longer we lived on the Bennington campus, the less I felt like a flourishing person. The guys in my school made it clear that I wasn't even a little beautiful, and the girls correctly tagged me as "different" — awkwardly precocious, opinionated, intense. At the same time, my enthusiasms were real and apparently on display, and I took satisfaction in presenting myself as a child about whom adults did not need to worry.

Chapter 7

Bennington Girl

◂+◂ ◂+◂ My father fell in love. I don't know just when it changed from his typical avuncular interest to romance, but he began corresponding with Arlene, a young literature student and aspiring writer, when she was off campus during our first Vermont winter. I became subliminally aware of his emotional absence and my mother's distress not long after. A few years ago, my mother told me that my father had not become fully sexually involved until after Arlene graduated in 1963, but who knows. Letters she wrote him during the summer of 1962, though without explicit reference to passion enacted, suggest that the heat was high. In one she tells him she's wearing earrings he's given her. During the summer of 1963, he traveled to Venice and apparently rendezvoused with her. I knew nothing explicit at the time. I cannot point to a moment of learning about her, only an atmosphere into which she, and her meanings to my father, materialized slowly, across years.

After my father died, my mother read through some of their correspondence. He had saved Arlene's letters and in the mid-1970s had had her photocopy his and send them to him. I suppose when he started writing *Dubin's Lives,* he wanted to refresh his recollections for the book. Mom was uncertain what to do with the letters. Her grief was fresh, and she didn't want them in the house. She wasn't ready to send them to any library; yet, respectful, she thought better of destroying them. On my suggestion, she mailed them to me. I put the unopened box on a shelf in a closet and left it there for almost twenty years. When I untied the string, the brown postal paper was so brittle that it crumbled in my hands.

I assume that the stack I have now read — Arlene's letters for twenty-two years, plus fourteen years of his — has been censored. Arlene could have tossed out or not photocopied some of his to her, and my father could have torn up some of hers to him, or some of the copies of his. Several are obviously missing. Certainly, the lovers wrote discreetly, guarding their privacies. So much so that in the late 1960s, Arlene angrily questioned my father as to why his missives were so short — and wondered whether he was worried about what posterity might see. It would have been his way to shield himself so. But as he pointed out to her, writing for him took time and effort, and the day's labor often left him little energy for more of it. At best, the letters are bits of spray cast by the tumbling of waves. They met in person regularly and talked frequently on the telephone. I reviewed a spotty archive.

The romance, once consummated, seems to have ended rather quickly, replaced first by angry silence, then by a stiff reticence with bits of quibbling, and then gradually by a warmer exchange, perhaps a continuing affair. Something — either friendship or love — reignited a dozen years later, when they were both spending time in New York City and he was writing *Dubin's Lives.* They seem to have become dear to each other again, or perhaps it was simply a continuing. He took her to dinner, to the opera, and to museums. They sent each other articles and books and exchanged gifts. She asked for — and he wrote — endless recommendations for fellowships, graduate schools, medical schools, psychiatric placements, and grants. The last such letter he wrote was on behalf of her child, who was applying to private kindergarten. (One of the few visceral reactions I experienced when reading the correspondence was at the ease with which she took up his time with such requests. As in some summer house with a fragile well, where showers have long been scrupulously rationed, she commandeered the bathtub, opened the taps wide and with abandon, flushed the toilet for the hell of it.) At one point, she asked for one or two thousand dollars to help pay for an analysis, and he gave it to her. He cared about her until the end of his life.

The last letter of hers in the folder, written two years before he died and more than twenty years after they had fallen in love, recounts a dream she had about him while she was traveling in Europe with her husband and child. She was pregnant at the time. In the dream, Malamud had become a poet and was reading her an anguished poem in which he wondered where his wife and child were. Where had they gone? (His wife and her husband were present in the dream.) Both she and Malamud knew that his poem was a disguised account of their love, written to her. She writes, "You were writing about the wife + child that we had never been to you, but were meant to have been." Then she adds, "Not the happiest night of this vacation, that wasn't . . . Anyway, you see I think of you."[1]

Earlier, with Rosemarie Beck, whatever their sexual encounters, it was the friendship that endured. Was it the same with Arlene? My mother believes that my father never had any intention of leaving her. My father's view died with him. Whether or not home held him fondly enough, had he contemplated a departure, he likely would have felt daunted by the guilt he'd bear, the stark violation of his sense of virtue. He no doubt recalled his experience after moving to Oregon, when he'd watched his brother collapse and his father die. I imagine that, whatever his feelings, he lacked the stomach to risk initiating such damage again.

HE BEGAN AS ARLENE'S PROFESSOR, teaching her to write. His early communications include an undated comment on one of her short stories:

> The story is an experience; it has great power. I still maintain that I've not read anything by a student that has this force. I am aware more clearly now of a certain monotony that derives from the force and perhaps excessive compression . . . It lacks at times transitional smoothness — a somewhat larger development of the man's mind and experiences, mostly the quality of *leading up* to what was bound to happen at the end . . . The whole is most impressive, most promising.

He lent her books and took an interest in the daily stories she recounted about her family and fellow students, as well as her reading. He debated literary ideas with her and continually encouraged her in her writing. He enjoyed telling her about his work and his social life. He took pleasure in her admiration of his growing fame. They corresponded regularly during the summer of 1962, and in the long letter he wrote to her in August 1962, one gets a sense that he might have been covertly discussing either with himself or her the terms of their engagement, defending the merit of instances where sexual feeling goes unexpressed. He construes *Jules and Jim* partly as a movie in which a woman's expressed sexuality wreaks havoc with men.

August 10, 1962

Dear Arlene,

   A week ago I was in Boston. We had eaten with Alex Inkeles and his wife (You remember his lecture here?) and were going to a movie when a girl came down the street, who I thought might be you. She greeted me and it turned out to be Diana R., Bennington '65. Small world.

The Movie was "Jules et Jim," one of the most interesting French movies I have seen in my life. In treatment, story, acting, photography, it is absolutely fascinating. It is a story of a woman who can't get her sex life straight and the havoc that wreaks in herself and the two friends who love her, Jules and Jim. The beauty of it is that it's a comedy with an exceptionally serious theme, and is done with such beauty it becomes a work of art. Look it up the next time you're in New York and do go to see it; I know you'll enjoy it. A few days later, at Wellfleet, Alfred Kazin, to whom I was talking about the film, said that he and his wife thought it a masterpiece. If you see it note the rhythm of the film and how the narrator manages to give it a novelistic quality of time. It is also of its times, the era shortly after World War I, the twenties (the girl reminded me of Zelda Fitzgerald) and the beginning of the period of the Nazis in Germany. The inner morality, or lack of it, is connected with the morality of the times.

On Friday we drove to Wellfleet, got a motel, and visited our friends the Lechays. Jim is the painter-in-residence in the University of Iowa; he took Grant Wood's place at his death. We spent most of our time with the Lechays and I had the pleasure of a private view of his paintings, and, on Sunday morning, being sketched by him. On Saturday and Sunday Maggie Roth appeared, Philip's wife. He is presently staying with William Styron, I think working on a movie script of one of Roth's short stories. Maggie is a petite, well-formed girl, who's been through a good deal and expects to be through a good deal more. She has a quality of strong will about her and reminds me of Martha Reganhart in *Letting Go*. We went swimming at Duck Pond, a lovely little lake in the woods — on the day we tried the ocean it was covered with fog yet there were many people on the beach — and then went back to the house, after drinks at Maggie's (she has two kids by a prior marriage, a boy of fourteen, and a nice girl, unsure of herself, of twelve) to meet the Kazin's who had come up on my invitation. They live at Wellfleet for the summer. Wherever Alfred is the conversation sparkles, and we enjoyed that and the barbeque dinner that Jim and Rose cooked up afterwards . . .

About Yeats: I think you'd have a hard time proving that the content of his poetry is "distorted" because of almost a generation of unsatisfied love for Maude Gonne, strange as that was. (The Irish say all men are boys till forty.) And what shines through his poetry is not distortion or poison but suffering, beauty, discipline, art. I am not arguing for his experience, would not want it for myself even to be great as he was, but you misinterpret what he made of it. It racked but enlarged his emotions; it filled him with longing, dreams, ambition, lust; with the vision of the most profound, most beautiful love. It made him a man in the highest sense of the word, as Gandhi was a man. Most great men are spiritual, profound, sex flames in their spirits. Maude Gonne was to Yeats the equivalent of Dostoyevsky's prison experiences. (He too contained his sex and it became part of his artist's spirit.) His references to her in his poems are not sickly but full of nostalgia, worship of her beauty, bitterness, perhaps hatred. In a way she entered into everything he wrote. It's good for artists to possess another self. Years later she said something like this: If I had married Yeats Ireland would have lost a great poet. At the worst his early verse was romantic, attitudinized, sentimental. His later poetry was magnificent, tempered to steel as his spirit was. He had loved her, been unfulfilled except as he fulfilled himself, and escaped her. Later he was to have a mistress, Olivia Shakespeare, a novelist who quickly taught him the facts of love. He was married very late, perhaps around fifty but he wrote about his wife that she taught him ecstasy. Ecstasy comes to very few; the opposite is boredom. And his poetry became miraculously great. Have you read "Sailing to Byzantium," "Byzantium," "The Second Coming," "Leda and the Swan," "Among School Children," "A Prayer for my Daughter," "Coole Park," the Crazy

Jane poems? If you like, in a free hour sometime I'll read them with you.

I sent out my "Naked Nude" story today: it's well built and very funny. Now I'll go back to a lecture I started writing. I'll be using it from time to time at different universities. I've accepted five engagements thus far: Oct., Washington University in St. Louis and Syracuse University. November, a reading at the YMHA in New York. February, the Esquire panel at Princeton, and March a lecture at Brandeis. I may take one more date in the spring and that will be it.

I'm so glad you liked *The Natural.*

And I'm pleased your second story is coming along; if you finish that and do one more that should be a good summer's work.

good things, Bern

He had thought leaving Oregon would be simply a relief and had failed to anticipate the loneliness of severed friendships and a new place. She was someone with whom he could speak, who might appreciate his sensibility anew. This bit, with its pleasure of sharing an observation, comes from a long letter he'd written two weeks earlier, on July 27, 1962.

What I shall remember most about the summer, I suppose, is Yaddo, for a while, where I snapped out of my end-of-term trance and began to work again. The wonderful Vermont summer cool, clear days that made working easy. And the discovery of the Marlboro Music Festival where Serkin played (three times) and Pablo Casals conducted. The most memorable experience was visiting a master class of Casals . . . He is a wonderful old man; humanism shines through him, and everything he says seems to have a wonderful quality of art. I remember his telling one student not to play Bach like Bach but as music. "Put some gypsy in him," he said; Lisa Tate told me that when she was there he said Bach had "the declamatory quality of a Jew." Isn't that interesting?

In the winter of 1962 and spring of 1963, falling in love, he wrote her brief, sometimes cryptic notes, mostly undated:

If you'd like to walk with me for an hour meet me in Commons at 7:30. Be warmly dressed, the country roads can be cold at twilight.

I hope you are yourself today, your lovely best self; you deserve to be.
    If you're not away come up for a while bet. 2–3.

At first I felt bad; regretting the asymmetry of the one-sided. But then I thought if it was one-sided I can depend on her generosity somehow to redress the balance. She will make it not bad.

They took the cat up the pole story: that should mean Europe sure . . .
    I've noticed I've been finishing work by 1:15. Please come up whenever you feel like it, at that time. I'm free every day except Tues when I counsel . . . This makes more sense. B.

How much I appreciate you.

You haven't said so but at this stage I'm convinced I owe you an apology for several unjust remarks and for involving you in some unpleasant emotions. My only excuse is the confusion of being myself involved.
    Thank you for the invitation to the party; we'll see.

Drop into my office when you get a chance. We'll arrange to meet. Unfortunately, I can't tonight.

Hi Baby, It was "a smashing success" I have much to tell you including my meeting two friends of yours. XOX

You are always kind, your soul glows in you.
    The matter is dropped with my usual apologies for certain ineptnesses; you notice how I fight them?

I see a long good period from here on in. We'll both come out stronger.

You're one of the most beautiful people I've met in my life. I want your life to be as beautiful, as lovely as you are.

I love you. B.

Apparently something went badly when they met in Europe in the summer of 1963. (She was on her way to spend a year abroad on a fellowship.) Her letter, between his two brief notes, which follow, is missing. The reference to the *New York Review of Books* is a gift subscription he'd sent her that needed to be rerouted to her new address.

September 23, 1963 — I shan't be writing. Have a good year. If you need help of any sort, please let me know. Best, Bern

October 22, 1963 — I appreciate your letter. I'm well and glad you are. I'll write sometime in winter or spring.

Now that you know your permanent address, will you write to the New York Review of Books and ask them to change it from the one I sent them last week? . . . Best, Bern

Once she returned, they began visiting. The letter that follows benefits from a little context. She had had her mother mail him a Saul Bellow novel, apparently his copy, which she had borrowed. She mentioned attending a production of *Hamlet* and seeing Philip Roth there. E., one of her professors in graduate school, had opined that Dad was snobbishly pro-Jewish, and she had unsettled E. with news of Dad's long marriage to a Gentile.

November 7, 1964. Dear Arlene,

If you can come on the twenty-first I can take the afternoon off. If on the twentieth, I can see you after work. I'll be in my old office at 2:00 P.M. Saturday, or 3:30 Friday.

I'm working on the book I told you about once: the novel of the ritual murder. It's coming along nicely now, though I had trouble before. I'm beginning the eighth of nine chapters and hope to have a first draft before the end of winter. After that another year should do it.

I've got the Bellow and thanks. Roth was at Yaddo until recently and visited me for supper one night. He has his troubles.

Sometime ask E. what he thinks I mean in saying, "All men are Jews." Best, Bern

In February 1966, they had dinner for the second time that winter, and he read her the first chapter of *The Fixer*. She was attending graduate school and teaching literature. She apparently asked to read the finished book.

March 26, 1966. Dear Arlene,

The book is done as of last Saturday. I had a carbon but it went off Wednesday to my English agent, who had requested it. However, galleys should be ready in May and I'll be glad to send you a set as soon as I can.

After three years of writing I feel depleted and down to bedrock nervousness. That consists in a sort of deep fatigue compounded by an inability to stop running. (I told one of my students that I felt as though a man with a sword were chasing me and she said, "Me too.") I hoped to rest a bit over the last weekend but had to go see my step-mother, who had had a stroke. I got to New York — Brooklyn, more exactly — on Sunday afternoon to learn she had died that morning, and I stayed on for her funeral. Perhaps I can rest a bit this weekend.

(Nemerov walks across the field with a girl. I can see his gray-haired head and hear a word or two. It's the end of that familiar sight here. I think you know he is going to Brandeis?)

I think your idea to write "plotted, economical and pointed" stories this summer is a good one. Don't worry the ideas, just jot them down as they occur. They will occur. Perhaps some of your difficulty is from almost always working from characters to plot? Why don't you concentrate a little more on theme? I say this with a certain amount of doubt because there simply is no one way, but for people on a treadmill there must be some sort of breaking out or away from the self's pattern. What do you stand for as a human being? Do you have a philosophy that goes beyond the need for emotional fulfillment? How do you see the world? What do you believe in other than the efficacy, or lack of it, of love? What, when you look at life is drama? How much of this sort of experience can you master — use as your own? . . .

All best,
Bern

February 16, 1967

Dear . . . ,

You have talent, brains, looks, so let me wish you love and accomplishment in your twenty-fifth year! Bern

March 31, 1967

Dear Arlene,

How nice it is to read so much good news. First there was a story acceptance, and now there is a new job, much more civilized than your last, and the invitation from Yaddo . . .

It's true that Howard [Nemerov] left Yaddo in a hurry but I doubt you will. He was frightened by the space, the quiet, the beauty and the people, perhaps too much of everything. Some of the rooms are magnificent. He sat down at one desk in his room — I think there were three — and looked out the window; then tried another desk and another look out. Then something possessed him, he packed his things and left. If someone had been there to make the room smaller I doubt that he would have left.

Yes, Dalton Trumbo is writing the script of the movie. I have seen the first draft and can tell you it's bad. One of his problems is not to make Yakov "too Jewish." And he's most eager to insert doings ("the worldwide protest") from the Beilis case, so I've just about written it off and have no intention of seeing the film. Hem-

ingway was right, it is as though somebody had pissed in your father's beer . . .

This is Friday; we're leaving for London Monday. I've put aside
a story and am rather looking forward to the beauty of the city and
some English sociability.

All best,
Bern

From a letter written July 11, 1967:

I'm sorry to hear about the ulcer. It's clear that you've been working much too hard . . . You ought to let down at Yaddo . . . even
though the place is massive and lonely at the beginning, and people
take to working at night in order to contain or forget it. If I were
you I'd quit at 4:30 at latest and go for a swim. Put on your Bikini
and let the boys admire your new slimness. And don't work at night
— read, go for a walk or to town for a movie, talk to people, play
croquet — get someone to teach you how if you don't know . . .

I'll be glad to come to Yaddo but not quite now, because I have a
strained back. When it cools down I'll call you and tell you when I
can come . . .

Take care, pace yourself more slowly, and trust in yourself even
though it seems a job.

My best,
Bern

Dad wrote the following letter on June 16, 1970. He was fifty-six
at the time.

Dear Arlene,

If you were my daughter I'd be close to sixty; spare me my
youth. You can be former student and present friend. Consider
yourself legitimized and stop worrying, after all the talking we did
on the subject, about a definition of status. If you relax about it a
comfortable relationship will ensue; you will no longer be Ana-
stasia. I'm very surprised that you feared my response to your deci-

sion to become an analyst. It was bound to be favorable — My goodness, how easily anxiety introduces unreal elements.

I've read a life of Soutine, among those of other artists, for Fidelman. Have you read *Life is with People?* a description of shtetl life in the Russian Pale. It's just loaded with the kind of information you got from the Soutine . . .

Best,
Bern

Dec. 29, 1971 [typed postcard]

Dear Arlene,

I'm hoping that in the new year we'll correspond more and see each other more often . . . Keep the faith, baby.

Your old friend,
Bern

October 6, 1972

Dear Arlene,

Your letter was waiting when I got back from a few days in the city. Congratulations on passing your National Boards! You have every reason to be proud. What a courageous accomplishment. I'm proud too.

Of course you're the special one, though the curious thing is I never really got to know you well. There was exchange but you hid a lot. You're a generous giver of not all.

What supports me? My accomplishment in writing, a certain wisdom in life, an ability to relate to a few people who make me think I could be more loved than I permit myself to be. And perhaps the feeling that if I give myself time I will do things right, even those things that do not come easily from a nature such as mine.

I live not badly.

And I *am* glad to be what I am to you.

Bern

Two years later, he wrote this letter. At the time, she was studying to become a psychiatrist, and he was writing *Dubin's Lives*.

October 10, 1974

Dear Arlene

I am secure in my feeling of your affection. If you can't write, though I miss hearing from you, I certainly understand.

I am well, which means, to some degree, that the book is well too, although I do have the feeling I am learning to write it as I go along, that is I am learning to rewrite it. You put something down, then you think of a better way to do it. That's what makes revision such a happy thing. If we could, after the fact, only revise our lives: — that would put you out of business . . .

See you soon — Bern

7/26/75

Dear Arlene,

. . . I should be down sometime in early September, with, if you like, another chapter to read to you. You and N. are the only two who have heard several chapters and you both seem to like what you've heard. That's invigorating, but I won't be sure of the effect until I've tried it on at least one enemy.

I had much pleasure with you at the opera even though you are an antsy type; on the other hand you make your living sitting and listening. Handball anyone? You owe me a letter. Abbracci, Bern

AROUND 1963 OR 1964, my mother more discreetly fell in love with a married friend of the Hickses and commenced her own affair. I was subliminally aware of her romance. I remember that he dropped her off at home late one night. At some point, she bought a movie soundtrack and played its romantic theme, "The Windmills of Your Mind," over and over on the hi-fi when my father was out. She'd take off to the Hickses' and return late. Suddenly, her friend took an interest in Paul and me, and we found ourselves gifted with an overnight sailing lesson with him on his sailboat on Lake Champlain (or maybe Lake George) along with several of his

children. I recall an outdoor cocktail party at his house when I
was twelve or thirteen. His wife, manic-depressive and drinking
heavily, started explaining to me that when a woman reaches a certain age, her breasts droop. To bathe, she has to lift them and wash
under them with a washcloth. I found the information more poten-
tially useful than most of what I garnered when boredom led me to
trail along at adult events. Was my father standing beside me? My
mother? I imagine the communication, or at least some metames-
sage, might have been directed at one of them.

The summer of 1965, my mother and brother and I spent ten
days in Rome while my father traveled to Kiev and Moscow. (He'd
written a draft of *The Fixer*, and he wanted to see if he'd imagined
the country accurately.) Rome was extremely hot; air conditioning
was still a rarity. My mother took us to cafés and bought us strong,
sweet coffee granitas topped with whipped cream to cool us off.
We were uncomfortable, slept poorly. My mother and I shared a
room — marble-floored, darkened, with its shades drawn against
the heat — and I remember her sitting on the edge of the bed and
weeping, frequently, for no reason I could fathom. A period of
anxiety, she explained, brought on by revisiting Italy — with all its
associations from her past. Maybe. But she may also have been experiencing, in her husband's absence, some larger sense of un-
steadiness about the two of them, or some coda of her own romance. When I try to recapture my sense of those years, I imagine
sourceless emotion unexpectedly filling the house, then ebbing just
as mysteriously, leaving me baffled.

I BELIEVE MY FATHER sometimes fantasized about an arrangement for himself like the one his Bennington music colleague managed for a while. He may have longed, hardly uniquely, to keep a
wife and a mistress and to be able to move between them more

openly, even as, in practice, he kept his particular actions hidden. He was a successful writer, and that raised the question for him of whether he might not be entitled to a polygamous life and a family that accommodated. If he felt like his character Dubin, his entitlement, though guilt inflected, was remarkably unequivocal and his rationalization well developed: "The biographer, as he read the newspaper, hefted and measured guilt, yet managed to sidestep it . . . Surely these years entitle me to this pleasure. In life one daren't miss what his nature requires. Only the spiritually impoverished can live without adventure."[2]

Dad also strove to live in a way he construed as moral, so the contradiction made him hesitant. In his Fidelman story "Naked Nude," there is an exchange between Fidelman and Ludovico, a pimp. Fidelman suggests that it is immoral for Ludovico to live off "the proceeds of a girl's body." Perhaps the author was struggling with his own conscience, seeking a more forgiving frame.

> The pimp leaned with dignity on his cane.
> "Since you bring up the word, signore, are you a moral man?"
> "In my art I am."
> Ludovico sighed. "Ah, maestro, who are we to talk of what we understand so badly? Morality has a thousand sources and endless means of expression. As for the soul, who understands its mechanism? Remember, the thief on the cross was the one who rose to heaven with Our Lord."[3]

The polygamous fantasy may well have appealed to him more than the practice. He put writing before all else. Although the possibilities of two relationships likely excited him, he was a man who wanted to breakfast each day at 7:15 and get to his desk by 8:30 or 9:00. The disruptive reality of two women's actual and impinging lives might quickly have become intolerable.

Furthermore, his relationship with Arlene seems to have so-
bered him about himself. In *The Tenants,* published in 1971, describing an imaginary character created by an imaginary character,
he set out succinctly what I see as an essential ruminative question
he had about the extent of his own ability to love. The writer protagonist, Harry Lesser, having stolen his housemate's girlfriend,
finally answers her question about the book he is writing. The
words jumped out at me. There was something familiar in them
that made me recollect my father, a language directly evocative of
many conversations.

Lesser explains that the novel is about a writer named Lazar
Cohen:

> Night after night he wakes in sweaty fright of himself, stricken by
> anxiety because he finds it hard to give love. His present girl hasn't
> discovered that yet but she will. He has always been concerned with
> love, and has often felt it for one or another person but not gener-
> ously, fluently, nor has he been able to sustain it long. It's the old
> giving business, he can and he can't, not good enough, too many
> unknown reservations, the self occluded. Love up to a point is no
> love at all. His life betrays his imagination.[4]

MY FATHER'S PASSION for someone so close to my age enacted
a kind of quasi-incestuous symmetry, which raised bad feelings
within me — though I'm not sure they surfaced into full conscious-
ness until *Dubin's Lives* was published. With a child's presumptuous vanity, much encouraged by him, I had assumed myself
adequate as the beloved alternative. So I felt quite particularly replaced. Moreover, Arlene and I overlapped. Not only did he endlessly instruct us both about literature; not only did she openly and
I quietly want to write, but we both eventually created work lives
with professional nurture as their center. He had told me since I

was little that he thought I was cut out to become a pediatrician or psychologist, someone who would become accomplished by healing. I disliked the pegging, which, though not inaccurate, felt like another statement of his basic belief — women should give care — together with what I took to be his silent wish — devote yourself to caring for me. Arlene also went the care route, though more ambitiously than I. I became a clinical social worker. She attended medical school and then pursued an arduous residency and psychoanalytic training. She now works as a psychoanalyst.

When Arlene married in 1979, she joined our family life more openly and was in it until my father died. At her wedding, to my mother's distress, he held a corner of her chuppah — the canopy that covers the couple and the rabbi. She and her husband attended events in Dad's honor, such as birthdays and book parties. I did my best on those occasions to keep some distance. The evening he died, I flew from Boston to New York with my four-month-old son, Zachary, in my arms. She was sitting in the chair next to my mother in the living room when I arrived. Was she the second wife or the incestuously accomplished older daughter? I suspect, in her mind and his, she had long since become a good friend, but I lacked a narrative of the transformation and felt alien in her weeping presence. I quickly decided it would be a good idea for me not to feel, so I froze into the too-cheerful good-daughter routine at which I was practiced and positioned myself by the telephone to answer the endless calls from friends and the press. My friend Deb Scott, whose father had taught history at Bennington and who understood what could happen there to families, came by the next day, and we went for a long walk. Within motion's sanctuary, grief briefly broke through numbness.

Several months later, Arlene mailed me a short piece she'd written about Dad as a teacher. She told me how much she missed hearing the phone ring at eleven on Sundays, when he had called

her each week. Then she sent me a story she'd published. I suppose she was reaching out to share the loss, unaware that in my
mind at that point, she, the sexual doppelgänger, was the loss. I
sent back a brief, superficial note on a postcard — a photograph,
black-and-white, perhaps by Doisneau, a scene that looked like
Naples, several men on Vespas teasing, whistling at, slightly harassing a pretty girl who is walking by. Perhaps the girl is a bit too
available. In retrospect, I regret my unkindness, but at that moment I simply wanted to shove her away. I did not hear from her
again and felt relieved. The summer before he died, my father had
taken me aside late one evening in Vermont and asked that I take
care of my mother after he died; she would move to Massachusetts
to be near me. I felt that backing Arlene off — as well as, for a
time, dodging biographers who might write about her and embar-
rass my mother — fell within the mandate.

THE RESULT OF my distancing is that I did not know Arlene and
cannot say who she was or what kind of love or friendship she offered. I'm sure my father sought in his affair all the usual suspects:
a new relationship, the pleasure of seduction, relief from his
chronic, self-critical aloneness, reward for his success, sex, excitement, companionship, youth, someone Jewish, someone admiring,
someone whose limitations he knew less well than his own and my
mother's. However much he fought it, he felt fundamentally deprived. He believed that poverty, the grocery store, his mother's
and brother's illnesses, and his father's failure of imagination had
limited his opportunity when he was young, that he was entitled to
make up for the loss. And then, too, he believed that writers and
artists particularly ought to "adventure." He taught Hemingway's
stories to his students and not only deeply admired the older
writer's clean prose but also appreciated the macho live-hard
writer template. He knew it was not remotely who he was, but its

braggadocio caught him. Later, in the 1970s in New York, he got interested in Helen Frankenthaler and took her out to dinner occasionally. One slushy winter night, he knocked at her door. When she opened it, she glanced at his shoes and ridiculed the rubber galoshes — "rubbers" — he had stretched over them. Whatever his desire, it seems that evening he flunked her standard. Real men never yield to weather — JFK coatless in January at his Washington inauguration. Deep down, however lusty, Malamud was a galoshes kind of guy.

One of Arlene's letters, written in 1975, recounts her running into Frankenthaler, who asked her to convey greetings to my father. "Dearest Bern, How are you? Let me tell you right off that I ran into Helen Frankenthaler at the Y the other day and she asked me to give you her greetings — precisely: 'Give him my love + tell him I miss him — if he's strong enough to stand it.'" The letter continues, "I have mixed feelings about delivering other women's sexual challenges to you. Maybe you can use it in your novel (I tell myself) — Time changes all the realities, but not the feelings."[5]

I ASSUME IT was significant to my father that Arlene was Jewish. Dad's interest in his own Jewishness increased with age and knowledge. He read more about Jews — their cultural, intellectual, and artistic heritage. He identified with his tribe's perennial homelessness and suffering. But there was also something more sentimental about his feelings. He may have had times when he wished he'd married a Jewish woman, but my bet is, safely away, he savored the longing: romantically, nostalgically, what might have been. Arlene in part represented that fantasy possibility.

A memorable surfacing of this feeling occurred in 1976 on the night before I married. David — Dutch, English, Irish blood, with a mild Congregational upbringing long since shed — and I were staying in my parents' house in Bennington in preparation for our backyard wedding the next afternoon. Family and friends were gathered. Earlier that evening, my parents had hosted a dinner for both families at the Rainbarrel and then returned home. My father and I sat alone reading in the living room; everyone else had gone to bed. He appeared to be concentrating on text but was ruminating. Perhaps the meeting with David's family, the rich food, the wine, had carried him somewhere unhappy. He liked David, but . . . He put aside his book, cleared his throat, fumbled. He had my attention. "You know," he said, "I wish you were marrying someone Jewish."

WITHIN TWO YEARS of our arrival in Bennington, my father had begun work on *The Fixer*, which, when published in 1966, won both a National Book Award and a Pulitzer and cemented his contemporary fame. I recall him writing it. Not the actual pages forming, but I have a strong mental image of watching him from a distance one winter day as he walked home from his office on campus along the plowed, snow-edged gravel path that ran by the frozen pond to our house in the Orchard — his head down; an off-white winter jacket, corduroy pants, a wool cap, hands in thick gloves; his mood somber. I remember hearing him tell people that writing the book depressed him. He talked about how hard it was to imagine Yakov Bok's suffering, to stay with him in jail. He based his story on a real case — a Russian Jew, Mendel Beilis, in Kiev, charged with the ritual murder of a Gentile child and jailed in 1911 at the height of a rabid anti-Semitic hysteria, then eventually released. He read Beilis's own account of his ordeal, and then read about Beilis and about Jewish life in the Pale.

I recollect how, when he joined us and the Inkeleses in southern France in the summer of 1965 after he'd visited Russia, he expressed relief that he'd imagined much of Kiev correctly. He had not been permitted to change his extra rubles back to dollars when he left and arrived with a large jar of caviar, purchased with the cash. For days, during the cocktail hour, we spooned caviar, grayish eggs in black ink, onto crackers and squeezed lemon juice over it. The adults drank red vermouth. I must have sipped from their glasses, for the taste still sometimes summons the scene. We were staying in a small, very old chateau the two families had jointly rented on a hill overlooking the Mediterranean in a village called Bormes les Mimosas. It had a lovely stone terrace with flowers and cypress trees. Europe was still poor enough that such rentals lingered within middle-class reach. I didn't understand at the time that, of course, he was returning to his family past. The same intense hatred that had jailed Beilis in 1911 had, six years earlier in 1905, caused Max Malamud and his brothers to flee their home not far from Kiev. Dad must have been curious to see where he'd come from, where his mother and father had lived. But I remember little mention of family — something vague about a cousin in the Soviet army. Once again, he talked about his invention, not his historic reality. Yakov Bok could have been kin.

As the book opens, Bok angrily leaves his shtetl to travel to Kiev in search of a better life — because his own is impoverished and prospectless, his marriage childless, and his "faithless wife," Raisl, has taken off with another man. *The Fixer*, the story of a man growing morally in the course of a torturous, brutal imprisonment, is a hard book to read, demanding an almost masochistic attention from the reader and writer — not to mention Bok — to absorb so much suffering. Bok, his father-in-law warns him at the beginning, should stay in the shtetl, and indeed he is punished for leaving home and entering the hostile world of anti-Semitic Gentiles. It was a world my grandfather Max particularly feared, and my father, thematically, drew from this knowledge. (In an undated letter Dad wrote to me while I was in college, he observed about his parents, "They lived in fear . . . of their ignorance of the unknown world, of gentile society.") In this way, the author was like his protagonist, the one who left against advice, married the Gentile, moved to Oregon. Living in America, not Russia, Dad had a better time of it. Perhaps in the novel, he was partly tracing out the alternative — his life had he been born in Ukraine. In Oregon, as the news of concentration camps and the devastation of European Jewry had emerged more fully, he had begun reading books on Jewish history and religion. Once, while tucking me in at night, he had announced that had I been living in Germany during World War II, the Nazis would have killed me because I was the daughter of a Jew. The memorable intensity of his comment makes me think that he may well have also spent time imagining his own fate in Germany, as well as in turn-of-the-century Russia, from which his parents fled.

Although the major events in Bok's imprisonment follow loosely upon Beilis's autobiographical account, the fictive experience was very much of Dad's own making. And my honest daughter's question was why my father would choose to turn his literary imagination to the graphic imagining and recounting of so much sadism. I know where my own sadism lies, and I know that, given time, I could probably imaginatively re-create many of the variations of horrific cruelty that people perpetrate upon each other. But why would I want to? What would it be like to spend three years, day in and day out, living there in my imagination? What would it do to me? And why choose it? I do not think I could or would. And perhaps I've discovered in this mental exercise the line between gifted fiction writers and the rest of us. My father spoke frequently about pushing himself, taking risks. Perhaps this is one example of exactly what he meant.

I suspect the writer put himself to the task of *The Fixer* because he wanted to challenge himself, wanted to see if he had the courage to explore human suffering created by political and social oppression and by the cruelty native to unchecked power. The more he lived and read, the more, as he aged, the past manifested itself to him, the more he must have recognized himself as a member of a particular tribe, as one of the human creatures whom the preceding decades had spent such great effort verminizing and eradicating. My father was, if you will excuse a cliché, a prototypical survivor. Like millions in his generation, he had somehow landed safe, on his feet, in America. But his familial anguish had been such that it drove the rest of his understanding. He had suffered deeply. He had seen up close the residual havoc of the pogroms and of immigrants fleeing — in his father's paralysis and his mother's madness, perhaps in stories of his grandfather's murder by Cossacks or the murder of his stepmother's first husband and children.

In 1938, as a twenty-four-year-old writing in his journal, he connected sadism and masochism with morality (see page 55). He was already working to manage these feelings in himself. Through Bok, my father was able to illuminate the transfiguration of intensely personal suffering — with all its attendant impulses — into an expanded empathy that included within it a deeply humanistic grammar of right and wrong, a comprehensive morality. He posed the big questions: What does suffering do to a man? What is its worth? And, more than that, how is it intertwined with a kind of ennobled humanness? In the Yeats letter to Arlene (see page 197), he singled out Gandhi as exemplar of man in the "highest" sense of the word. Most of us no longer speak so grandly. Although we still recognize the greatness of some people, such as Nelson Mandela, we tend to shy away from setting them as exemplars of larger ideals or articulating their place within a larger moral context. Public discourse is fractured on this score. Many serious artists and intellectuals, particularly in post–Vietnam War, post-Watergate, post–cold war America, have become more ironic, guarded, and chastened, have dropped all "capital letter" concepts as if they were polluted by the radioactive residue of Hiroshima.

But my father believed in the human creature Man, with a capital *M*. A Man, as he saw it, was someone who sought knowledge; someone who would work very hard, devote his life to learning — intellectually, morally, and personally — and through that effort grow into something more than his birth-given self. A Man might summon moral courage to become if not great, then more substantial than he had been. He would transmute suffering into something redeeming, sometimes privately, other times through a vision publicly offered to sustain a community. To a degree, the Brooklyn boy turned writer accomplished exactly what he described for Bok. He learned, through writing stories, to voice a human view that was, at its best, morally centered, tragic, and comic, and that readers found deeply affecting. Still today, I regularly encounter people who want me to understand how reading Malamud changed their lives.

YAKOV BOK'S EFFORT to make peace with his feelings about his wife, Raisl, is a significant subplot in *The Fixer*. I don't believe my father knew about my mother's "faithlessness" at that time, so perhaps he was on some level dealing with his own. In fact, I cannot help wonder if the book *in part* draws energy from his unconscious guilt about his emotional "setting out" from his marriage. Perhaps one additional, intimate psychological strand driving the book was his need to do penance, to punish himself, for his illicit passion and pleasure, an act that violated his own notion of himself as teacher if not as husband and father. He had behaved badly by involving himself with a student. Still, affairs are quotidian. What made his significant was his effort to metabolize it within his devotion to his own intense moral code, particularly the suffering and contradiction that effort entailed. I realize now that the harsh period of depression I had associated with his writing the book may well have had to do less with creating Bok and more with love (or sex) gone wrong — although the two were likely intertwined.

THE FIXER ARRIVED on the scene at exactly the right cultural moment and caught two waves. One was the civil rights struggle. The theme of anti-Semitic dehumanization translated well into the contemporary American effort to confront its own apartheid. Toward the end of the book, the once apolitical Bok challenges in fantasy Tsar Nicholas for his cowardly inhumanity toward the Jews and, in an often quoted line, states the moral fruits of his own prison torture: "One thing I've learned, he thought, there's no such thing as an unpolitical man, especially a Jew."[6] However much Dad was harking back both to the pogroms and to Nazism in choosing Bok's words, he was also speaking to his admiration for Martin Luther King Jr. and other contemporary civil rights leaders, and expressing his absolute certainty that desegregation and equal opportunity were necessary for the nation. Writing to Rosemarie Beck in 1959 about Ralph Ellison's rumored work on a second novel, he observed, "I like his thesis of the moral canker of America. I think America is immoral to the Negro, and, indeed, it does make us sick, sicker than we should be. Every society has its weakness and failures but it hurts particularly badly when a democratic society can be so cruel to a particular people. Stendhal's remark fits: 'We commit the greatest cruelties but without cruelty.'"[7]

The second wave *The Fixer* caught was the moment of arrival of American Jews. Dad's generation of Jewish immigrant children, and the more recent war émigrés, shared with him — inchoate for some, explicit for others — an understanding of their collective near-miss encounter with annihilation. At the same time, in their daily lives, they had often done well. They had started businesses or worked their way up corporate ladders, becoming bankers, professors, lawyers, and doctors; they had bought houses in the suburbs, built synagogues, and successfully moved their families into the middle or professional classes. They could afford to buy new furniture, new cars, the infamous "nose jobs" for their "princess" daughters, books, records, and theater tickets. I remember Murray Malament, Dad's cousin who'd become an accountant, describing a walk they took together in the early 1980s. They compared notes about wealth. They were both schoolboy-pleased by their prosperity. Once poor and alien, they had won a place at the table. And they were fairly typical of their generation.

More directly to Dad's benefit — and Saul Bellow's and, slightly later, Philip Roth's — many Jewish Americans found themselves ready to entertain, needing, unconsciously desiring as a means of signifying their arrival, public narratives of their collective past. Indeed, they were able to pay good money to witness their own stories. In 1964, two years before Dad published *The Fixer*, *Fiddler on the Roof* opened on Broadway with the incontrovertibly Jewish, marvelous Zero Mostel playing Tevye, the dairyman and father of a very poor family in Anatevka, a shtetl in Russia. The musical is set in 1905, the same year so many Jews fled Russia to avoid wartime conscription into the tsar's army, "conscription" itself a euphemism for profound suffering and likely death. My parents took me to see *Fiddler* in 1965, when I was thirteen. The production had become a huge hit, and I remember the buzz of seeing Lucille Ball, red hair dyed redder, in the audience that night. After the performance ended, Dad brought me backstage to meet Mostel. He was in a long robe, a towel tucked around his neck, sweat still beading all over his balding head (with long gray strands of hair flattened across the top), trickling down the edge of his expressive face.

When I asked him for his autograph, he took a pen with point retracted and grandly scribbled his name across my forehead. Then he belly-laughed, grinned, and signed my program.

The huge success of this musical was no accident. It was for many Jewish Americans their unspoken, untransmitted, obliterated, individual family pasts cleaned up, sentimentalized, with all the too-messy traumas polished to a mirroring, salable shine, made loving and bearable, and offered up onstage to a nation as something respectable and comprehensible. *The Fixer* offered serious literature and fine writing. Yet in a sense, it also provided a more intelligent, painful, likely version of the same sought-after narrative, a plausible past, an awkward progenitor transformed into someone for whom one could feel empathy and in whom one could feel pride.

By THE MID-1960s, my parents had decided that it was time for me to exit the North Bennington school, but they weren't ready to have their last child leave home. They decided to move to Cambridge, Massachusetts, in 1966 for two years so they could keep me company during my sophomore and junior years at the Cambridge School. I think they also wanted time away from Bennington. The move coincided nicely with Dad's growing success. It was when we arrived in Cambridge that I realized he had become famous. *The Fixer* not only won both major national literary prizes, but it also visited the bestseller list, was optioned for a movie, and was translated into many languages. Dad was written up in magazines and newspapers, interviewed and visited by scholars and journalists from all over the world. Protecting family privacy, though enjoying the offer, he turned down a request from the *Saturday Evening Post* to do a feature spread on him at home. My new, more worldly schoolmates immediately pegged me as "Bernard Malamud's daughter," a status I sometimes relished, sometimes detested.

For the most part, I loved living in Cambridge and found it a relief from Bennington. We rented the Inkeleses' Acacia Street duplex from them for the year while they were away. Not quite fifteen, I found myself on the edge of Harvard Square, with movie theaters, bookstores, and record stores galore within walking distance; a university full of events and museums; and a subway system that allowed me the run of Boston. My parents subscribed to the theater and the opera, and when one could not go, I would sometimes accompany the other. My father took me with him to Sarah Caldwell's very sixties radical production of *The Rake's Progress*, wildly updated with motorcycles onstage and girls in vinyl, op art miniskirts. While such stagings are clichéd now, it was bold in its day. I also remember a production of Bertolt Brecht's *Caucasian Chalk Circle*. I believe that Dad and I saw *Blow-Up* together at the Brattle movie theater, and that Mom and I saw Michaelangelo Antonioni's *Red Desert* there. My mother and I would occasionally trek into the Italian North End, where the skinned lamb and rabbit carcasses hung whole on hooks in front of butcher shops, the dried salt cod was piled high in precarious stacks, and we would buy fresh mozzarella and ricotta, in those days produced by small-scale Italian cheesemakers for their neighborhoods and otherwise not widely available.

DAD HAD AGREED to teach one freshman seminar a year in creative writing at Harvard. Someone else screened the young applicants, but he made the final selections himself. Among his ten talented students the first year was the novelist Jay Cantor. The poet and social critic Katha Pollitt studied with him the second year. He knew he was lucky to be teaching writers of such caliber and enjoyed it. He occasionally let me read their work, and I still remember the opening line of a hilarious story by Cantor about being stoned and getting into trouble in a grocery store.

My parents had a very good time in Cambridge and a very active social life. They were in their early fifties, and their marriage had, though banged about, made it through Bennington. They had success, adequate money, intellectual curiosity, energy, and health. They quickly fell in with a whole new group of friends.

The Cambridge years coincided with the growing Vietnam War and the social turbulence over war and civil rights. I remember one night in the spring of 1968, when my friend Andy Ruina and I, hearing the siren screech and the shout and clatter of student riots, walked together into Harvard Square and found it in frightening chaos: store windows shattered; massed police, wearing gas masks and with batons in hand, thundering through to clear streets. We flattened ourselves against a building and watched first rioters and then police charge back and forth. It must have been close on the assassination of Martin Luther King Jr. A few weeks later, I went camping overnight at a beach with a young teacher at my school. We woke early at dawn, turned on the car radio to get the time, and heard of Robert Kennedy's murder in California.

I recall, before we moved to Cambridge, picking my brother up at school, probably in late 1964 or early 1965, and during the car ride home debating the war. My father wrote to Arlene, on April 9, 1965:

> I may stay on in the city to the 25th to attend a seminar on writers and the prevention of war. The Viet Nam thing has me bothered, and since some good people are sponsoring this — Robert Lowell, [Philip] Rahv and others — I think I'd like to hear what's going on, although I confess I take a dim view that artists can be directly effective. Perhaps they can be as people — in the way that Jean Paul Sartre and Camus are and were — but one's work can't be directed

to that end. Once you do that there's no art. In a way it's a frightening paradox.

I also remember a lot of commotion when we went to New York City in 1967 for the National Book Awards ceremony. Vice President Hubert Humphrey was to speak, Secret Service agents were everywhere, and a good number of writers — I believe Dwight Macdonald and Norman Mailer among them — shouted hard at Humphrey in protest of the war, and then stormed out.

When each academic year ended, we returned to Vermont for the summer, and in 1968 my mother found a white, 1930s, colonial-style house on several acres in Old Bennington and talked my father (who never, after Corvallis, sought to own property) into buying it. It was a beautiful home, light, airy, and with a lovely treed lawn, set on a hill with a view over the town to the Green Mountains. They both quickly grew to love it. In the winter of 1969–1970, they also rented an apartment in New York and began spending winters there. After trying several places, they leased, and my mother eventually bought, a two-bedroom apartment at Lincoln Towers on Sixty-eighth Street and West End Avenue.

It was also, I believe, in the summer of 1968 that Felicia and Ben Kaplan invited us to spend a week in the little guesthouse on their property in Chilmark, on Martha's Vineyard. We visited several times, and the visits have converged in my mind into one gilded moment. I loved the island — who doesn't, or at least didn't in the sixties, when it was still half empty? But I loved it so particularly then that I have only gone back once — just after Dad died. The time at Felicia's with my parents felt glorious. Not only the great, duned, sun-struck beauty of their property, with its long, half-empty, white beach, the gentle waves lapping up on it, blue sea spreading endlessly beyond. But also because it felt like exactly the right place at the right moment. If some part of me is fixated as the happy daughter of my famous father, it is here. A combination of things — being somewhere that evoked the Oregon coast, being well cared for, feeling relaxed, feeling welcomed into the social life — created a fine family moment. Dad would write in the mornings but was ready to relax after lunch. He'd sometimes even make his way onto the beach with my mother, where they'd walk, talk with friends, and sit for a while in the sun. I remember one day Nick Delbanco, who'd just started teaching at Bennington, came by with his girlfriend Kate. I'd volunteered that summer with Kate teaching art to low-income kids in North Bennington. Nick owned a sports car, a Volvo modified into a convertible. The two of them decided to show me around. We zoomed off, me stuffed in the tiny seatless back. We buzzed along the island roads, swam at the nude beach at Gay Head, and bought mussels that we steamed with red onion and white wine. I felt completely at ease, sun-glazed.

FELICIA LAMPORT KAPLAN was a memorable hostess, a great entertainer, and the mistress of a kind of floating intellectual/literary/political salon. A short, blond/silver-haired, sharp-featured woman, she had intense blue eyes that met you directly and a deep voice. She had a drink often, a cigarette always, in hand. She would not wear a dress or pair of pants that didn't have pockets, so that she could rest her empty hand in one as she talked or walked. She was very smart, possessed a constant, droll sense of humor, and was an astute raconteur and a close observer, interested in all who crossed her path. She was able to supply a full, detailed history about absolutely everyone. When I complained to her how harshly a particular professor had treated me during my undergraduate orals, she described her early view of him, how he'd gone to write his own graduate thesis at a borrowed house in the mountains and kept binoculars at hand to watch cars smash up on the icy highway below. I remember visiting her once in the 1990s and getting the update on a teaching "fellow" on whom I'd had a crush in college twenty years earlier. She knew all he'd done well and badly since, noting particularly his bungled public career and his failure to bathe. If you needed a wife or husband, she was at the ready to consult and to arrange a date for you. She published an autobiographical account of her wealthy childhood called *Mink on Weekdays,* but mostly she made her reputation on her ironic verse, clever and sometimes hilarious, which was published on the *Boston Globe*'s op-ed page. Sometimes she collaborated with Edward Gorey.

Felicia was unusually generous. Having heard about Dad from Alfred Kazin's sister, Pearl Bell, whom she knew, she invited him to stay with her and Ben for a few days in 1961. She then regularly invited him and Mom to dinner when they returned to Cambridge a few years later. She preferred to write late at night and asked her many Vineyard or Cambridge houseguests only that they not attempt conversation with her before noon. She was a fine gardener and took pleasure from raising fruits and flowers that won prizes at the Martha's Vineyard fair. The summer nights we spent with her and Ben included beach encounters, cocktail parties, and dinners with writers and politicos who'd worked in Washington for Kennedy or Johnson.

One evening we were invited to Lillian Hellman's house for dinner. Hellman, over sixty and not svelte, was wearing a pink one-piece knit jump suit. My memory, perhaps to be doubted after almost forty years, is that while the guests were of both genders, she spoke almost exclusively to the men. I am positive that she did not address a single word to me. I picture an elaborately set table, and I believe she had a uniformed maid and butler, but I may have moved them onto the scene from another occasion during the same era.

I sat quietly and watched Hellman as if she were one of her

own plays. Someone later told me that for years, as a young woman, she had worn a veiled hat to hide her nose, of which she was ashamed. Certainly, her face made an impression. She held court, bantered with the men, pronounced on all subjects — poker, Vietnam, Lyndon Johnson, theater. The dew had already fallen when we left. Felicia pointed out the neighboring house where Dashiell Hammett had lived, and I remember conspiratorially, deliciously, comparing notes with her about the evening and the pink jump suit as we drove home.

Chapter 8 ⫷⫸

Thanksgiving

⫸ ⫸ THANKSGIVING DAY 1968 in Old Bennington barely dawned into a cold, gray drizzle. The weather was ugly, the clouds so low they obliterated the mountains. I was briefly home from school, where I had begun boarding for my senior year. It was my first time staying in our new house, which my parents, back from Cambridge, had just moved into. The place felt unfamiliar to me, echoey, rooms unsettled, some windows curtainless, a few boxes still unpacked. To fill the spacious living room, my mother had purchased a handsome pale blue-green sofa, a grayish print loveseat, and a pair of upholstered chairs, low-armed and well suited for reading. Bennington had good woodcrafters, and she hired one to make cherry bureaus for their bedroom. Later, she had someone craft a coffee table by framing in cherry a handsome piece of brown Vermont marble my grandmother had bought her at a quarry. I remember that the freshly built bookshelf in my room was mostly still without books, although my father had unpacked and shelved some for me.

Their lives were full. Dad wrote to me at school:

Dear Janna,

Ma says you would like your November check and I am sending it along with the gentle reminder that you[r] allowance has been raised by five dollars and that you are supposed to make it last until the first of December. Naturally, I will pay bus ticket expenses on your Thanksgiving Weekend holiday.

We're having guests soon: Howard [Nemerov], after a reading in Albany, is due for a visit and party for him on the 15th. The Erlichs are due the same date; Howard goes on the sixteenth but they will stay over a day or two, partly to be with the Inkeles, who arrive on the 16th. We look forward to this visit.

My proofs for Fidelman have arrived and I am busily at work. Mother has been doing interviews — even boys — and is pounding away on reports. I had hoped she would hold off until we had the house further along, but her help was needed and she pitched in.

I am sorry I missed your phone call the other night. I would have liked to hear of your interview and other adventures. Ma says Mr. —— is going to help you pick your camera. That's right nice of him.

My reading went very well; the kids were most enthusiastic and I enjoyed myself.

Much love, Dad[1]

My mother was working part-time interviewing for Bennington College admissions. A couple of weeks later, my father responded to two pieces of my writing in the school newspaper and chronicled their settling into the house:

We read both articles — the one with Cilla, which was fair enough and nicely written (how does one collaborate with another writer?), and yours on the Wallace rally, which was very good: a superior piece of personal journalism — graphic, vital, very well written. I hope you write more in this vein; it becomes you.

The house continues to make progress. Mr. Mead was around

yesterday to do some cleaning up and spot painting. From a D job of painting we have persisted in our efforts to raise it to a B. The book cases in the guest room — really additional space for me — are completed and I'm getting some of my books packed away. The shelves still remain to be built in my study. That will be slow going because Bill Crosier is a hunter and the deer season is on. And the kitchen is now fully papered, with cabinet installation promised for this week. . . .

I've been reading *The Glass House,* a new biography of Ted Roethke. The title of the book refers to Ted's father, Otto, who grew flowers in hot houses. Obviously it has another meaning. I liked Roethke very much and once taught his poetry at Bennington. He was the true wounded poet — as in the legend of Philoctetes. He tried to push a tremendous vitality through a cracked life, and its amazing how much he was able to achieve. He wrote poetry, he taught exceptionally well; and in the end I think he loved someone other than himself . . . Love, Pa[2]

I was in the midst of applying to colleges and knew that this home would be transient for me. Summers and school vacations for a few years, maybe. Yet it was a lovely physical space, quietly New England; not pretentious, but elegant, nicer than anything we'd inhabited, with large open rooms, lots of light and windows, a guest room and extra bathrooms, all freshly papered and painted. They'd paid around $35,000 for it. It was the first time my mother had enough money to take a free hand. She preferred uncluttered space, Shakeresque, furnished in blues and browns, with friends' paintings hung on white walls and Oriental carpets laid upon hardwood floors. Over the years, she'd haunted used furniture places and had become adept at refinishing tables and chairs that she'd purchased for tiny bits of money. That summer, or another not long before, she'd scoped out a big estate auction in Bennington and spotted a beautiful burnt-umber and deep-blue Chinese rug.

My father, a bit surprisingly, returned the next afternoon with her to help her bid. They'd had a good time, gotten into the spirit, and enjoyed winning the rug over the competition. The living room was big enough to display it well, and its dense colors defined the space beautifully.

The success of *The Fixer* had put a different life at hand, and at moments you could feel their pleasure: at their dinner parties; when they bid for the rug; when they decided to live winters in New York, bought a subscription to the Metropolitan Opera, tickets to concerts in Lincoln Center, and tickets to plays. They began to travel more and spent some months in London in 1971 and again in 1978. If there is such a thing as living a "literary life," they often laid claim to it.

In May 1978, Dad wrote to me from England:

Ma and I were in Sussex with the Inkeles over the weekend. The most exciting part of the trip was our visit to the Cathedral in Canterbury, and later, stopping off in Rye to see Henry James' Lamb House. In the Cathedral, as many have done, I stood in the transept where Thomas a Becket ("Who will rid me of this tempestuous priest?" — Henry II) was murdered; and later in the same day stood on a quiet clean street, before the redbrick house where Henry James lived and worked. Mother and I looked — or tried to — through the white-curtained windows, and peered, lifting the lid — not lifting — the slot was perpendicular — but looking in to see the staircase to the second floor. We were both moved to be this close to James' actual presence even though it is more than 60 years since he died.[3]

From another letter a week earlier:

Thursday night Mother and I went to Claire Bloom's and Philip Roth's for dinner and had a rather good evening there. Ms Bloom is very lovely — about as tall as Mother, very good to look at — a woman of 45 or so. She is absolutely unpretentious, cooks well; they are obviously in love, I think a first for him. (We kissed on the lips when I came in. He couldn't have done that two years ago. The kiss, which he sought, was to signify I had forgiven him for the foolish egoistic essay he had written about my work. He's a good reader as a rule but certainly misinterpreted *The Assistant*.) Anyway, we talked, had dinner, and talked for hours at the dinner table. Claire is not secure in intellectual talk but handled herself with dignity. Mom was, as usual, very good. Philip was funny. I said not much until the last hour or so when he complained nobody read literature any more. No one understood it. Who was there to write for? I was as eloquent as I've been in years. I don't have to rehearse the argument because you know it — and I'm sure he does — but I do remember advising him — a personal note — to think less of literature and more of the cosmos when he was writing. I called literature a "sweet [strain?]" and said some moving lovely things about it. A good time we had of it. Love, Dad[4]

UP EARLY on that Thanksgiving Day of 1968, my mother set about stuffing the turkey and preparing the meal. We often spent the holiday with friends, several times with the Inkeleses, once in Seattle with the Erlichs. But this year, it was to be just the four of us.

After my father finished breakfast, he announced that he wanted to be taken to his office at the college to write for the morning. I'm not certain why. We owned a single car, a tan Valiant station wagon, and my mother had a last-minute errand still to do, something needed for the meal. There was more food to prepare. Pressured for time, possibly irritated that everything fell to her, she did not want to spend thirty minutes dropping him off. (Perhaps there were other tensions between them; I don't know.) Paul, home from college, was still asleep. So I was told to make the trip and reluctantly obeyed. I resented not only that my father was writing on Thanksgiving but also that he refused to work in his study at home. I knew well by then that he saw no point in Christmas or Easter (though he tolerated my mother celebrating those holidays with us in her understated, secular way) and observed no Jewish ritual or holy day. Yet I sometimes took his aversions personally — not as a dislike of holidays for which he lacked affinity, but as a slight devaluing of family. I would guess, thinking on it now, that he found the days difficult, occasions more to be endured than enjoyed. I have sometimes since shared this view. I can imagine that his pain might have been large, but at the time I experienced his stance as a refusal to bring goodwill, a withholding of effort.

His demand, as I construed it that morning when I was sixteen, was about the way his writing needs trumped all other hands, the way he lived in time so obsessively that settling himself other than by sitting down at his desk and beginning to place words upon sheets of yellow paper was often beyond him. Likely, he was trying to finish proofing *Fidelman,* or to start or finish some story, and having both children home from school disrupted his routine. He felt uneasy facing a morning of interruptions.

The new house in Old Bennington was about five miles away from Dad's campus office. I more or less knew the route. Our family friend Pat Beck had been hired the summer before to teach me to drive. A somewhat eccentric failed writer in her late forties, Pat lived in North Bennington. By then she was long divorced from the blind jazz musician she'd married and driven to and from gigs at clubs. She had attended Bennington, then stayed on in town. She lived mostly by doing odd jobs, and my parents liked to hire her, both because she was companionable and as a way to help her out. She would sometimes drive my father to Rensselaer, New York, to catch the train to New York City, or to the airport in Albany.

I think my father met Pat when she audited his first writing class

at Bennington. Not long after, she sat next to me at a college concert — blond-brown hair cut short, friendly blue eyes, a face more
delicate than her sturdy body — good-humoredly commiserating
with me, a restless ten-year-old, while a music professor sang
badly an interminable program of lieder. Dad liked her, but he
never believed that she was meant to write. Indeed, she'd papered
her bathroom with hundreds of rejection letters from *The New
Yorker*, the *Saturday Evening Post*, and many other magazines. She
finally got one short story published in *Vermont Yankee*, but that
was it for a lifetime of trying.

She'd been diagnosed with diabetes when she was young. It was
corrosive, and she didn't take care of herself, didn't watch what
she ate or drank. As I came into adulthood, she began to have ugly
complications: first one leg amputated, then a second. I visited her
in the hospital, and she recounted the horrors of trying to get her
prosthetic legs to work together. Finally, her eyesight started to go.
She had always loved reading, bird watching, painting, and driving
and insisted on living alone. To her, vision loss was intolerable. It
occurs to me now that her marriage had likely taught her too much
about living sightless to leave adequate illusion. So she walked out
to the car in her garage one winter day after swallowing a lot of
pills, stuffed the tailpipe, turned on the ignition, and sat there
drowsily until the carbon monoxide killed her.

That happened almost a decade after the driving lessons, during
which we'd spent many hours together in the car. Pat had worked
me hard, taking me out on dirt roads and highways, then through
the center of town, forcing me to master a range of circumstances
— passing trucks on country roads, making U-turns, backing up
and down hills. By the end of that summer, I'd not only passed my
driving test easily, but I'd also learned my way along a number of
local roads.

*   *   *

THANKSGIVING MORNING, my father got into the passenger seat. He placed his manuscript, in a folder, carefully on the back seat. What I didn't yet understand, having not driven in winter, was black ice. The ugly sky misted a very fine rain that hit frigid asphalt and gradually accreted into an invisible slick shell. Our station wagon had lap belts, but they were a newish thing, and we didn't wear them. The first few miles went fine — up the hill from our house, left in front of the tall granite monument commemorating the Battle of Bennington, and on down a tranquil, winding road that passed houses and fields and even crossed a picturesque red covered bridge. I can't recall what we talked about. Perhaps not much of anything. I might still have been resenting my assignment. Dad might have been thinking ahead to his morning's writing. But we often chatted together amiably about our lives: what he was reading; what I had been studying — that autumn it included Matthew Arnold and John Dos Passos, and I was writing a paper on modernist painters (Arthur Dove, Marsden Hartley, Charles Sheeler, and others); my thoughts about college; which of their friends in Cambridge I might have seen; who'd come to dinner lately in Bennington; the despised Nixon's upcoming inaugural; the war.

ALMOST TO THE CAMPUS, I stopped at a stop sign. When I accelerated again, I lost control of the car. We skidded toward the big stone gate — deadly — that marked the entrance to the college. I managed to veer and miss it, but the steering wheel did nothing predictable, and the brakes did nothing at all. We spun around — caught in one of those timeless and interminable warps that define disaster, hurtled too fast — and crashed full force, head-on into a solid tree — metal crunching, glass shattering — as loud as anything I've ever heard — totaling the car. Both our heads smashed into the windshield. I bent the steering wheel back into a U, slow-ing my thrust. In the passenger seat, my father had his hands on the dashboard, and the impact broke two fingers and a rib. When his head hit the windshield, he suffered an internal head wound, a brain bleed, a big hematoma that over the next few weeks drained down through his eyes and face.

Too shocked yet for pain, we managed to exit the car and stand upright. We couldn't find words right away. Blood must already have covered my face. I remember looking down at my blue parka, jeans, and black suede boots and seeing the dark red from my head flowing onto them, soaking into them, then thinking, bizarrely, that I now knew what the police-clubbed protesters had experienced in Chicago at the Democratic convention the summer before: *So this is what it feels like.* The convention had been violent, alienating, beyond my ken — a deeply confusing, torturous culmination of the spring assassinations of Martin Luther King Jr. and Robert Kennedy. The association made a certain sense.

Stunned and quietly frantic, my father looked at me and finally spoke. "Where is my manuscript? Where is my manuscript? I need my manuscript."

He somehow opened the back door, retrieved his pages from the car, and clasped them to him as we stood by the side of the deserted road, knowing that aid would have to come from a motorist. I'd nearly killed him, and I wondered years later if his difficulty in inquiring after me came not only from the shock of the accident but also from finding that I, so particularly trusted and heretofore innocent, had joined the ranks of endangering, near-deadly women.

An ex–Bennington girl did pick us up and drove us, skidding herself and squeezing from me the last bit of terror I could feel, the six or seven miles to the hospital. I remember only the slippery roads, the suffocating dread mixed with the relief of being on the way to succor, and her handing me a big Kleenex box that I held ineffectually under my forehead to catch the blood until the box was itself quickly saturated and overflowing. I don't think Dad was bleeding much, but he was dazed and miserable. The surgeon, Oakley Frost, who that morning put seventy stitches in my head, still spoke about me years later whenever he ran into my parents: my humor, the curiosity and interest I'd taken in his sewing work. And perhaps it was his perspective, together with my habit by then of simply being "fine," that let me return to school several days later, my state of mind unplumbed, my vast horror at the near patricide silently intact. I assumed my parents were furious at me for having put my father so in harm's way, although the notion was likely a fantasy of my own making, guilt for harming him and for the anger I had felt as chauffeur setting out. Within a day or two of the accident, my mother bought a Saab, and they assigned my brother to take me out and teach me to shift its manual transmission. I remember feeling touched by his patience.

After a week, Dad wrote briefly to me at school, enclosing a check for one of my college application forms: "Dear Sweetie, I enclose the check to Yale. I'm all right but continue to look like hell. However I'm going to teach tomorrow even if it scares the girls out of their seats. Love, Pa."[5]

WHEN, THREE WEEKS LATER, during the Christmas break, I joined them in their apartment in New York, my father was ill with the flu. His face was a sickly yellow and bruised. The blood from the hematoma was draining internally, and his eyes had big, dark half circles under them. It was afternoon, but he was, so unlike himself, still in his pajamas and a dark maroon wool bathrobe. He seemed a frail, withdrawn man, rendered old at fifty-four by me. They had a sublet on Gramercy Park that winter, and I remember sitting in its small living room, deep in my own camouflaged despair, imagining that the superficial shell of cityscape I could see through the window would shatter and leave a black void.

When the holiday ended and I returned to school, I poured my feelings out to the white-haired, fatherly English teacher I so loved. I'd taken several courses from him. He was deeply, broadly literate and had introduced me to poetry and taught me photography. I would slip up to his classroom and talk to him at any opportunity and felt with him like a friend more than a daughter. We looked at paintings and photographs together. He was an accomplished photographer, and I learned a lot about seeing and making art from him. But more than that, he listened to me and helped me elaborate my own nascent ideas. Although he instructed, he was less relentless than my father about instilling knowledge. "Ah," I remember him observing after the accident, "the Rock of Gibraltar has become a clinging vine."

Rather than turning me over to some more professional hands or holding himself to a fiduciary role, throughout the winter and spring he urged on our intimacy until he'd fallen in love, returning my speedball of misplaced passion, kissing and caressing me every moment we had alone. Having smashed one father, I suppose I sought another, though I'm not sure I was that purposeful. Certainly, I yearned for a sheltering adult. Some part of me had simply, temporarily, given up and sought relief through a mix of dependency and passionate abandon.

I TURNED SEVENTEEN in January 1969 and was admitted to Radcliffe in April. That spring found me unexpectedly grown from awkwardness into a moment of sexual arrival that others noticed before I did. An ophthalmologist had freed me from the glasses I'd worn from kindergarten, uncovering my blue eyes. My thick auburn-brown hair had grown long and wavy, and I pulled it back.

When I wore a short white dress and high-heeled sandals to a cocktail party given for Dad in Cambridge that May, to celebrate the publication of *Pictures of Fidelman,* one of my parents' middle-aged married friends invited me to bed. I reported the offer to my "teacher"; he was indignant at the impropriety and warned me away from the interloper. But no one — either by my invitation or their own — warned me away from him. Through the following summer, imprinted like some traumatized duck, I experienced him as the single spar on my ocean, the only source of oxygen and light. I did not flee him until autumn, when I began my freshman year in college. He, having left his wife, transformed before me into a grotesque, incestuous apparition. Sensing my sudden shift, he became frantic, wrote long letters, telephoned weeping from a phone booth, and turned up unannounced at my dormitory room, pleading that I stay with him, that I finally make love to him.

I closed the door several times until it held and sort of went about my college life. But the accident, and the cloud of confused, unspeakable, miserable feeling that mushroomed in its wake, demoralized me for a long time.

BY THE FOLLOWING SUMMER, 1969, my father was back to himself — head, rib, and fingers healed, healthy except for chronic high blood pressure and back problems. He bought a slightly sporty yellow Plymouth Barracuda with a bright red interior to drive himself to and from work. Proving that his confidence in me was so different from my perception of it, he happily loaned his car to me for ten days and provided money so that two girlfriends and I could take a road trip and camp in Nova Scotia and New Brunswick. Indeed, he offered constant support for all my many projects: a summer of travel in Europe, a month building a raft with friends and floating down three hundred miles of the Mississippi River, a multimonth trip with David to Africa and Europe, a

1,200-mile walk with David from Pennsylvania to Wisconsin. I worked steadily as soon as I graduated from college and paid a good chunk of my way, but he was happy to fill in many gaps. He delighted in offering me opportunities he had not had. Weeks before I was due to visit them in New York City, he'd want to know what play or opera I'd like to see. He would suggest some museum exhibit for us to visit together. On a postcard he sent right before I returned home for Christmas in 1971, he wrote, "You have dates for Fri Dec 22 (Vonnegut, Krementz, Roger + Nina Straus at Dinner); Tues Dec 26 (Madame Butterfly) with family at the Met. and Thurs. Dec 28 'Much Ado about Nothing': with me at the Winter Garden. Love, Dad."⁶ When I went to Vermont, he offered tickets to the Marlboro Music Festival or the Williamstown summer theater.

He would clip articles he thought I'd like to see and even sent David baseball scores while we were traveling in Africa. He always bought me books: a gorgeous volume of maps of Revolutionary War America I'd asked for as a graduation present from college; the complete Freud when I became interested in doing psychotherapy; and many others that he simply thought might interest me. A number are still on my shelves decades later: a biography of the photographer Margaret Bourke-White, *The Female Eunuch* by Germaine Greer, *Three Guineas* by Virginia Woolf. Although the premises of feminism grated against his emotional grain, he grasped its importance to me and to his young female students, and he tried to comprehend it. He read Kate Millett and Adrienne Rich, among others, and appreciated that he was witnessing a new conversation that was intellectually novel to him, though emotionally untenable.

AS I MADE MY WAY through college, my parents moved between Vermont and New York and occasionally traveled. In the late fall and winter of 1971–1972, they lived in London, on Eaton Place. My father arrived ahead of my mother.

Dear Janna, We'll I'm here. The house is in a posh neighborhood and comfortable but not really gracious (as Gramercy Park was) and somewhat too noisy . . .

I saw Paul on Saturday night; he came down from Oxford . . . [w]e had a good meal at a fine Italian restaurant in Chelsea and he patiently answered my questions . . .

I have put the place in order and am awaiting mother's arrival on Wednesday. I've seen Michael Thomas, my literary agent, and Harriet Wasserman (from Russell + Volkening) who happened to be here when I arrived. I missed Roger Straus by a day or so. (Before leaving for London I had lunch with Nina Straus and we had a wonderful talk. She's registered at NYU for a master's and would like to teach.) Tonight I shall see Ralph Richardson in a new John Osborne play, and the night before last I saw Michael MacFriammoin [illegible] do a one-man reminiscence about Yeats. He's not always attractive — a bit queenish — but the performance on the whole was moving, particularly when he recited some of the poems.

Tomorrow I'm going to try to begin a story. I'm already making notes about the caretaker here, a mister Choppel, a Chekhovian sort with bruised eye, whiskey breath, and pure Cockney. I was concerned about the heat and he offered to give someone "a ding dong." I've just about worked up a story about someone like him and an American renter.

The weather here has been beautiful. Yesterday I walked in St. James Park . . . At night I had a bit of supper in a pub close by. Then I read *The Observer* and the [illegible] section of Updike's *Rabbit Redux*, which is very good, and so to bed — With Love Dad[7]

I visited them at Christmas. Dad had bought tickets for me to see Laurence Olivier in *The Merchant of Venice* and again, the same week, in *Long Day's Journey into Night*. Earlier, seeing *Merchant* himself, he'd written:

> The play was very interesting though we all thought Jonathan Miller was making more of the Jewish historical tragedy than the Bard had left room for. The last thing you hear is a cantor singing a Kaddish for the dead. Olivier's performance, considering a recent heart attack, was passionate and daring — daring, let's say, the passion is part of anything he does. Temple Smith finds him mannered and that is there but it doesn't bother me because the feeling is so strong.[8]

After I returned home, he wrote (undated letter) to thank me for the copy of Ted Hughes's book of poems *Crow*, which I'd given him for Christmas and about which he felt mixed. My mother was in Naples for a week visiting friends and family.

> I had a drink with C. P. Snow and his wife last night (Lord + Lady, but you wouldn't know it) and went away almost potted. They are kind people. She, poor thing, had had a stroke last year and can't write by hand — "holograph," she called it — but now works well at the typewriter although afraid of the fluency of the machine. I confess I was a little bothered at the way she hopped up when he said, "I'll have a cigarette," or "will you fill my glass," and was the one who let me in and out. Perhaps this is the old-fashioned way, but it made me understand quite clearly why I approve in principle of women's lib.

On February 3, 1972, he wrote:

> Not very much new here: the weather has been comparatively cold for a week, but is milder today. And I've worked up some kind of a painful swollen ankle that may be gout; therefore I'm making my first visit in England to a doctor tonight. Otherwise, I've completed a long story, "The Silver Crown," and have begun a new one, "The Talking Horse," both, you will be pleased to hear, comic. I've spent

a couple of days with the Constables in the Victoria and Albert —
hours of the day, that is — and yesterday I took in the impression-
ists and post-impressionists in the National Gallery.

OVER THE YEARS, my father gradually metabolized the car accident, and when it appeared in *Dubin's Lives* almost a decade later,
Dubin had become the driver, his car skidding out of control while
he is doing a trivial grocery errand for his wife. The driver's irritation, once mine, had become his. *Dubin's Lives*, set in Vermont-like
rural New York State, is a novel about a middle-aged, married biographer who falls in love with a younger woman. In part it's a
meditation on the writing of lives, in part on marriage and affairs. I
read it in 1979, when it came out, and managed to find things to
praise in the mandatory note home, something made easier because David liked the book. In truth, I could make no objective as-
sessment of the literary work, for I experienced it as a continuation
of the accident aftermath and as a way-too-intimate view of my
father's confused feelings. Lately, as I reread it for the first time, I
felt again a vague nausea, and the notion "virtual incest" came to
mind. Reading a parent's fiction is rarely simply a literary experience; it is, or can be, much more bizarre. The characters often
share intimate traits but then go off on their own. That's the more
recognized truth, and the easier one. But the underlying themes
possess an uncanny, sometimes creepy familiarity: they are the
spooks of the familial unspoken returning to haunt. They know no
walls and can invade with ease across years or decades.

When Dubin arrives in Venice with his mistress, Fanny, he believes he glimpses his daughter, Maud, with an older teacher.
Later:

As he was falling asleep Maud appeared in his mind; Dubin awoke.
Was it she he had seen in the fog with a man old enough, ironically,

to be older than her father? Whoever he was had been past sixty. "My daughter is not for thee": Brabantio. Yet, could Dubin despise an aging man who desired the company of a young woman — endless insistent hunger? The old gent, he guessed, would have to be one of her teachers . . . So soon out of the crib, so quickly grown — bleeding, breasted, gone — lost to me. Out of the house at eighteen; at nineteen as deeply as he into amorous intrigue? . . . He figured her age with her friend's would average a good forty; his with Fanny's, less. Himself less culpable — if one were to use the word — than Maud's male friend — if it was Maud . . . Life responds to one's moves with comic counterinventions.[9]

Well, not entirely comic. (And I was barely seventeen.) When Dubin is about to bed Fanny in Venice, she develops the diarrhea I had repeatedly as a child the year we lived in Rome, so he paternally wipes her clean instead of making love. Were Dad alive, he'd prefer to think of my still too-troubled reaction as simply documenting the power of his fiction (I initially typed "faction") for one reader. A daughter's solipsistic squeamishness. Of course. But however literally accurate, he would be being cagey, as he so often was when queried about the literal basis of his work. He defended his artist's prerogative ferociously to anyone who tried to finger the place where creative transformations started and ended. Yet to a family member, some fictions feel like a view through a misaligned stereoscope, where two separate images overlie each other, never reconcile, and leave you a little queasy.

I must have raised some part of my reaction with my mother, complained to her how so many aspects of our family life, never mentioned among us, had shown up in print. She wrote back to me expressing relief that I'd acknowledged that the book was good. For had I reported otherwise, she allowed, "it would have had to be 'entre nous.' Any adverse criticisms of course have to be relayed directly, as I am not about to get into that." She added:

There's a reason [the biographical element is] not discussable among us in the family — I guess by now, after 7 novels, I do accept the fact that if you know a writer, you may become part of one of his characters. I suppose my feeling towards Kitty is — well, whatever parts of her are me give me the only immortality I'm likely to have! But time has to some extent inured me — I can understand that you might feel less used to the idea — Talk about it with Dad + get the writer's view.[10]

She did not spell out the reason for the "undiscussability," but I decided I'd had enough of the writer's view and did not take it up further.

Chapter 9

Heart

⤙⤙ ⤙⤙ I ASSOCIATED MY FATHER'S angina attacks with loss. My youthful theory, only slightly tempered now, was that his heart took the hit whenever sorrow overwhelmed him. He hated the great vulnerability loss awakened and attempted to minimize it. He forbade himself open response and feared seeing his distress reflected back at him from others. His heart condition worsened after Eugene died, and again immediately after Ida, his mother-in-law, died in January 1982. Long before it became a truism, I understood, observing him, how false was the notion of physical health unaffected by emotional circumstance.

He sought care from his doctors and sometimes used medical attention as a way to comfort himself. I remember, as a very little girl in Corvallis, visiting him in the hospital, watching someone crank his bed. I also remember, one day on a beach in Spain, getting assigned the task of pulling off thick, sticky tape a Spanish doctor had wrapped around his stomach and hairy back to support a pulled muscle. He was not a credulous person, but he sometimes granted medical authorities more than their due.

He minimized the seriousness of the angina to me, the heart disease generally. I knew he took blood pressure pills and attempted to modify what he ate, though he struggled with his sense of deprivation from the restrictions. Occasionally, in later walks when I was visiting, he would have to pause for a moment on a hill. And sometimes when I phoned, he would offer me studied clinical accounts of his pain: I did well yesterday. I walked for half an hour; the sidewalk was level; no cold wind blew.

ON JANUARY 5, 1978, he wrote the following letter. I cannot remember the conversation to which his first paragraph alludes. I believe I'd given him a book of Robert Frank's photos for Christmas.

Dear Janna

I was very much moved by our talk that night in the café. How easy it is to let things drift, and how kind and wise you were to call for definition. I shall remember "latitude" and "change" and hope you will remember that I have loved you from long ago and expect to go on doing so past all words.

I am back from a visit to Dr. Laragh, my Irish friend at New York hospital. He says he's no maverick but believes food never killed anyone — so I can eat all the eggs, ice cream, salt, butter I want. But he'd like me to lose eight pounds, so give up, please, one quarter of my present food intake. And if I feel like eating a pint of ice cream, okay, but skip dinner. That's how it goes: everytime you win one you lose one. But he's taken me off one pill and has cut another in half, wanting me to drop pills altogether. He thinks medical practitioners are from five to a dozen years behind research.

I'm glad to have a look at him but I don't much take to Robert Frank. He is too easy a buff for the slightly odd, the commonplace, almost accidental candid shot. His faces are the faces of a moment, rarely relaxed enough to be dignified. I do like his touches of misty poetry, the wetness of streets and rivers; also rare moments of comedy and some of his panoramas.

Harriet [Wasserman] told me that Rust Hills, who is again fiction editor at Esquire, has sold to a dealer letters by writers written to him at the magazine. You can buy one of my letters for $135. He's also selling, or has sold, Wright Morris, Updike and Jack Hawkes. I don't think I'll ever answer any of his letters again. I'm told he has money so his enterprise seems to be a form of kleptomania.

Happy New Year to you and David. I know we've said it over the phone but I want to say it again. Much love, Dad

HE SAW VARIOUS medical experts, often receiving contradictory advice. During 1981–1982, he and my mother spent the winter in Palo Alto, California. Dad was a fellow at the Center for Advanced Study in the Behavioral Sciences, and they wanted to spend time with the Inkeleses and with Ida, who was in a nursing home dying of ALS. Knowing that he was near one of the best hospitals for heart bypass surgery, he consulted a cardiologist there. At first it seemed as if he could wait to have the bypass operation, but then Ida died, and his heart pain worsened. Suddenly a consensus built — a stress test and an angiogram showed that he had occluded arteries. He must have the procedure at once, then and there. So one night in early March 1982, a month before his sixty-eighth birthday, he telephoned me from the hospital and told me the surgery was set for the next day. I cannot recall exactly what he was writing at the time. He may have been working on short stories. I remember he was reading Margaret Brenman-Gibson's biography of the playwright Clifford Odets. Since she had a connection to the Cambridge Hospital, where I worked, and to my own slight involvement in the antinuclear effort, we talked a bit about her as well as the book.

He carefully reassured me that all would go well, and I, naive about the risk, believed him. As I learned later, the procedure from its inception had carried a high incidence of strokes. Although this had improved somewhat over the years, no one could find a way to keep bits of plaque from falling off artery walls during the great cataclysm of cut-and-graft. They would slide into the bloodstream and make their way to the brain, where, within its immense network of small capillaries, they would become stuck and wreak their particular havoc. My father, six hours after the long triple-bypass surgery, had a stroke that almost killed him. And while I doubt he would have chosen not to live his last four years, the ones the surgery may have bought him, the damage caused him suffering in some ways worse than death. He lost many of his words or at least his ability to summon them at will. He could drive himself mad of an afternoon simply trying to remember a noun. His language, oral and written, became impoverished, tentative. He would reach for something that had been there but now eluded him. The absence where his talent had been haunted him and drove him into a depression. His whole life balance tipped, and all that he'd held at bay since boyhood seemed to collapse in upon him. He became to himself a diminished, frail, uncertain man.

He attracted loving care in the hospital. The doctors kept him there for a good while, set him up for physical therapy, retaught him as much as they could. Young residents and nurses befriended him, making a special effort to work with him. His body had some damage, but it had not been paralyzed. His mind was scrambled. Across days, he reoriented enough to know where he was, who he was, and more or less what he'd been about. Gradually, he settled into himself. My mother, having only weeks earlier lost her mother, not being grounded in either of their homes, and perhaps already experiencing the earliest, undiagnosed symptoms of multiple sclerosis, found herself in a free fall. I remember we talked once about money. She realized she had to learn how much they had, where it was, and how to pay the bills.

It took me a while to grasp his peril. I'd gotten a phone call: things had not gone well; he was in intensive care. I don't think I understood right away that he'd spent a day on the edge of death. That day, David and I had tickets to a Peter Sellars production of Handel's opera *Orlando*. Sellars had updated the eighteenth-century piece, had placed a big, shiny, silver Airstream trailer on-stage, constructed a drinking fountain that at some point rose up slowly out of the floor midstage. The production's screwy dislocation resonated with my own, and I sat in my seat, there and nowhere, brokering shock. I was four months pregnant. I had been certain the operation would repair him. My mindset had momentum and turned only slowly, reluctantly, toward reality. I flew west.

IN ONE OF ARLENE'S LETTERS to Dad, years before the surgery, she told him of going to dinner with a friend and reminded him he had once met this person and had referred to her as "a fresh piece of lettuce." Describing an early girlfriend in his journal, he finds her kisses "as cold as forgotten cereal." Or writes, "My days are filled with a sort of cream cheesy pain." Another time, years later, talking to David about the Plymouth Barracuda, he observed that it drove "like a young truck." He described Roethke as trying to "push a tremendous vitality through a cracked life." He had a genius for slightly askew juxtapositions and metaphors. They are everywhere in his writing. His word use — in this sense — functioned like a good joke, apparently simple and straightforward, yet surprising. Who knows where he got the gift, but now, finally contemplating the meaning of his having learned English late, in grade school, I imagine the second language might have met the Yiddish, rock against flint, and sparked this energetic pidgin discord. Part of the mastery of the craft for him must have been in turning the hybrid possibilities to his purpose, fusing them with his sensibility. The stroke mostly ended the knack, burst that part of his mind, and then resettled his words so they rested together more limply.

Writing was everything to Dad. Without his work, he could conceive of no life he would be willing to live. He had no sense of laurels on which he might rest. (Seven years earlier, in 1975, he'd written to me, "About myself it's pretty much the same thing: the book coming along, though not entirely satisfying. Everytime I do something well I want to do it better. But my mood is 'at peace.' I shan't mind time going so long as I have mobility and can work as well as I do. I feel young even though the mirror catches me as I pass by.")[1] To make matters worse, he initially had double vision, which made reading difficult; his stroke-damaged fingers struggled with writing and typing; his memory faltered.

A MAN OF EXORBITANT WILL, he returned to his desk and pen and daily fought to retrieve what he could find. He began with very short stories and gradually worked his way to a novel he'd wanted to write about a Jewish Indian, called *The People*. Long before he became ill, he sometimes told a joke that began, "Once there was a Jewish Indian . . ." He would grin at the outset, kid-delighted with the silly concept. And, of course, it mirrored his own foreign/native being perfectly — Yozip, the novel's protagonist, seems loosely based on Max Malamud.

As months passed, he gradually recovered some of who he had been, and he returned to a more active life. To people who did not know him well, he looked like his old self, perhaps slightly more hesitant. On September 25, 1983, he wrote David and me a letter, among the last I have from him. He and my mother were spending a month in residence at the Villa Serbelloni in Bellagio, Italy, a center for scholars and writers.

Dear Janna and Dave,
We've settled in at this beautiful villa above Lake Como in the Alps. I'm doing short fiction as Mother wanders around shopping

and otherwise holding the fort. We walk in the woods from time to time, and have already taken the hydrofoil to Como. One night there was choral singing in a nearby church, very well done by a mixed choir of about fifty voices.

Tomorrow the routine changes somewhat when a few dozen scholars begin meetings on Central European problems. We have no plans to attend any of them, but if something interesting should pop up, we may make an exception. My own feeling is that I can do without the academic stuff. I've had so much of it during my lifetime. On the other hand, there are some first-rate scholars around and its often a pleasure to hear them talking on their specialties. I've made the acquaintance of a biblical scholar, a Mr. W. D. Davies (I'm not sure of the D.) whom I like to chat with on religious subjects. He is a Welshman who has made a career for himself in America . . .

Yesterday we went across the lake with another scholar, a young man from Oxford, a delicious person, who laughed raucously at some of my anecdotes, and made a point to kiss mother on the head when he came in for breakfast. He knows Carolinean poetry and is about to embark on a work about Charlemagne and some of the poets he cultivated. Last night at dinner he delivered a farewell appreciation partly in medieval French, partly in classical Latin. I must confess these people impress me. What extraordinary memories.

Our plans are to stay on until about mid-October and then go to Milan for a few days. We hope to see Flavia and Vera [Ponzi] who will be coming up from Naples, as well as Annamaria and Elio [Palombi] and Manuella, their daughter . . .

Almost at the end of the month we will return to New York and take up life there.

We often talk of you and friend Peter. Mother shows his pictures around. What is he up to? Love, Dad, Bern

Peter, David's and my first son, had been born in August 1982.

Between caring for my family and working, I was immersed in my own life, and for several years my memories of my father lack much distinctness. I know we traveled to Manhattan to visit him at Christmas and on his birthdays, and that my mother traveled by train to stay with us in Milton and see Peter. My father may have come with her once or twice. Otherwise, we talked on the phone. He was depressed but enjoyed hearing about our lives and about his grandson.

In July 1980, a year and a half before the surgery, Dad had written two versions of a villanelle. In the first, the opening couplet read: "As you are grooved / by wind, by tooth / so you are grieved." The revision ten days later changed one word: "As you are grooved, / by wind, by tooth, / so you are graved." I read the lines as a conversation he was having with himself about his sense of limitation — the parts of himself he could not change. In spite of his extraordinary achievement, he could not quash his disappointment and regrets — self-criticism about his difficulties loving and feeling loved; frustration at his inability to relax and take easier pleasure in his life. He was aware that grief — and grievance — had "grooved" him, cutting channels that would remain until he was "graved." In the years after the stroke, his internal conversation became sadder. He felt more alone. I still have the small, white, three-by-five-inch notepad that was on his desk the day he died. In green ink: "I am difficult" and "Who else can I confide in? I can no longer listen to myself."

OUR SECOND SON, Zachary, was born in November 1985. My mother visited after his birth, but Dad did not meet him until year's end. They flew up for Christmas, joining David's family and us for the afternoon. I had not seen my father in several months, possibly not since the end of the summer, when I'd visited Bennington. I took one look at him and knew absolutely that he was about to die.

I do not know why, but I grasped his situation completely, and I felt stunned — my neck hairs literally on end. I focused on keeping up the conversation. He seemed tired. I remember noticing his eyebrows had become unruly. Their hair grown whiter and longer, they hung over his eyes and needed trimming. But how death particularly emanated from him I cannot say. He spoke with me and David for a while, with Peter, and he gently held Zack in his lap. He was quiet, perhaps a little flustered by two families in a small space. Sometime during the next weeks, I wrote to dear friends in Amsterdam and to his goddaughter, telling them both that if they wanted to see him again, they must come soon. They probably thought me a little nuts. Such forecasts are no doubt as confusing for the recipient as for the sender. What I recall most is that I could not take the advice myself. I felt frozen in a silent cry, senses hanging open, aghast, unable to act. I did not travel to New York to see him. I did not attempt to take my leave. I could not imagine how to do it, what I might say.

ON MARCH 18, 1986, my mother briefly left their New York apartment to meet a friend for lunch. My father was writing. She had set out a plate with some tuna and tomato and lettuce for him. (She recalled later how much he disliked the enforced salt-free diet, the low-fat mayonnaise.) When she returned an hour or so later, he was lying dead on the living room floor: a massive heart attack. She telephoned the police, my brother, and me. Right after I hung up, I looked out our second-floor window and saw David and Peter in the backyard, the three-year-old boy hosing water onto a sodden, half-frozen, brown lawn, his father raking away old leaves.

Not knowing close death, I was, in that first instant, deeply uncertain whether I would survive his. Sometimes I had longed for him to die: to free me of him, to make the burden of fearful waiting end. But in that moment, though it wasn't ever a conscious thought, I was unsure whether his beating heart had also pumped my blood. Some minutes later, I crossed the street and knocked on the door of a friend who had lost her father. I looked at her intently and asked, "Will I survive this?" She met my eyes and answered, "Yes." The question was utterly real, the answer completely, almost ridiculously, settling.

FROM HIS NOVEL *God's Grace:*

> Cohn lay on the floor of the cave waiting to be lifted into the flames. By the golden dark-light of the fire he could see that his long white beard was flecked with spots of blood.
>
> "Merciful God," he said, "I am an old man. The Lord has let me live my life out."
>
> He wept at the thought. Maybe tomorrow the world to come.[2]

I read these lines at Dad's memorial service later that spring, in New York City at the 92nd Street Y. Musician friends played the stately, aching "Adagio" movement of Schubert's String Quintet in C Major, a piece Dad particularly loved. My brother spoke, as did Robert Giroux and the writers Daniel Stern and Cynthia Ozick. The tenor Paul Sperry sang the mourners' Kaddish. I believe Cohn's words reflect Bernard Malamud's own surprise — and gratitude — at having lived out his life, at having realized his preposterous youthful claim that he would become a fine and famous writer.

MY CLEAREST IMAGE of my father writing is in the house in Old Bennington. He must have been in his late fifties or early sixties. By that time, success allowed him to arrange his teaching schedule around his work. He rose at about seven, before my mother. He dressed upstairs either in their bedroom or, so as not to disturb her, in the broad open hall and stairwell next to it. During mild weather, he preferred a short-sleeved sport shirt. I see him in one with blue and white checks; his pants a fine-wale, dark green-gray corduroy; a Shetland sweater against the morning chill; comfortable brown leather shoes with rubber soles. He'd grown a mustache by then. Once his doctors had warned him about his heart, he took a daily walk, usually in the late afternoon before he napped. Later, ill with angina, he added a second walk in the morning. When I'd come home, I'd join him sometimes in the afternoon. It was a good time to talk. The motion and privacy relaxed him; he doubtless felt his time pressure eased by the efficiency of accomplishing talk and exercise together.

He usually breakfasted alone, eating each day a small bowl of cold cereal, a half slice of toast, orange juice, instant coffee with a little milk. I remember, for some number of years, he'd carefully, at night before he went to bed, set his own place with a spoon, napkin, and white teacup and saucer, neatly cutting and placing half a banana beside the cereal bowl. He'd put water in the kettle. He wanted to arrive the next morning and find everything ready, the table receptively set for him as if by a loving other — a little jump gained upon the day.

We had a succession (five across almost forty years) of cats. Before feeding himself, Dad would let whichever ones were current up from the basement or in from the yard and scoop kibble into their bowls. He was often tender with them, amused, speaking back when they meowed, coaxing them to eat if they were aged or unwell.

His study was off a hall, in a two-room back wing behind the kitchen. When my mother had urged him to let her buy the place, he had initially feared the space would be too small. But it was a good corner room, high-ceilinged and pleasant, with two large windows. He had had a carpenter build floor-to-ceiling bookshelves along its inside wall and across the back to the window. In the far corner, he had placed first one, then another file cabinet. He liked making order.

It's been a while since we dispersed his books, but I believe they started at the left top with nineteenth-century America — Hawthorne, Melville, Twain, Henry James; then on to twentieth-century America — Faulkner, Hemingway, Fitzgerald, some novels by his contemporaries (Bellow, Mailer, Roth, Updike, Nabokov), works by critics (Kazin, Wilson, Trilling). After that was English and Irish literature — several volumes of Dickens, some Hardy, Virginia Woolf, Joyce; followed by other European literature — Flaubert and the Russians (Dostoevski, Tolstoi, Chekhov). Literary biographies were often placed next to the corresponding authors' fiction. (When he read Richard Ellmann's biography of Joyce, it amazed him. I can't remember whether he gave David and me Walter Jackson Bate's *Samuel Johnson* or we gave it to him, but he loved it. He also loved Bate's *John Keats.*) He had plays — Shakespeare, of course; Ben Jonson and John Synge. On the back wall were several oversize shelves in which he kept large art books — Picasso, Cézanne, Matisse, and Rembrandt, among others. (Had he been made to choose a favorite artist, it would have been Rembrandt. I remember going with him to the National Gallery in London and enjoying his excitement each time upon seeing the Rembrandt room. He loved *Belshazzar's Feast*, all the self-portraits, and any painting with Saskia in it.)

A smaller bookcase on the wall next to the door held poetry and a mishmash of contemporary ephemera — books by friends, some respected, some held politely. Most nonfiction was shelved in the guest room next door. Among those, I recall Alex Inkeles's books on sociology, also Lynd's *Middletown*, Jung and Freud, Sandburg's biography of Lincoln, a book on Stalin, and a history of the Jews. His whole collection was small, maybe two or three thousand volumes, and he pruned ruthlessly, giving to local libraries most of what came in the mail. He kept only books he considered classics and occasional volumes by good friends or former students.

My mother refurbished a cane-seated maple rocking chair with comfortable arms that fit easily between his desk and the far window, and he liked to sit in it and read for a while in the afternoon. The chair eased his sometime back pain. He hired a carpenter to mount, on a narrow space between door and bookshelves, a thin, vertical bulletin board on which he pinned photos of family, friends, and favored students, as well as several postcards of portraits from the National Portrait Gallery in London, including Virginia Woolf and D. H. Lawrence, and several others of Rembrandt paintings: *Belshazzar's Feast*, Saskia dressed as Flora, Hendrickje bathing in the river. The paintings on his walls included three small oils by his friend Ben-Zion.

He wrote at a large, spare, teak desk that sat midway into the room, facing the door, one end flush against the side window. An Oriental rug, deep red and blue, covered some of the floor. Turning his head slightly left, he could look east out the window. The house was on a hill at the edge of town, so his line of vision traveled along the sloping back lawn and across downtown Bennington to the Green Mountains that loomed behind it. The backyard was a couple of acres, with abundant green lawn. There were old maples, a young crab apple, an elm, maybe an oak, and other trees. Tutored in perennials by Dottie Hicks, my mother had constructed a bright, curving flower bed midway down the slope. Near it, out of Dad's view, was a very large hydrangea bush, memorably mauve and golden in the autumn. If I sat outside, as I often enjoyed doing, on the porch off the living room, the most prominent mountain across the way looked to me like the belly of a pregnant woman, lying back, distorted, as if sculpted by Picasso.

Dad would go to his desk each morning on weekdays, and he wrote from 8:30 or 9:00 until 1:00. Sometimes he'd write on Saturday, too. He was a man of habit, firm in his wish for morning quiet. And although he disliked interruptions, there were inevitably some. My mother would filter telephone calls; his agent, editor, and publisher might get put through. Occasional others. If the day's mail brought something of sure interest — such as a letter from a magazine purchasing a story — she would knock and bring it in to him. Crises — a cat with a half-dead bird or a car stuck on the steep, icy driveway — pulled him briefly out of his study.

I figured I had one free *billet d'interruption* any morning I was at home, though I did not daily use it. If I did knock, he would almost always look up from his page, smile, welcome me, ask about my day, and wait to hear what I wanted from him or had to say. A second interruption required good cause, and, of course, his receptivity depended on his mood and how deeply he was into his work. When I wanted his companionship, I was adept at finding ways to visit with him without raising his ire. I'd muster some compelling literary question or urgently need to know the derivation of a word — a quest that would spark his interest and create solidarity. Occasionally, hearing me nearby, he'd call me in. If pleased with a few sentences he'd just written, he might read them aloud. More often, he simply greeted me, or perhaps queried me on a contemporary phrase. We had an exchange about some slang my friends and I were using: For a brief period in the 1960s, I made a distinction between "That's his bag" and "That's his thing." The former referred to a day job, the latter to a passionate interest. Mine was a casual usage. Dad wanted to borrow one or both of the expressions for *The Tenants* or *Dubin's Lives*, and I remember his running through any number of examples with me, then grilling my friends as they dropped by, hoping he could find a hard-and-fast rule where none existed.

*   *   *

ON FEBRUARY 3, 1972, while living in England, he wrote:

> Dear Janna
>
> For a new story I'm writing I need some conundrums of the:
> "What's black and white and re(a)d all over" type. Even jokes like
> "Why does a chicken cross the road?" etc. And I'd like a couple of
> good elephant riddles, such as "Why does the elephant wear green
> sneakers?" Will you take a minute to write down a few things of
> this sort — and anything else that sounds appropriate, like some
> of the "knock-knock" questions if you know any — and send them
> to me?

He wrote in blue or black ink, often in later years with a Bic
ballpoint pen, on yellow unlined paper, a pile of which he kept in a
desk drawer. He spaced the lines intending correction and would
begin each morning by rereading and editing what he'd written the
day before. I have an image of his handwritten pages, with words
neatly crossed out and replaced by others. I believe he felt that half
a page a day was a good yield. His process was so private, so easily
interrupted, that I rarely witnessed him putting words on paper.
My mother or a college secretary he hired after hours would type
up the finished stories or chapters. Then he would rewrite. And rewrite. Usually two or three times, occasionally into the double dig-
its of drafts. His sentences and paragraphs were hard won, the result of considered thought and constant revision. He understood
that effort and discipline made up his strong suit, and at least once
he said that his success had come from 10 percent talent and 90 percent hard work. Intensely competitive in spite of himself, acutely
aware of his contemporaries, and always weighing and sizing his
own talent, he liked to retell to dinner guests a story Philip Roth
had told him probably in the early 1970s: On days when Roth
pulled himself out of bed with difficulty, lingered over breakfast
and newspaper, and tried to push himself reluctantly, late morning,

to his desk, he would goad himself on. "Malamud," he'd growl, "has already been working for three hours."

Wherever Dad was — writing, reading, walking, sleeping — he kept a pen and a three-by-five-inch notepad with him, often in his shirt pocket. When an idea or a word came to him, he'd write it down to try in his manuscript the next day. Sometimes we'd be in the middle of a conversation, and he'd stop talking, take out the pad, apologize, and write a few words. I remember many times over the years being called to the bathroom door when he was in the shower. "Janna," he'd shout over the water, "could you please write this down for me?" I'd grab the nearest pad and pen and scribble out the phrase he uttered. I imagine that sometimes, after laboriously arranging words in his head until they were just right, he panicked if he could not immediately set them down.

The summer I was sixteen, I did my first serious reading, books borrowed from his library: the five volumes of Leonard Woolf's autobiography, Walter Jackson Bate's biography of Keats, and van Gogh's letters to Emile Bernard, among others. I'd interrupt him in his study to replace one and take another, or to tell him about something I was learning, recite a poem I had lately memorized, or simply get him to explain some idea. He delighted in my intellectual awakening. I enjoyed holding his attention. But more than that, I found *him* then, at his quiet best. They were moments of deep compatibility; easy, comfortable closeness; conversations with a friend. His study is still where I cherish him most; where he is exactly my loving, beloved father. To this day, I find it difficult to return there in my thoughts without entering thick emotion, an incommunicable mix of sadness and sustenance.

I RECEIVED THE following undated letter (probably written on a Sunday in September 1970) right after I'd returned to college to begin my sophomore year. My mother was away, possibly visiting my grandmother.

Dear Janna,

I hope you're entirely well and that your room meets your expectations. I'm sure you can make it suit your needs and taste.

I was walking this morning and remembering you walking with me. It made me think of the "poverty and insanity" thing that I had brought up — you say more than once. Of course I was talking about my own background; yours, once removed from your parents' is something else again. And of course, referring to myself, it's not the whole story. It leaves out the love I got from both my parents, and their quality of goodness, simplicity, honesty. And their ability to endure life, if not live it — I mean it more positively than it sounds. I think I translated their endurance into my discipline. I thought they lived with a kind of discipline; they had to. Of course they settled for too little: there was no music in the house — we weren't that poor — no books except a few in Yiddish. We had little family life. There were few visits to us and we visited people rarely, on the Jewish holidays when the store was closed. The store was rarely closed. I know they were concerned about Eugene and me, but they were convinced we had a way out, no matter what they were able to give us or not give us, and the way out was education. If you were educated you could earn a living and had nothing to fear. They lived in fear mostly of not being able to make a living, of sickness, of their ignorance of the unknown world, of gentile society. Of course some of their fears have remained with me. In a way I've spent much time making myself strong against what they feared most. I got the education they wanted me to have. I learned to work well. My most important strength, my imagination, without their knowing it, came from them.

Last night turned out to be nice. I went to the Florys alone . . . Later, Peggy and Bill, Shelley and Ruth and I went to the Vt. Steak

House for Dinner . . . Afterwards I went home and read Borges' little autobiography in the New Yorker.

Today is a beautiful day, as it must be in Cambridge, and I intend to walk again this afternoon. I miss you. It was a pleasure to have you here most of the summer. At the same time I'm glad you're back at college because I know that's where you want to be, at least a good deal of the time, and I'm sure, despite some pessimistic predictions, that you will have a good year. You're one of the happy few who can make their own world.

Love,

Pa

A Chronology of Bernard Malamud's Life

APRIL 26, 1914–MARCH 18, 1986

April 26, 1914	Bernard Malamud born in Brooklyn, New York.
1917	Brother, Eugene Malamud, born.
1922	Malamud family moves to Flatbush section of Brooklyn. Bernard enters P.S. 181 in third grade.
1928–1932	Attends Erasmus Hall High School.
May 1929	Mother, Bertha Fidelman Malamud, dies.
1932–1936	Attends City College in Manhattan; B.A., 1936.
1937–1938	Attends Columbia University; M.A., 1942. Dissertation subject: Thomas Hardy.
1938–1939	Unemployed; odd jobs, including tutoring German refugees in English.
1939	First teaching position, Lafayette High School, Brooklyn.
1940	Clerk, U.S. Census Bureau, Washington, D.C. Publishes first nonfiction vignettes in *Washington Post*. Returns to Brooklyn to teach at Erasmus Hall Evening High School. Starts writing during the day.
1941	Begins writing short stories.
1943–1944	First short stories published in *American Prefaces, Threshold,* and *Assembly.*
November 1945	Marries Ann deChiara. Moves from Brooklyn to Greenwich Village.
October 1947	Son, Paul Francis Malamud, born.

1948	Completes first novel; eventually burns it. His later terse comment: "dark; no dice with publishers."
1949	Teaches at Chelsea Vocational High School and Harlem Evening High School. Moves to Corvallis, Oregon, to join faculty of Oregon State College.
1950	Stories appear in *Harper's Bazaar, Partisan Review,* and *Commentary.*
1952	First novel, *The Natural,* published.
January 1952	Daughter, Janna Ellen Malamud, born.
March 1954	Father, Mendel "Max" Malamud, dies.
1955	Publishes, under pen name Peter Lumm, a children's novel, *Kim of Korea,* coauthored with Faith Norris.
Autumn 1956–	Receives *Partisan Review* fellowship in fiction. Lives with
Summer 1957	family in Rome; visits Austria and France.
1957	Second novel, *The Assistant,* published.
1958	First collection of short stories, *The Magic Barrel,* published. Receives Rosenthal Award from National Institute of Arts and Letters for *The Assistant.* Spends summer at Yaddo.
1959	Wins National Book Award for *The Magic Barrel.*
1961	Teaches creative writing in summer school at Harvard. Moves to Bennington, Vermont, to teach at Bennington College.
1961	Third novel, *A New Life,* published.
1963	Second collection of short stories, *Idiots First,* published.
1966	Fourth novel, *The Fixer,* published. Moves to Cambridge and becomes visiting lecturer at Harvard University.
1967	Wins National Book Award and Pulitzer Prize for *The Fixer.* Becomes a member of American Academy of Arts and Sciences.
1969	Fifth novel, linked stories, *Pictures of Fidelman: An Exhibition,* published. Moves to Old Bennington. Begins spending winters in Manhattan.
1971	Sixth novel, *The Tenants,* published. In London from late autumn to following spring.
1973	Third short story collection, *Rembrandt's Hat,* published.
1974	Death of Eugene Malamud.
1979	Seventh novel, *Dubin's Lives,* published.

1979–1981	Serves as president of PEN American Center.
1981–1982	Spends winter as fellow in Palo Alto, California, at Center for Advanced Study in the Behavioral Sciences.
January 1982	Mother-in-law, Ida Barbieri, dies.
1982	Eighth novel, *God's Grace*, published.
1983	*The Stories of Bernard Malamud*, published. Wins Gold Medal from American Academy and Institute of Arts and Letters.
March 18, 1986	Bernard Malamud dies of a heart attack in his apartment in New York City. Cremated; ashes buried in Mount Auburn Cemetery, Cambridge, Massachusetts.
1987	Malamud family and members of PEN/Faulkner board establish PEN/Malamud Award for excellence in short fiction.
1989	Unfinished novel, *The People and Uncollected Stories*, published.
1997	*The Complete Stories* published.

Appendix: Other Voices

Herbert Wittkin

Excerpts from "Bernie, the Early Years: A Memoir,"
October 1986

We were about eight or nine years old when, in the mid 1920s, we became friends at Public School 181 in Flatbush, and began what became a lifelong relationship through elementary school, high school, college and adulthood. The school was three blocks from my home in Flatbush, and five miles from his in the Gravesend area of Brooklyn. I lived within the school district, he did not. I had about a five minute walk to school; he had to ride two trolley lines for about three quarters of an hour on a good day. However, it isn't the distance alone that's significant: it's that he attended P.S. 181 at all. What was he doing at a school situated miles outside his official district? . . . [Perhaps, Wittkin speculates, one of his teachers recognized his abilities and wanted him in the new, more progressive school.]

In any case, P.S. 181 changed his life. He was thrown in with a collection of youngsters who ran at a pace that tested him intellectually and moved in an environment that widened his social horizons. Early in the game he began to play a central role in our small group of six or eight boys and girls. He drew attention to himself and was ready to stand in the spotlight. He was assertive with us and venturous and bold, bordering at times on the brash in his relations with adults . . . I marvelled at his composure when he conversed with my parents in my home. And when it came to teachers, he took them captive. All the teachers in the last three years at P.S. 181 — Mrs. McDermott, Mr. Squires and Mrs. Ahner — fell under his spell.

The nature of his attachment to his teachers was unique. It was not truly that of a teacher's pet . . . It was engaging more than ingratiating. He volunteered his services, initiated projects and mixed in a healthy amount of seduction, so that he became more of a child affiliate of the teacher than a pet.

He talked himself into most of the choice positions involving extracurricular activities that provided him with some measure of prominence and authority. This characteristic, this tendency to find his way into his teachers' hearts remained a constant throughout his school years . . . Interestingly enough, when it came time to choose an occupation, he turned to teaching. He remained a teacher at the college rank all his professional life, long after he had attained towering success as an author . . .

While some of us in the class were secretly jealous of his penchant for collecting teachers, and while we may even have expressed derision among ourselves for his barefaced forwardness, we were quite willing to accept the favors he could bestow . . .

[He and I] both attracted the attention of adults as naturally and as needfully as the air we breathed. He, because he got too little at home; I, because I got too much. In his home, it would appear that so much devotion had to be paid to the daily struggles of making ends meet that little was left over for him. Hence *his* great need . . .

The need to be noticed has innumerable facets. To Bernie it meant a healthy dedication to the work ethic and a mighty will to succeed. Nowhere was this more evident than in his wish to play baseball. He was not well coordinated and consequently not endowed with much athletic talent. Yet he yearned so desperately to play the game that during the summer vacation period, he would make the long trip to Flatbush to play catch in the street in front of my house. I would equip him with a worn, misshapen first baseman's mitt. We would stand about seventy-five feet apart and throw a baseball to each other . . .

What started as recreation would turn into a grim exercise in frustration, as he strove determinedly to master the technique of throwing and catching a baseball. It was not to be: his body couldn't respond . . . Yet, he would sweat, strain and punish himself unmercifully, unwilling to accept defeat. After awhile, we stopped those practice sessions, and the subject of baseball was seldom a topic of discussion . . .

Bernie laughed easily and often. He had a soaring sense of humor, which would break out in hearty laughter. At times he would smile knowingly as though he were being amused by a private joke. As a youngster, he was buoyant and energetic, one might say action-oriented. As he matured, some of the exuberance faded, to be replaced by a kind of controlled imperturbability. I can only guess that much of that outward vitality was being diverted to the printed page. He could grow angry when ruffled, and fight back; but rage was never a motivating emotion, and I never recall his resorting to personal invective or vicious abuse when someone might have offended him. Mostly he defended himself with biting sarcasm and sharp jibes, which left one slack-jawed and tongue-tied.

During those early school days he displayed few of the scholarly qualities he developed during the high school and college periods . . . What did come through, however, was the strong undercurrent of a ruminative, curious mind, seriously penetrating and filled with the magic of things. He was not what could be called happy-go-lucky. None of us in our small tribe fit that description. We were children of the Great Depression, anxiety-ridden and tense, particularly Bernie and me. We were worriers . . .

We were allied in our Jewishness. Our roots had been planted, centuries ago, somewhere along the Russian-Polish border, and our inherited similarities were evident to us both . . . We may have been Jewish more in the cultural than in the deeply religious sense, but there was never the slightest doubt about our heritage . . . As far as he and I were concerned, the coincidence of our Jewishness was a bond that helped fasten our emotional ties.

This was apparent in my home where he was a familiar and welcome figure. I believe he felt relaxed in surroundings that had firm, Jewish underpinnings, where an occasional Yiddish expression would be interposed with English, and where old-world hospitality was conveyed through food, drink and laughter. He liked my mother's chocolate cake, and she held him in high regard. After his visits and after he had conducted a grown-up conversation with her, she'd say, "He'll get some place, that boy." . . .

Though we may not have been prize-winners at baseball, we were champions at a home-grown competition we called Jousting. This was a title for a rough and tumble activity several of us had devised in what we called our Friday Night Club . . . Friday was the only night in the school week we were permitted outdoors after dinner. There were six of us who, under cover of darkness, would cavort about the neighborhood, playing such games as Ring-a-eave-ee-o and stealing Concord grapes from a nearby vine. Jousting was modelled after the tilts on horseback engaged in by the fabled, armored knights of the Middle Ages. We formed three teams consisting of one person perched precariously on the shoulders of another — not piggy back, but high astride the shoulders. The objective was to topple the opposing teams in whatever way possible — bucking, bumping, butting, mauling or manhandling. The team left standing at the end was the winner . . .

Bernie and I were a team, with me on top because I was lighter. The horse was the key, inasmuch as the one on the bottom had to maintain his balance while under attack from all sides. He had to support a tottering rider whose legs were wrapped around his head, while warding off the charge of the other teams . . . There we were, three grotesque creatures from outer space, in a quiet residential neighborhood, in the eerie light of a street lamp, lumbering at each other to commit mayhem . . . As a team, Bernie and I were the self-proclaimed, undisputed champions of the Friday Night Club . . .

We were on common ground in another vital and emotionally charged area, our youthful sexual appetites . . . [Wittkin describes how, in seventh grade, Dad was put in charge of the mimeograph room and selected Wittkin as his assistant. He goes on to describe how the two of them frequently got themselves sprung from the classroom.]

Suddenly the classroom bell would ring twice. This was a signal from the office for Bernie to go downstairs for a stencil to be reproduced on the mimeograph machine . . . He would rise, a model of solemnity, and in the midst of a lesson, leave the room, at a deliberately measured pace so as not to reveal the jubilation he felt at getting away. Five minutes later the bell would sound four times. This was my call to join him downstairs.

Once in our lair, we were free . . . Mostly our talk would turn to sex and our erotic fantasies. We would estimate the proportions of our teachers' bosoms and review the physical assets of the various girls in our class, rhapsodizing over the shape of their legs, the curve of their buttocks and the size of their budding breasts . . . This led nowhere but to arousal and an instant erection, against which we would each place an ink-stained wooden ruler to see whose was longer. There was never any question. His was.

Bernie was a ladies' man from his youngest days. Girls were attracted to him, and he to them. From his earliest conquests in elementary school through high school and college, he not only had an eye for women, he knew inherently how to win their favor. He was seldom without a female friend . . . As with his teachers, Bernie's manner was direct, persuasive, gentle and seductive. In addition, he was, in those pre-teen times, somewhat more free-wheeling, more assured than the rest of us. He travelled alone long distances to school, seemed more liberated and much less concerned than we about parental restrictions. He was coping on his own; and while it evoked envy in boys like us, still trailing apron strings, his posture of youthful independence left many girls breathing hard. If that weren't enough, he projected a strong sense of vulnerability which, given his circumstances, was to be expected . . .

Somewhere along the line in high school, during our junior or senior year, Bernie joined the Drama Club and cultivated a new company of bright attractive people. He brought along some of us from P.S. 181 . . . Though this attempt to have me join his newfound friends was only moderately successful, it illustrated the sense of loyalty he felt for his earliest companions. He maintained long-time relationships, tried to bring together friends of different eras and varied stations. He stayed connected all his life with several of the people from P.S. 181, besides me. He was rooted in friendship and valued it like few people I have known . . .

The first Malamud story ever published appeared when he was in the eighth grade: he put out his own newspaper. That may be a gross overstatement, but it was his sponsorship of the project, his idea primarily that culminated in an eight or ten page rough hewn publication carrying stories written by the pupils in our class . . . It took uncommon initiative for a youngster to persuade teachers and staff members to help design a format, devise a masthead of sorts and arrange for the stories to be typed . . .

The title escapes me, but I recall the paper was made up of standard size 8½″ by 11″ sheets, stapled down one side, and printed on the infamous mimeograph machine. To call it a newspaper was stretching things. In content, it was more a magazine than newspaper, but, in appearance, it resembled a tabloid. Lacking as it did the semi-stiff covers of a periodical. His was the opening story on page one. I have no memory of the narrative, but because the style was so idiosyncratic, it has always stayed with me. Bernie's phrasing, already at the age of eleven or twelve, was of the same nature that distinguished the prose of his mature years . . . Only a few years ago, I told him that I thought he still wrote as he did when we were kids. He knew I meant it as a compliment, implying that his language retained the purity, lucidity and enchantment of childhood, unencumbered by the paraphernalia of age. He thought about it quizzically for a moment, smiled and asked if I really meant it. When I assured him that I did, he was pleased . . .

There was a time during our high school days when we became addicted to dice. There were about eight to ten of us involved in the action. We had a roving crap game which moved from one house to another as we wore out our welcome. We were nickel and dime gamblers in an era when a penny bought three green-leaf gumdrops . . .

A game held one Saturday night at Bernie's home is especially vivid. It took place in an area behind his father's delicatessen, the same store that became the backdrop for *The Assistant*. I believe the room served as the family's kitchen; the rest of their living quarters were upstairs over the store. The walls and the linoleum floor cast a pale green aura, which was brightened by the light from a lone, bare bulb hanging from the ceiling. We gathered in an uneven circle . . . At the start, we stood around, but as the action grew heated some of us got down on our haunches, others bent in half or dropped to their knees. Coats off, we were in shirts and ties, which we converted to casual dress by the simple maneuver of opening our collars.

The game had a rhythm of its own, growing out of the movements and sounds of the players. There were those who shook the dice while holding them high and some who rattled them low. As the contest gathered momentum, there were sounds of pleading — "Come to me baby"; sharp demands for a natural — "Seven! Eleven!"; mournful prayers for a number . . . and impatient requests, "Shoot, you're faded!" . . . This was a rite of youth with overtones of teen-age sexuality, raw competitiveness and cultism — tumultuous emotions letting go.

Each of us had his own personal style of handling the dice, and Bernie was no exception. He may not have been any more colorful than others in the game, but he was on his home court this night and was performing with authority. His tendency, while waiting for his bet to be covered was to hold the dice between his hands chest high, with the palms flat as though in prayer. He would warm them by rolling them up and down. His face would be flushed; and when his bet was faded he would burst into action by vigorously shaking the dice in his right hand as though they were being masturbated. He would toss them, snap his fingers loudly and yell for a natural. If he made his point or was on a roll, he would sink to his knees and complete his turn in that position. As the pot built, so would his passion until he either hit it big and withdrew some of his winnings or threw a seven and lost it all. In either case, it was a release and he would be spent, until the dice again came his way.

We played well into the night until exhaustion or bankruptcy overtook us. Midway through the evening, Bernie provided sandwiches and soda from the delicatessen, which topped off a memorable evening for a gang of hungry teen-agers . . .

[Bernie] was hard on himself, a trait that lasted all his life. He persevered working with undiminished patience until he was satisfied with the job. Although he was outwardly animated and ready for a romp, he was basically a profoundly serious, reflective and analytical person. Above all, he made friends, held on to them, and was deeply interested and curious about their lives.

Hannah Needle Broder

Excerpts from "Reminiscences"

April 20, 1986. New York. Dear Janna, Here are the recollections I promised to record for you. They evoked a lot of emotion and thought. I hope you find them interesting. It was a happy time! Fondly, Hannah

I met Bern in Miss Mastin's English class. She was a poet of some note and had an ability to convey her enthusiasm for literature and creative writing to the members of her class. Learning from her was a rewarding experience and Bern often gave her credit with kindling his original desire to become a writer. One day, Bern came up to me and said, "I like your dress." (It was a pretty dress.) The next day I returned the compliment by telling him, "I like your poem." That is how our friendship began . . .

We did not have many classes in common at Erasmus. Recently, I was discussing Greek with Bern only to find out that he never took Greek at all. It was probably Latin that we shared. So much for the accuracy of my recollections!

Bern was a member of the Erasmus Dramatic Society and I went to see him play the lead in "The Man Who Married a Dumb Wife." He was really great as "The Man" and received quite an ovation at the end. This evoked my sincere admiration because I was an excessively shy teenager and could never have performed as he did. Listening to Bern read at the "Y," I again marvelled at his poise and ability to project, and the memory of this play returned. I reminisced, "Of course. He was an actor in high school. No wonder!"

Eventually, we began to go out with one another, usually to a show because the theater continued to fascinate him. I gained new insights into what we had just seen in our discussions that followed each performance . . .

One of the shows we enjoyed together was "Cyrano de Bergerac," which we saw at the Majestic Theater on Fulton Street in Brooklyn. Afterwards, Bern gave me a lovely illustrated copy of the play. In the front he wrote, "Page 47 —

the last two lines." It was the scene where Cyrano duels with the Viscount and declares that as he duels, he will simultaneously compose a poem. The designated lines read:

> "I warn you, dear Myrmidon,
> That at the end of the refrain, I shall thrust."

Our friendship continued throughout Erasmus. At graduation, lined up in alphabetical order, "Needle" was close to "Malamud." For some reason, Bern asked me to wear his wristwatch during the ceremony. It was huge for me and flopped around my wrist with every move. But I wore it proudly and returned it afterwards. He seemed pleased.

Then, I went away to Vassar and Bern went to City College. Early in Freshman year, he came to visit me in Poughkeepsie. During the day, he asked me to become engaged to him. This made me terribly flustered. I had never thought at all in terms of getting married to anyone . . . I was certainly too immature for a commitment at that time, and truthfully, I don't think Bern was ready for one either. However, it hurt me to see him so upset. I explained that I was dedicated to completing college and to studying Psychology in depth in preparation for a career. We were both sad when he boarded the train back to New York. Years later, I told Bern that it was lucky that he never married me, because my father would have fought hard to make him into a stock broker. Probably, he would never [have] been able to write at all! Bern just laughed and said that we would have moved to California and never opened our mail.

Some time later, I received an eight page letter from Bern, beautifully written, recapitulating our relationship and ending with the sentence, "You'll have your Psychology, and I have my fragment of lace." Even though it contained tinges of anger it was an unusually poignant narrative. I treasured it for many years and would love to share it with you. However, when my daughter, Nan, was a freshman in college, she was visited by a girl whom she knew in Erasmus. This young lady was attending Reed College in Oregon, and by then, Bern had a strong cult following which included her. Nan showed her friend the letter and tears poured down her face. She said it was the most beautiful thing she had ever read, and alas, neither Nan nor I ever saw the letter or her friend again. It was a great loss and would have been a unique memory for you.

Happily, the friendship between Bern and me did not end when he left Vassar that day. I saw him over the years and when I transferred to Barnard for my Junior year . . . we spent time together . . .

Early in his career, also, Bern taught in night school — in Erasmus, I think. He must have been involved with teaching English to foreigners, because he told me this story (he said it was true), which will enable me to end on a light note. After class, a little lady came up to him and asked, "Tell me, teach, which is right to say — 'piss' or 'shit'?" Good teacher that Bern was, he did not panic. He commented that he was not sure what she meant and could she explain her inquiry a little more. The lady replied, "I never know whether to ask for a 'piss' of paper or a 'shit' of paper." Bern relaxed!

Miriam Milman Lang

Excerpts from "The Young Malamud: Age of Innocence"

November 11, 1986 Dear Janna, When I heard you were interested in gathering memoirs of your father, I set my recollections to work, and as they coalesced, I was able to put this together. It's by no means complete because I don't have Dad's early letters to refresh my memory. However, it should give you some idea of the sensitive, vulnerable teenager that he was in the context of the circumstances in which we were growing up . . . Cordially, Miriam Lang

We met in 1930, when Bernie was sixteen and I was a year younger, innocents in an age of innocence such as the world will not see again . . .

Bernie lived above his father's grocery store on Gravesend Avenue, which literally ended in a cemetery; later the name was changed to MacDonald Avenue. Small businesses suffered most under the economic blight, and while Bernie studiously avoided talking about his home life, I sensed a deep melancholy in him. Only much later was he able to reveal so poignantly in *The Assistant* what his family must have endured.

Actually, Bernie was hypersensitive about his background, for we children of the Depression had an egalitarian attitude . . . Bernie [and I encountered each other] at the Youth Group at Temple Beth Emeth, to which my family belonged.

He was slightly built and not much taller than my five-feet-four; in fact, we were almost level when I wore high heels. His fine, black hair waved slightly, and his clean-shaven face was shadowed by the darkness of his beard. The expression in his brown eyes could change from melancholy to mischievous to inscrutable, depending on his mood, which shifted mercurially. His voice had a theatrical range, from soft to deep, with a slight intonation. He once told me that, coming from a Yiddish-speaking home, he didn't speak English until he went to kindergarten where he caught on quickly that in order to survive, he had to talk like the other kids.

The first year, Bernie and I didn't actually date . . . As a compromise, we'd arrive separately at the Sunday evening Youth Group meetings, after which Bernie would walk me home along the maple-lined streets of our quiet neighborhood. On the way, he liked to clown with the irrepressible spirit of a Groucho Marx ad-libbing melodramatically in iambic pentameter alternating with a convincing Hebrew chant. Between laughter and embarrassment, I'd try to hush him, for fear of what the neighbors might think . . .

Since he avoided direct talk of his personal life, I could only surmise from bits and fragments that his mother had died tragically, and in the background was an *éminence grise* of a stepmother. About his father he was strangely silent, and for years I wasn't aware that he had a brother. To all intents and purposes, then Bernie seemed like an orphan in need of family closeness. He enjoyed stopping by our house of an afternoon to visit with anyone who happened to be around: me, my two younger sisters and brothers, even my parents. And as time went on, he acquired a circle of friends who also served as sibling substitutes.

This was subordinate, though; foremost in all our minds was getting high grades and preparing for college. A year after our first meeting, Bernie entered City College, by which time we'd progressed to dating, usually with a group of friends. Because money was so scarce — even with the subway a nickel and City College tuition free, Bernie had to work part-time to maintain himself — we were limited to the movies at ten or fifteen cents and on rare occasions, the second balcony of a Broadway theatre at ninety-nine cents. Sometimes, after the movies we'd splurge at Joe's Spaghetti House in downtown Brooklyn, where we'd order one bowl of pasta for all of us.

. . . As a group, we were politically liberal and, later on, very much concerned over the rise of Fascism and Nazism. I recall once going with Bernie to a meeting of the Committee Against War and Fascism, but while we sympathized with the Spanish Loyalists, we had neither the time nor the temperament for activism.

. . . Our favorite English teacher at Erasmus, Dr. Clara Molendyk[e] enjoyed us so much that she became part of our social group. Though only a few years older than her students, she was the first to recognize Bernie's talent and encourage him. As he wrote in a letter to me in 1983, "She (Clara) actually told me that she expected to be remembered because of what I would accomplish. That sounds unbelievable, but I still remember the time she said it. And if what I remember is correctly remembered, then I proved something to both of us. If I could embrace her now, I would." . . .

During my sophomore year (1933–4) Bernie seemed to experience a delayed adolescence in his attitude toward sex. A kind of immature exhibitionism. Since I had all the repressions of my generation and he was inexperienced, our intimacy didn't go beyond primary necking. Actually, I'd say that, based on the fact that he never pressured me, Bernie was remarkably chaste for the era. At the same time, he was governed by the age-old male chauvinism: he put the individual woman on a pedestal, while at the same time he regarded sex and the sexual woman as degraded.

In the apparent hope of witnessing a strong reaction, he took my best friend, Bunny, a very proper Bostonian, to see the notorious *Tobacco Road*. When she stoically failed to respond to the play's depravity, Bernie took me to see it, and I also disappointed him by sitting through it poker-faced . . .

In another effort to shock, one evening while we were out on a date, Bernie suddenly pulled an unrolled condom from his breast pocket and flapped it in my face. Though I'd heard about such things and their function, I had never actually seen one . . . Still, I wasn't going to give Bernie the satisfaction of outraging me, so I merely looked puzzled, putting him in the embarrassing position of having to explain.

In a less prurient vein, he claimed that after he brought me home from a date, or sometimes when I'd been out with someone else, he would station himself across the street from our house and look up at the windows of the front bedroom I shared with my sister. Since we always drew the shades, the most he could have seen, if anything, were silhouettes. I never tried to verify it by giving Bernie the satisfaction of my looking out the window. In fact, I was inclined to blame his overwrought imagination — until I came across a parallel in Frank's voyeurism in *The Assistant*.

. . . He was never really coarse in word or deed, just immature, like a small boy trying to make an impression by behaving outrageously . . .

By my junior year at college, Bernie had declared himself in love with me. I, on the other hand, was dating several different boys and not at all ready to limit myself to one. Still, regarding me with the eyes of a lover, he wrote increasingly passionate letters, even though mine to him remained at a fond but friendly level . . .

I recall especially one letter he wrote while working at a summer resort in the Catskills. Perhaps to make me jealous, he described in flowery detail an episode in the woods with one of the female guests, climaxing with, "And then I honored her with my body." Far from being jealous, I was amused, and somewhat annoyed — even in those pre–Women's Lib days — that any man dared to assume a woman should feel honored by his sexual attentions. During that period, he also wrote to my sister, Doris, describing similar escapades, and to Bunny, who recalls his reference to "Miriam's comforting breasts." That piece of gross exaggeration really amused her, since I was always bemoaning my size 32A bra . . .

Despite his feverish rhetoric on paper, when Bernie was with me in person, he communicated quite normally . . . When I came home for Christmas vacation that year ('34–5), he had a surprise for me. Having worked overtime after classes, he had accumulated enough money for a "formal" date, complete with taxi, theatre and dancing afterwards. To live up to his expectations, I passed over my own evening dresses in favor of my mother's more sophisticated silver lamé gown. Wearing a tuxedo, also borrowed, Bernie arrived with an orchid corsage, and off we went to Manhattan by cab. I can't recall the name of the play we saw or of the hotel where we went dancing, though I have a general memory of the excitement of the evening, heightened by the fact that Bernie had gone to such trouble to make it a success.

On returning home in the not-so-wee hours, I went straight upstairs to bed, then realized I had forgotten to put the orchid in the refrigerator to preserve it. Bernie had made a date for the next afternoon, and naturally he'd want to see me wearing his corsage. Too tired to go downstairs, I placed it on the window sill, relying on the cold air to keep it fresh. I hadn't reckoned with the winter wind and woke to discover the purple flower with its sparking silver bow perched conspicuously on a bare branch of the maple tree in front of our house. In vain did I plead with my brother to go out onto the porch roof and retrieve it . . .

Lacking the *savoir faire* to handle the situation gracefully, I met Bernie at the front door *sans* corsage and *sans* explanation, praying that he wouldn't look skyward when he left the house. To my horror, he did glance up, but since he made no comment, I couldn't be certain whether he noticed what seemed like blatant evidence that I'd tossed his beautiful, expensive flower out the window. And so I remained tongue-tied, though it haunted me for quite a while afterwards. Twenty-odd years later, my guilt was revived when I read in *The Assistant* (pp. 192–3) the episode where Frank sees in the garbage the carved rose he has given to Helen. I resolved to ask Bernie some day whether it was in fact based on the affair of the orchid and at long last to apologize. Alas, the opportunity never arose, and I'm left with the uncertainty . . .

Though Bernie was indeed serious about me, there were checks and balances. At a time when most young people dated simultaneously, not serially, there was no fertile ground for "relationships." In addition, all occasions informed against sexual intimacy . . .

The only approved alternative was marriage, not undertaken lightly in the mid-thirties, with financial prospects so bleak. Add to that the fact that my parents were in the vanguard of those who sent their daughters to the best colleges not for status, but because they believed women should have the same educational and career opportunities as men. They'd have taken a dim view of a premature son-in-law, even if I'd wished to marry, which I didn't.

Undaunted by such obstacles, Bernie proposed to me, college student though he still was with no visible future. His driving motivation, as he confessed at a party I gave for Doris's anniversary in 1966 was simply, "I was nutty about her." I believe also that, bolstered as he was by the conviction that he would become a famous author, he wasn't completely irrational in his desire to marry, just unrealistic.

This all consuming belief [that he'd become a famous author] colored his entire outlook, both verbally and non-verbally. I remember his reaction after we visited my cousin, Sidney Kingsley, who, in his late twenties, had recently won the Pulitzer Prize for his first play . . . After we left, Bernie was silent, but I sensed as though he had uttered the words, "Some day *I'm* going to win the Pulitzer."

This faith in himself may have been a cover-up for his insecurities; I never knew for certain because with Bernie, as with me, so much lay beneath the surface. Sometimes that faith could be contagious. I remember walking with him along Church Avenue, listening while he expounded for the umpteenth time on his dream. In a sudden flash, I saw the future: Bernie a prize-winning novelist and I, his wife, proudly facing those who had belittled his ambition. But that vision didn't bear close inspection. I was not the special woman who could give him the support and encouragement he needed to fulfill his dream. By the same token, he was unable to give me what I needed: a sense of my own identity. Despite by attempt to let him down gently, Bernie was hurt to the point of tears. Accustomed as he was to mask his feelings with wry humor, this time he couldn't rely on that defense . . .

Subsequently, the tenor and frequency of our dates changed. School, work, play and his increasing circle of friends kept Bernie quite busy. Meanwhile, Ben [Loeb] and I were growing closer . . . Thus, I didn't have much time for Bernie that Christmas vacation, and he reacted with characteristic dramatic flair. When I refused him that all-important New Year's Eve date, he invited my sister, Anne, instead. They went to a masquerade party, she dressed as a gypsy and he as the ragged, unshaven Jeeter Lester of *Tobacco Road*. As Bernie relished telling the story later, they managed to get to the party, but long after midnight, when he tried to summon a cab to take them home, no one wanted to stop for such disreputable-looking characters . . .

After getting his degree, Bernie was appointed to teach at Lafayette High School at the request of Clara Molendyk[e], who had become English Chairman there . . .

In the autumn of 1939, I met Ted, my husband-to-be, and the following February I was appointed to take over Bernie's job at Lafayette High School. He had decided to teach at night so that he could devote his days to writing. From then on, our paths crossed erratically, sometimes by design, sometimes by happenstance. This may be apocryphal, but I have some recollection — though I don't know who could have told it to me except Bernie himself — that on the June evening when my future in-laws first came to dinner to meet my parents, Bernie was stationed across the street, watching.

Though it would have been a typically dramatic gesture on his part, the story might not fit in timewise. At some earlier period, between 1936 and '37, Bernie had deliberately managed to make Ben's acquaintance, whether to assess the competition, discomfort me or add to his own discomfort, I could never tell . . . Bernie and Ben, so opposite in personality, became friends, and I know definitely that some time in 1940 they roomed together in Washington, where they both found other jobs . . . At the time, Ben says, Bernie, while he talked about writing, didn't seem to be producing any stories . . .

Subsequently, I met Bernie twice, by chance, on Church Avenue. The first time, in 1941 or '42, I invited him to visit with me in my apartment. In addition to the usual three rooms for a newly married couple, we had a study with a built-in bookcase wall complete with work desk for me. When Bernie saw it, I recall vividly his sighing, "Oh God, I'd give anything for a room like that!" His naked longing made me feel guilty for sublimating my own writing aspirations to the boring tasks of making lesson plans and correcting themes . . .

Memory, distorted by hindsight, is notoriously unreliable, and unfortunately, I have little documentation for the period I've tried to recreate. After I was married, my mother asked me [to] clear away the "junk" I had stored in the attic. Since a newlywed's apartment was no place for such memorabilia as college notes, pressed corsages, Playbills and boxes of letters from family, friends and lovers, I decided to throw everything away. But first, I carefully tore up all the letters — as though the garbage men might be interested in reading them!

To my surprise, Bernie phoned me some years later asking that I return his letters. Since legally they were mine, to do with as I chose, I wondered why he set such store by them. Did he really believe that he would become so famous that his youthful effusions might become valuable, or conversely, prove an embarrassment to him? By that time, he'd had some stories published, but I had not yet seen them, so I couldn't judge. Still, it wasn't my place to question the value Bernie placed on his letters, so I simply told him how I'd disposed of them. He sounded a little upset, and I couldn't tell whether he was insulted, relieved or skeptical. Speculation was put to rest finally when he wrote to me in 1963, "Thanks for your letter; I'm grateful to you for having got rid of mine of an earlier date. Sometimes I shudder at what a romantic kid I was." . . .

In defense of those of us who did not give Bernie his due early-on, I must point out that he didn't show us the work that Clara saw. Thus, when all I had to go by were his letters, I was astonished at the discipline and economy of style he displayed in his published work . . . As for the subject matter, it was logical, if surprising, that he drew on his Jewish roots — which he attempted to ignore as a teenager . . . As I read each new book that he published, I could see more and more the old Bernie in the new Bernie. I dare say that had I preserved his early letters, we might recognize in them now their latent promise: "The child is father to the man."

Murray Malament

October 30, 1988. Dear Ann, . . .

Janna would like my recollections about her Dad's growing up, about my Uncle Mendel [Max], about Eugene, and about Bertha. It is precious little that I can tell her.

About Bern's early years I learned from our mutual Aunt Frima that he was a wonderful young man, that he was acting in a repertory group, and that she was in awe of him.

My uncle Mendel as an unmarried immigrant lived with my mother and father as a boarder in a five-story walk up in Brooklyn. My mother not only prepared his food, but also washed his clothes. My recollection of Bertha comes from my mother's talking about her, that she was a sweet, kindly woman.

Years later I was sent to my Uncle Mendel by my father, Doodya, to collect some money which had to go to Russia to our grandmother, Zlotta, and three aunts. Money needed to bring them to America. At this time both Bern and Eugene were in the kitchen, in back of the grocer store. We had a friendly, lively talk, and then I was on my way. Bern must have been about 14 and Eugene 12 . . .

Edward Engelberg

December 6, 2003. Dear [Ms] Malamud Smith,

I was a student of your father's — no, not at Bennington nor in Oregon, but at Erasmus Hall Evening High (we called it "night school") from which I graduated in 1946 . . .

Your father was a fantastic teacher (something you've heard before, I'm sure): this was wartime and I have several distinct memories of that time. In re-reading "The German Refugee" . . . I noted that in the volume with the introduction by the editor there is no mention of that stint at Erasmus. I do recall talking frankly with your father about why they could not appoint him to the "day session" and I think he felt it to be both jealousy (his degree), and his liberal politics, and a dose of anti-Semitism. I can't say he was bitter — too strong — but not happy. Perhaps that period was something he did not want to remember. Who knows.

But as I said it was war time. We had frequent air raid drills and sat against the walls of the hallway and he relaxed and entertained us with Bulldog Drummond and Ellery Queen (I may be misspelling) stories. He was so modest that he seldom claimed authorship, only when people asked. And then some did not believe him, thought he was kidding!

I also recall him reading the opening pages of *The Return of the Native*, and I am sure that was part what sent me on to study literature, though at heart I wanted to be a writer (having actually written a novel about German refugees). One day he came in with *The Magic Mountain*, and I read some Mann stories, and he said it was a terrific book and he was reading Freud, too. Well *The*

Magic Mountain became one of my cherished novels — I have published quite a bit on it . . .

When FDR died we had an assembly and your father delivered the most moving eulogy I can recall. The whole huge hall was silent, and even his arch enemy, Mrs. McKenna (memory after all this time!) told me that this was a very fine speech, as she called it. I am certain she was a Republican who hated both FDR and probably Eleanor even more.

Notes

The following abbreviations are used for frequently cited sources.

Brg: Berg Collection of English and American Literature, New York Public Library, Astor, Lenox and Tilden Foundations

Rnsm: Harry Ransom Humanities Research Center, University of Texas at Austin

PREFACE

1. "Where Does a Writer's Family Draw the Line?" *New York Times Book Review,* November 5, 1989.
2. "My Father Is a Book" was originally written for the Panel on Patrimonies, Jewish Identities and American Writing Conference (Rothermere American Institute, University of Oxford, England, October 2001). It was published in *Threepenny Review* no. 94 (Summer 2003) and reprinted in *The Best American Essays 2004,* ed. Louis Menand (Boston: Houghton Mifflin, 2004).

1. EARLY STORIES

1. Bernard Malamud, *The Assistant* (New York: Farrar, Straus and Cudahy, 1957), pp. 228–29.
2. Bernard Malamud, *Long Work, Short Life,* Chapbooks in Literature (Bennington, Vt.: Bennington College, 1985), p. 6.

3. Bernard Malamud, *A New Life* (New York: Farrar, Straus and Cudahy, 1961), p. 200.

4. Dad listed Max's death as 1953, but the death certificate says 1954, which fits with family correspondence.

5. Amos Elon, *The Pity of It All: A History of Jews in Germany, 1743–1933* (New York: Henry Holt, 2002), p. 251.

6. Bernard Malamud, "Armistice," in *The Complete Stories* (New York: Farrar, Straus and Giroux, 1997), p. 3.

7. Elon, *The Pity of It All*, pp. 250–51.

8. Letter, Murray Malament to Bernard Malamud (hereafter BM), July 25, 1976. "Tante Boontsah" was apparently the daughter of Shepsil's brother Kalman, so Max's cousin.

9. Letter, Mathis Silverman to BM, undated. Mathis was the son of Zlotta's sister Zisle. Zlotta was Shepsil's wife.

10. One scribbled, unsigned, and undated note implies twelve children in all. Did some die or stay in Russia?

11. Telephone conversation, Florence Hodes and Ann Malamud (hereafter AM) November 1986. In Dad's family history folder, there is also a letter, dated May 16, 1967, from Ben Schmookler mentioning that he had read about Dad in the paper: "My name is Ben Schmookler and your father and I conducted a grocery store in the years 1915 up to 1918 at 15th Avenue and 38th Street in the Borough Park section of Brooklyn." In Dad's own notes, someone named Morris Wolin became a partner to Max in his next store: "When my father sold the 15th Ave. store he bought another on 1111 Gravesend Ave (now McDonald Ave. — I own the house) with Morris Wolin as his partner. He had met Wolin through Mattis Cohen . . . Wolin, I'd heard, was clever and shifty. My mother didn't trust him." Therefore, the portrait in *The Assistant* likely had several sources.

In the same conversation between my mother and Florence, the daughter of Max's brother Mattes (or Morris), Florence mentioned that Mattes eventually brought their father, a schochet, to the United States, where he lived into his nineties. By this account, Shepsil was not killed by Cossacks. All other family recollections state that Shepsil was a secular butcher, not a schochet, and no one else mentions his coming to America, although it's clear that Zlotta, his wife, eventually came.

12. Malamud, *The Assistant*, pp. 204–5.

13. Ibid., p. 230.

14. Telephone conversation, Hodes and AM, reporting on a conversation with her cousin.

15. Notes from conversation, BM and "Aunt Anna" (Anna Fidelman), March 14, 1976. Anna was married to Dad's uncle Casile.

16. http://www.geocities.com/~alyza/Jewish/shachita.htm.

17. Letter, Silverman to BM.

18. Bernard Malamud, *The Natural* (New York: Harcourt Brace, 1952), p. 191.

19. Malamud, *A New Life*, p. 217.

2. THE EARLY JOURNALS

1. Bernard Malamud, *Pictures of Fidelman* (New York: Farrar, Straus and Giroux, 1969), p. 172.

2. Personal communication, Alex Inkeles to Janna Malamud Smith (hereafter JMS), September 12, 2003.

3. Bernard Malamud, *Dubin's Lives* (New York: Farrar, Straus and Giroux, 1979), p. 141.

4. Ibid., pp. 311–12.

5. Bernard Malamud, "Life — From Behind a Counter," *The Erasmian*, February 1932, pp. 148–51.

6. Ibid., p. 149.

7. Ibid., p. 150.

8. Malamud, *Long Work, Short Life*, p. 6.

9. Herbert Wittkin, "Bernie, the Early Years: A Memoir," personal communication, October 1986. See more excerpts in the appendix, p. 266.

10. Letter, Hans Kerber to JMS, September 4, 1987.

11. Hannah Needle Broder, "Reminiscences," personal communication, April 20, 1986. See more excerpts in the appendix, p. 272.

12. Miriam Milman Lang, "The Young Malamud: Age of Innocence," personal communication, November 11, 1986. See more excerpts in the appendix, p. 274.

13. I have distinguished the two journals as Notebook 1 and Notebook 2 in the following notes. I have not corrected spelling or punctuation errors in the journals.

14. Bernard Malamud, "A Summer's Reading," in *The Complete Stories* (New York: Farrar, Straus and Giroux, 1997), p. 173.

15. Notebook 1, pp. 1–2.

16. Ibid., p. 4.

17. Ibid., p. 12.

18. Notebook 2, p. 1.

19. Ibid., p. 18.

20. Ibid.

21. Notebook 1, p. 27.

22. Ibid., pp. 21–23.

23. Notebook 2, p. 11.

24. Ibid., pp. 38–39.

25. Ibid., p. 57.

26. Lang, "The Young Malamud."

27. Ibid.

28. Letter, BM to Miriam Milman Lang, October 14, 1963.

29. Notebook 2, pp. 52–54.

30. Ibid., p. 56.

31. Notebook 1, pp. 68–69.

32. Ibid., pp. 51–56.

33. Notebook 2, pp. 25–26.

34. Ibid., pp. 21–22.

35. Ibid., pp. 31–32.

36. Ibid., pp. 32–34.

37. Ibid., pp. 40–41.

38. Ibid., pp. 42–43.

39. Bernard Malamud, "A Lost Bar-Mitzvah" (unpublished, 1982).

40. Bernard Malamud, "The Refugee," The Post Impressionist, *Washington Post*, late July or early August 1940.

41. Letter, BM, c. 1938. A copy of this letter was found in his journal.

42. Notebook 2, pp. 60–72.

43. Letter, Ben Loeb to Miriam Milman Lang, July 23, 1986.

3. COURTSHIP

1. Letter, BM to Ann deChiara (hereafter AdC), July 29, 1943, Harry Ransom Humanities Research Center, University of Texas at Austin (hereafter Rnsm).

2. Letter, BM to Rosemarie Beck (hereafter RB), May 7, 1959, Berg Collection of English and American Literature, New York Public Library, Astor, Lenox and Tilden Foundations (hereafter Brg).

3. Letter, BM to AdC, undated [Spring 1942], Rnsm.

4. Letter, BM to AdC, November 1942, Rnsm.

5. Bernard Malamud, "The Lady of the Lake," in *The Magic Barrel* (New York: Farrar, Straus and Giroux, 1958), p. 105.

6. Bernard Malamud, "The Girl of My Dreams," in *The Magic Barrel* (New York: Farrar, Straus and Giroux, 1958), p. 27.

7. Letter, BM to AdC, October 29, 1943, Rnsm.

8. Letter, BM to AdC, August 2, 1943, Rnsm.

9. Letter, BM to AdC, undated [1943], Rnsm.

10. Letter, BM to AdC, July 21, 1943, Rnsm.

4. THE YEAR I WAS BORN

1. Letter, BM to AdC, April 1942, Rnsm.

2. Letter, BM to AdC, undated, Rnsm.

3. Letter, undated [December 1951?], Rnsm.

4. Bernard Malamud, "The Grocery Store," in *The Complete Stories* (New York: Farrar, Straus and Giroux, 1997), pp. 14–21.

5. With thanks to Vicki Kirsch and others at the Cambridge Health Alliance, who translated this sentence for me.

6. Notes from conversation, BM and Florence Hodes, undated [1976?].

7. Eulogy for Eugene Malamud, undated [Autumn 1973], Rnsm.

8. http://www.nypl.org/research/chss/spe/rpe/faids/fsg/fsginven.html, accessed October 15, 2004. See also Robert Giroux, *The Education of an Editor* (New York: R. R. Bowker, 1982).

9. Letter, BM to AM, June 30, 1952, Rnsm.

10. Letter, BM to AM, July 22, 1952, Rnsm.

11. Letter, BM to AM, July 24, 1952, Rnsm.

12. Letter, BM to AM, July 5, 1952, Rnsm.

13. Letter, BM to AM, July 4, 1952, Rnsm.

14. Letter, BM to AM, July 8, 1952, Rnsm.

15. Letter, BM to AM, July 5, 1952, Rnsm.

16. Letter, BM to AM, July 10, 1952, Rnsm.

17. Letter, BM to AM, July 11, 1952, Rnsm.

18. Letter, BM to AM, July 24, 1952, Rnsm.

19. Letter, BM to AM, July 19, 1952, Rnsm.

20. Letter, BM to AM, July 28, 1952, Rnsm.

21. Letter, BM to AM, July 30, 1952, Rnsm.

22. Letter, BM to AM, July 11, 1952, Rnsm.

23. Letter, BM to AM, July 20, 1952, Rnsm.

24. Letter, BM to AM, July 20, 1952, Rnsm.

25. Letter, BM to AM, August 4, 1952, Rnsm.

26. Letter, BM to AM, undated [August 6?, 1952], Rnsm.

27. Letter, BM to AM, July 2, 1952, Rnsm.

28. Letter, BM to AM, July 8, 1952, Rnsm.

29. Letter, BM to AM, undated [August 6?, 1952], Rnsm.

30. Malamud, *The Natural*, p. 9.

5. CORVALLIS

1. Malamud, *A New Life*, p. 25.

2. Ibid., p. 15.

3. Letter, BM to Miriam Milman Lang, August 21, 1951.

4. Letter, Bernadette Inkeles to JMS, March 21, 1986.

5. http://osulibrary.oregonstate.edu/archives/chronology/chron_1950 .html, accessed January 10, 2004.

6. Chester Garrison, "Bernard Malamud: An Instinctive Friendship" (Unpublished, c. 2000), p. 3.

7. Letter, BM to RB, April 15, 1960, Brg.

8. Letter, BM to RB, April 28, 1960, Brg.

9. Letter, BM to RB, August 21, 1959, Brg.

10. Letter, BM to RB, July 13, 1959, Brg.

11. Letter, BM to RB, November 30, 1959, Brg.

12. Letter, BM to RB, March 7, 1960, Brg.

13. Letter, BM to RB, October 26, 1960, Brg.

14. Letter, BM to Janna Malamud (hereafter JM), undated [Summer 1958].

15. Letter, BM to JM, November 16, 1975.

16. Letter, BM to RB, May 29, 1959, Brg.

17. Letter, BM to RB, June 1, 1961, Brg.

18. Bernard Malamud, *The Tenants* (New York: Farrar, Straus and Giroux, 1971), p. 6.

6. BENNINGTON AND ITS COLLEGE

1. Letter, BM to RB, September 17, 1961, Brg.

2. Letter, BM to Arlene, January 6, 1962, Rnsm.

3. Letter, BM to Arlene, February 6, 1962, Rnsm.

4. Letter, BM to JM, undated [Winter 1972].

5. Bernard Malamud, "A Choice of Profession," in *Idiots First* (New York: Farrar, Straus and Giroux, 1963), p. 71.

6. Letter, BM to RB, December 30, 1961, Brg.

7. Letter, BM to Arlene, January 6, 1962, Rnsm.

8. Letter, BM to RB, September 5, 1964, Brg.

9. Howard Nemerov, "The Blue Swallows," in *The Blue Swallows* (Chicago: University of Chicago Press, 1967), pp. 89–90.

10. Letter, BM to RB, August 19, 1960, Brg.

11. Letter, BM to Arlene, June 20, 1962, Rnsm.

12. Eric A. Gordon, *Mark the Music: The Life and Work of Marc Blitzstein* (New York: St. Martin's Press, 1989), pp. 526–27.

13. Letter, AM to BM, July 29, 1963.

14. Letter, BM to RB, March 6, 1964, Brg.

15. Letter, BM to RB, February 14, 1967, Brg.

7. BENNINGTON GIRL

1. Letter, Arlene to BM, June 13–14, 1984.

2. Malamud, *Dubin's Lives*, p. 210.

3. Malamud, *Pictures of Fidelman*, pp. 110–11.

4. Malamud, *The Tenants*, p. 192.

5. Letter, Arlene to BM, July 24–25, 1975.

6. Bernard Malamud, *The Fixer* (New York: Farrar, Straus and Giroux, 1966), p. 335.

7. Letter, BM to RB, May 1, 1959, Brg.

8. THANKSGIVING

1. Letter, BM to JM, October 28, 1968.

2. Letter, BM to JM, November 10, 1968.

3. Letter, BM to JM, May 10, 1978.

4. Letter, BM to JM, May 1, 1978.

5. Letter, BM to JM, December 3, 1968.

6. Letter, BM to JM, December 7, 1971.

7. Letter, BM to JM, November 1, 1971.

8. Letter, BM to JM, November 12, 1971.

9. Malamud, *Dubin's Lives,* pp. 64–65.

10. Letter, AM to JMS, February 2, 1979.

9. HEART

1. Letter, BM to JM, September 27, 1975.

2. Bernard Malamud, *God's Grace* (New York: Farrar, Straus and Giroux, 1982), p. 223.

Acknowledgments

I thank my mother, Ann deChiara Malamud, for reading and consenting to my publishing this book, and for granting me permission to read and quote my father's journals and family letters. I thank my agent, Miriam Altshuler; my editor and publisher at Houghton Mifflin, Janet Silver; and her editorial assistant, Meg Lemke. I thank my manuscript editors, Barbara Jatkola and Peg Anderson, for carefully reviewing and preparing the manuscript. I thank Robert Friedman, director of the Center for Jewish History Genealogy Institute in New York, for his help with Ukrainian geography.

For supplying and/or permitting me to quote letters in their archives, I thank Richard Workman, research librarian at the Harry Ransom Humanities Research Center, University of Texas at Austin; and Wayne Furman, Office of Special Collections, the Berg Collection of English and American Literature, New York Public Library, Aston, Lenox, and Tilden Foundations.

For sharing and permitting me to quote stories and privately held letters, I thank Arlene, Hannah Needle Broder, Phebe Chao and Roger Sorkin, Edward Engelberg, Louise Garrison, James Groshong, Alex and Bernadette Inkeles, Miriam Milman Lang, Sylvia Malament, Henk and Molly Meijer, Norman Selverstone, and Herb Wittkin.

I thank my dear and tolerant friends. I thank Jacqueline Olds. I also thank my colleagues at Cambridge Hospital — particularly those of you I fondly refer to as "my-psychoanalytic-guy-reading-group."

I thank Michael T. Gilmore, Deborah Valenze, Paul Malamud, and Peter Malamud Smith for reviewing the penultimate draft.

Finally, I thank my husband, fellow traveler, and first reader, David M. Smith, who continually braved the marital equivalent of *mare mosso* to offer his astute opinions.